D0890021

A MODERN COMPANION
TO THE
EUROPEAN COMMUNITY

A Modern Companion
to the European Community

Erratum page 111
12.2 Economy 1989
The Figure for inflation should read 5.3%

A MODERN COMPANION TO THE EUROPEAN COMMUNITY

A GUIDE TO KEY FACTS, INSTITUTIONS AND TERMS

ANDREW COX

PAUL FURLONG

Edward Elgar

© Andrew Cox, Paul Furlong, 1992

Published by
Edward Elgar Publishing Limited
Gower House
Croft Road
Aldershot
Hants GU11 3HR
England

Edward Elgar Publishing Limited
Distributed in the United States by
Ashgate Publishing Company
Old Post Road
Brookfield
Vermont 05036
USA

CIP catalogue records for this book are available from the British Library and the US Library of Congress

ISBN 1 85278 516 0

Printed in Great Britain by
Billing & Sons Ltd, Worcester

CONTENTS

PREFACE

This work is intended as a practical guide to the institutions and terminology of the European Community and of its 1992 project. It originates from our concern at the lack of an accessible work of reference intended for people who have no previous acquaintance with the EC. All those who have had to teach in this area will be aware of the perplexities and difficulties presented by this unfamiliar and sometimes daunting subject. The European Community is in the process of radical change and expansion. Its attempt to create a single market for goods, services, labour and capital from 1992 puts it in the forefront of international economic and political relations. What we try to provide here is a basic introduction to the institutions, together with a guide to the political and economic structure of the member states, supported by a glossary of key terms and acronyms.

A work of this kind inevitably involves its authors in debts of gratitude to a very wide number of people. We wish to thank all those who have helped us in writing the *Modern Companion*. We are particularly grateful to Sally Harris and to Joe Ingle for their work on the glossary and on the guide. We would also like to thank Frances Lamont, Sheila Longbone and Sandra Whitcomb for their help in completing the final manuscript.

CHAPTER 1

EC INSTITUTIONS

EC INSTITUTIONS

1. The Establishment of the European Economic Community

Few political institutions can claim a history which pursues a straight line without pause, but that of the EC is more than usually littered with deviations and unscheduled halts. European federalists like to refer to precursors from centuries ago - early Medieval writers who called for a United States of Europe, and many since then for whom the idea seemed a perfect but distant solution to the problems of a Continent apparently doomed to periodic domestic strife. In the 19th century, the fervour of free trade doctrines gave an added dimension, that of economic advantage, to the notion of a guaranteed peace in Europe. In late 19th and early 20th century Europe, East and West, schemes abounded for institutional engineering aimed at bringing about a European supranational government, though they generally made little headway against the cold realities of competitive European national identities.

The immediate origins of what is now the European Community lie much closer to the present. The aftermath of the 1939-1945 war found Europe economically exhausted and militarily divided. On one side of the divide, Eastern European nations were firmly anchored to Soviet designs and to Soviet economic and political needs. On the other side of the fault line, the Western Europeans were economically dependent on the United States to enable them to rebuild quickly, and after the Brussels Treaty of 1948 their military priorities were for the most part subsumed under those of NATO (established in 1949). But both of these factors actually pushed them into closer cooperation with one another. Also, competitive nationalism was widely blamed for the 20th century wars, and the dominant political forces in the new post-war states were for the first time speaking with similar voices about supranational collaboration. The new dimension which they brought to the debate, which they added to the traditional objectives of peace and prosperity, was that of morality, of justice, of Europe as an instrument of social equity. This combination of themes has run through European integration since then, sometimes in contradiction with one another, sometimes complementary.

The first European regional economic agency after the war was the Economic Commission for Europe (ECE), established in Geneva (Switzerland) in 1947 as a branch of the United Nations. The pan-European aims of the ECE were quickly revealed to be unachievable because of the rigid economic separation of Eastern Europe from the West. The ECE was intended by some to be the coordinator of the US-backed Marshall Plan for the reconstruction of Europe, but Soviet disagreement blocked whatever prospect there was of this. With US support, the Committee for European Economic Cooperation was established to channel Marshall Plan funds, and this led to the founding of the Organization for European Economic Cooperation (OEEC) in 1948. The setting up of the OEEC was the occasion of the first of many disagreements between the British and various other European countries (on this occasion, it was France) over the issue of supranationalism. What this meant in practice was whether the OEEC should have genuine coordinating powers over and above the sovereignty of the individual states, as the French sought, or whether it should be controlled by a ministerial council nominated by delegates from individual countries, taking decisions on the basis of unanimity. Despite US support for the French position, it was the British view which predominated in the structure of the OEEC.

This division was also clearly visible at the creation of the Council of Europe. The founding Congress of

Europe held at The Hague in May 1948 gave formal support to European political and economic union. But efforts by the French and Belgians to make this effective by adopting majority voting in a European Parliamentary Assembly were defeated. This dispute over the form and direction of European integration is sometimes regarded as a difference of principle between two approaches to European integration. The position adopted by the French and Belgians in 1947 and 1948 (not one the French have maintained consistently since then) is referred to as the federalist approach, in which union is to be achieved by the creation of a supra-national political organization to which real power is ceded by the nation-states. The alternative is the functionalist approach, which sees integration as a process of gradual extension of cooperation between governments, particularly in the economic sphere. Though the French strategy immediately after the war was quite close to federalism, it would be difficult to argue that the British were 'functionalists' from this point of view, since they never had political or economic union as a real aim, and they certainly had great difficulty in accepting constraints on national sovereignty in the economic sphere.

The Marshall Plan funds were scheduled to be spent over four years, which meant that the OEEC would lose its original purpose in 1952. The British held that the OEEC should be reduced in size and some of its functions handed to NATO, which would have held back the pace of integration by curtailing one of its institutional levers, albeit one with limited powers. Before this could happen, six Western European countries established a new supranational organization with enhanced powers over a much more restricted range of policy. This was the European Coal and Steel Community (ECSC), whose founder members were Belgium, France, Italy, Luxembourg, the Netherlands and West Germany. The ECSC, which originated in the

Schuman Plan of 1950, established a customs union in coal, iron and steel, and set up a High Authority with direct independent powers to oversee the union. The ECSC was formally approved by the six countries in the Treaty of Paris in April 1951.

The ECSC worked as expected and with some success - in fact the UK, which initially declined to join as a full member, signed an agreement of association with it in 1954. But the years immediately after its establishment were marked by uneven progress.

The outbreak of the Korean War in 1950 brought military issues higher up the agenda. In particular, it raised immediate questions about the need for West German re-armament and possible NATO membership. The French demurred, and instead proposed (with the Pleven Plan) a European Defence Community (EDC) controlling a European army. With the momentum created by the ECSC, this proposal made rapid headway among the six ECSC members. In May 1952 they signed the EDC Treaty, which agreed to common parliamentary, ministerial and judicial structures to direct the EDC. The UK stayed out, but raised no objection to the new organisation.

The six quickly moved on. The integration of defence policy inevitably raised issues of foreign policy. Also, the Benelux countries, already operating a customs union since 1948, were keen to make further progress in economic integration with the rest of Western Europe. There was considerable debate about the need to bring the military structures under real representative democratic control. Using the ECSC, the six 'core' states drafted a proposal for a European Political Community (EPC). After a transitional period, this would have established a new institutional framework subsuming the ECSC and the proposed EDC within a European Political Authority. This would have consisted of a supranational executive government, a European Parliament, a European Court and a Council of Ministers from the member states. The proposal included economic integration in the form of a common market of goods and services.

These ambitious plans needed the approval of the Parliaments of the member states. Five of the six approved the first stage, the EDC Treaty, but vigorous disagreement emerged in France. In particular, rightwing parties objected to supranational control of the French Armed Forces, while parties on the left were opposed to West German re-armament. A further difficulty was the refusal of the UK government to participate in the EDC. After unsuccessful attempts to have the EDC Treaty amended, the French government, headed by Pierre Mendes-France, submitted the original document to the French National Assembly, which refused to consider it and thereby finished off the EPC as well as the EDC.

A side-effect of this failure was the re-emergence of British minimalism as a factor in European integration. After the collapse, the UK government proposed new intergovernmental structures to deal with questions of defence and foreign policy in Europe. These eventually resulted in the renegotiation of the 1948 Brussels Treaty, the admission of West Germany into NATO in 1955, and the establishment of the Western European Union as a consultative defence and foreign policy institution for the European members of NATO.

So by the beginning of 1955, a battery of multi-national sectoral organizations existed within or including Western Europe: NATO, the OEEC, WEU, ECSC, Council of Europe. But there was no agreement about overall methods of control, or about the next steps. The response within the 'European movement' was to shift objectives. In June 1955, the Messina Conference attended by the six ECSC member states resolved to seek economic integration through a general common market. In view of the increasing importance of nuclear energy, it also agreed to consider a common atomic energy pool. Political integration of the kind attempted in the draft EPC treaty was relegated to the status of long-term objective. The Messina Conference set up a committee chaired by the Dutch politician Paul-Henri Spaak to draft treaties accordingly.

The British were invited to join in the work of the drafting committee, and substantial differences soon emerged between Britain and the six. The British favoured a free trade area coordinated by an enhanced OEEC, whereas the six had already agreed at Messina to a customs union and powerful independent institutions. The UK government withdrew its representation in November 1955. The Spaak committee continued, with some internal disagreement still evident, particularly between France and the rest. Its report was considered by the foreign ministers of the six in Venice in May 1956. After detailed negotiations, the two treaties, one on the common market and the other on atomic energy, were signed in Rome on 25 March 1957. Their signatories were the six member states of the ECSC. The treaties were ratified without major problems by the Parliaments, and the European Economic Community (EEC) and Euratom came into being on 1 January 1958.

2.   Development of the EEC from 1958 to 1969

The objectives of the EEC were laid out in Article 3 of the Treaty of Rome. This required the member states to proceed to economic integration in the form of a common market within twelve years. So by 1969 the EEC was expected to have removed all internal trade barriers such as customs duties and quotas, to have established a common external tariff for goods coming from outside the common market, and to have abolished internal obstacles to the free movement of factors of production - not just goods and services, in other words, but also labour, capital and enterprise.

Article 3 also provided for a variety of other developments, including common policies for agriculture and transport, common commercial policies towards the outside world, special arrangements for relations with former colonial dependencies, institutions to prevent distortions in competition, and funds aimed at helping less-developed regions or those suffering short-term consequences of competitive restructuring. There was also reference to the need to coordinate macro-economic policies, but this was intergovernmental rather than supranational.

By 1969, the six had clearly established a customs union, since internal tariffs and quotas had been removed and a common external tariff adopted. The Social Fund (ESF) and Investment Bank (EIB) were in place, and a common agricultural policy was also in operation. Progress towards a common transport policy had been much slower, and serious problems remained in the form of non-tariff barriers to the free movement of factors of production.

Political institutions had also developed at variable speeds. Outside the framework of the EEC, the OEEC had found a new role after the end of the Marshall Plan. In response to international needs for an intergovernmental forum for coordination of policy, it was relaunched in 1961 as the Organization for Economic Cooperation and Development (OECD), based in Paris, with a membership including all the Western European Countries, the US, Canada, Japan, Australia and New Zealand. Within Western Europe, the non-EEC countries including Britain established the European Free Trade Association (EFTA) in 1960, with limited economic objectives relating mainly to the removal of tariff barriers and quotas. This had long been the objective of successive UK governments, whose intention for some time in the 1960s seemed to be to try to draw the EEC as a block into a free trade association with EFTA.

Within the EEC itself, the difficulties of the transitional period, serious as they were, never reached a sufficient pitch to make this a likely proposition. The difficulties, as might have been expected, related to the political mechanisms for implementing common intentions, not to the principle of economic integration as such. The Treaty of Rome laid down complicated rules about voting procedure in the Council of Ministers, which caused much dispute. In some areas of policy, such as admission of new members, unanimity was needed in the Council, but after the early stages of transition a system of qualified majority voting was applicable in others, such as agriculture. The voting system gave France, Italy and West Germany four votes each, Belgium and the Netherlands two each and Luxembourg one. The 'qualified majority' needed for measures in the appropriate areas was twelve, including at least four member states on some kinds of proposal.

The purpose of this was to prevent individual member states holding up progress indefinitely during the transitional period, and to encourage compromise and consensus. But at a crucial stage in the EEC's growth, qualified voting had to be shelved. In 1965 the Commission (in effect, the EEC's executive) proposed to the Council of Ministers a package of radical measures which would have extended the powers of the European Parliament, increased the independent budget of the Commission and completed the financial aspects of the agricultural policy. The French government objected to much of the package and adopted what became known as the 'empty chair' strategy - the French absented themselves from the Council meetings for over six months. Eventually, agreement was reached to respect the weight of 'very important interests' of individual member states by seeking solutions agreeable to all even where majority voting was applicable. This agreement, reached in January 1966, was known as the

Luxembourg compromise (not to be confused with the very different Luxembourg Report of 1970, nor with the Luxembourg Accord of 1985). The Luxembourg compromise resulted in the effective abeyance of majority voting on most of the important issues.

A further change during the transitional period occurred in relations betweeen the three communities (EEC, ECSC and Euratom). From 1958, the European Parliament and the Court of Justice acted for all three jointly, though they retained separate Commissions and Councils. In 1967 a new treaty merged the Commissions and Councils of the three. Formally, three communities still exist, but they are now usually referred to as the European Community without distinction.

3. Development of the EC from 1969 to 1986

At the end of the transitional period, the heads of government held a summit at The Hague, in Holland, to review progress and to decide what further action was necessary. At this point the EC could have decided to go no further in economic integration and merely to maintain existing institutions, completing the agenda set by the Treaty of Rome as appropriate. In fact they agreed to attempt an ambitious relaunch of the EC, including in their final resolution the objective of economic and monetary union (EMU), regarded as the next and final stage in economic integration after the common market. What actually happened in the 1970s has often been referred to, perhaps a little misleadingly, as a broadening rather than a deepening of the community.

The 'broadening' certainly did occur. The community extended its membership, with the accession of the United Kingdom, Eire and Denmark on 1 January 1973. Norway had been included in the negotiations but pulled out after a national referendum on membership.

Negotiations between the United Kingdom and the EC had been particularly difficult and prolonged, both because of the complexities of the issues and because of political uncertainties on both sides. There were several major problem areas. One of the most complex was the issue of relations between the UK and the other countries of the Commonwealth, particularly sugar producers such as India, and the lamb and dairy product exports from New Zealand. Other more general issues were the international role of sterling, the UK budgetary contributions, and the position of remaining members of the European Free Trade Area.   There was also suspicion on the part of some member states, particularly France, that Britain was not committed to being a 'good European', that it really wanted a radical reform of the Treaty of Rome before it would join, and that its foreign policy was more strongly linked with that of the United States than of the EC members. Despite these problems, and after suffering one spectacular public rebuff from the French President Général de Gaulle in 1963, Britain and the member states persevered, compromising on some issues and leaving others to be resolved after accession.

In 1974, the incoming Labour government in Britain sought a thorough renegotiation of the terms achieved by its Conservative predecessor. The renegotiations particularly concerned the objective of economic and monetary union by 1980, which might constrain national economic policy. But they also involved a wide range of other issues, including Britain's budgetary contributions, which were disproportionately high because of the British pattern of trade with third countries, and the common agricultural policy, which did not favour traditional British farming. On the issue of EMU, British fears about speedy progress proved groundless, and compromises were reached on the other issues without radical reform. A national referendum on

EC membership in June 1975 supported British membership overwhelmingly.

These episodes left a legacy of doubt about the cohesiveness of the newly enlarged community. They also made it difficult for much progress to be made in the 'deepening' of the EC, and those developments which did occur were mainly filling the gaps in policy areas remaining from the transitional period. The most important of these developments were in 1970, when a common fisheries policy was set up, though the policy itself was not completed until 1983, and in 1972, when the Paris Summit agreed a general approach on industrial policy, and called for coordination of science and research policy. The same Summit agreed the establishment of a European Regional Development Fund, to promote a more active involvement of the EC in regional development. The commitment of the community to Third World countries was reinforced through the Lomé conventions, the first of which ran from 1975 to 1980.

However, there were some significant developments in the role of the community institutions. For the most part these amounted to a series of small steps rather than to any great leaps forward, and in some cases amounted to the institutionalization of existing practice - a process seen by some as vindication of the functionalist approach over federalism. The main changes related to the European Parliament, to foreign policy coordination, and to the development of the Council of Ministers.

It was agreed to enhance the authority and powers of the European Parliament by introducing direct elections and by giving it greater powers over the budgetary process. The first direct elections to the European Parliament were held in 1979 across all member states. Cooperation in foreign policy was formalized through the political cooperation mechanism adopted after the Luxembourg Report of 1970. There were two significant features of this mechanism. First, it was set up as an exercise in cooperation between the governments of the member states, having a membership identical with that of the EC but formally entirely separate from it. Second, there is no provision for majority voting - its aims are to ensure better understanding of international problems and to strengthen the solidarity of the members, through common action if possible. Third, defence policy is excluded from the procedures, as were in practice other foreign policy issues which concerned the internal politics of individual states. With regard to the Council of Ministers, this developed an unusual shifting membership of relevant ministers and sometimes of civil servants empowered to deal with the routine negotiations by which the work of the EC advanced. But increasingly the major decisions were being taken at the summits of heads of governments held at least twice a year in the capital of whichever country happened to be holding the Presidency of the Council for that six-month period. These summits became known as the European Council, though they were not formally integrated into the institutions until 1986.

The final development to be mentioned from this period relates to the goal of economic and monetary union. The adoption of this as an objective in 1969 was reinforced in 1972 (again at the Paris summit) by the call for its achievement by 1980. For a variety of reasons, not least the increasingly uncertain state of world currency markets, this proved over-ambitious. The first stage was the 'snake in the tunnel', a coordinated float of European exchange rates within agreed internal and external bands, but this suffered periodic defections and unilateral re-alignments. In December 1974, the heads of government agreed to take note of the difficulties of the preceding two years, and thus metaphorically speaking put EMU into the capacious EC drawer marked 'Forget For Now'.

The issue re-emerged in more modest garb in 1977 and 1978 with proposals by the then President of the Commission Roy Jenkins and by the West German Chancellor Helmut Schmidt. The emphasis in this case was on coordination for monetary stability rather than on an eventual common currency. The immediate objective therefore was the practical one of minimizing the destabilizing effects of speculative flows into and out of specific European currencies. After typically complex and contentious negotiations, agreement was reached on a European Monetary System. This had several features, but the two most important were the adoption of the European Currency Unit (ECU) to replace the traditional European Unit of Account, and the setting up of the Exchange Rate Mechanism (ERM), to which the new ECU was tied.This was initially referred to as a 'supersnake', since unlike the previous snake it worked by fixing each currency against a central currency (the ECU), using this to establish a grid of bilateral exchange rates from which only prescribed deviation was possible. The EMS also provided for credit and deposit arrangements to fund the new ECU and to enable governments to manage short-term currency fluctuations within the ERM. The EMS was agreed at the European Council in December 1978, and came into operation in March 1979. Of the member states at the time, only the United Kingdom chose to stay out of the ERM, but it did agree to participate in the other aspects of the EMS.

The development of the EC in the early 1980s was a great disappointment to the long-suffering optimists in the European movement. In 1981, the EC was further expanded by the accession of Greece, and negotiations were put in train following the membership applications of Portugal and Spain. But the community as a whole suffered bitter and protracted disputes about two key issues, and in both of them the United Kingdom played a leading role. The two issues which bedevilled the progress towards further integration were the Common

Agricultural Policy and the budget. It is not relevant
here to go into the details of the disputes, but their
connection with one another, and their impact on other
institutions such as Parliament and the Council of
Ministers, blocked reform in other areas and prevented
the further development of supranational elements in the
EC's framework. In 1981 the price and income support
mechanism of the CAP accounted for 62.9% of the EC's
budget. It was difficult to envisage enhancement of
other programmes within the Community's budget
without some rescaling of the weight of the CAP.
Social and regional policies in particular suffered
because of the financial constraints.

A further problem was that the UK benefited
relatively little from the CAP because of the small size
of the agricultural sector in the British economy. For
this reason and for others, at the beginning of the 1980s
Britain was the largest net contributor to the EC budget,
though it was only the third largest economy. The
problems of the CAP and the budget assumed a major
political significance in Britain which they did not
necessarily have elsewhere. Other EC countries viewed
with some impatience the efforts of the Thatcher
government to hold up major changes until the problems
at the top of the UK agenda were resolved. Britain
wanted a radical reform of the CAP aimed at curtailing
its price support system, cutting back on the repeated
farm surpluses through quotas on production, and
putting ceilings on agricultural support expenditure. For
other countries such as France and West Germany, the
political importance of the CAP far outweighed the
financial burdens involved, and the British objections
were regarded at worst as a pretext for wider
disagreement over the objectives of the community.
Though the CAP continued to provide the occasion for
annual conflict throughout the 1980s, the problem of
UK budgetary contributions was at least partly resolved
with the Fontainebleau agreement of 1984, which

provided for a UK rebate proportionate to the difference between its contributions through VAT payments and its receipt of Community expenditure.

4. The Single European Act

It was in this acrimonious and inauspicious climate that the EC made a bold attempt to break out of its institutional stalemate. Again, it was a shift of objectives which unblocked the position, through the adoption of a radical programme designed to reform the Treaty of Rome, to re-introduce majority voting, and to agree a range of measures needed to push Europe rapidly towards the completion of the single internal market. The impetus behind the new drive for economic integration came from a variety of sources. Not least among them was the increasing frustration of some of the heads of government with the political obstacles to reforms aimed at enhancing the powers of EC institutions. Some, particularly the Benelux leaders, correctly reckoned that success in direct economic integration would improve the prospect of political changes. Others such as the increasingly vocal and influential heads of European multinationals like Philips and Volkswagen, senior figures in European industry, together with free-market politicians such as Margaret Thatcher, sought the removal of all remaining barriers to trade as a means to improve Europe's capacity to compete in world markets. These ideas found their institutional expression in a 1985 White Paper produced by the EC commissioner for competition policy, Lord Cockfield, which identified the remaining barriers to free movement of goods, services, capital and labour.

The programme outlined in the Cockfield White Paper was developed by the Commission, discussed by a special intergovernmental conference in December 1985 (the Luxembourg Accord), signed by the heads of government in February 1986, and agreed by the national parliaments. It came into force in July 1987. The European Parliament had sought a completely new Treaty, but the programme adopted a different approach. It involved a radical reform of the Treaty of Rome, contained in the Single European Act. The reform set a deadline of 31 December 1992 for the completion of the internal market. It covered all the measures held to be necessary to remove internal frontiers, without exception, and it provided for the extension of majority voting in the Council of Ministers on issues relevant to the single market programme. Unanimity in the Council of Ministers was retained for particularly sensitive issues, including indirect taxation, fiscal harmonisation, and labour relations.

The Single Market was defined in the SEA as an area without internal frontiers in which the free movement of goods, persons, services and capital is assured in accordance with the provisions of this Treaty.' As well as reforms directly relating to the SIM, the Act also introduced a new cooperation procedure between the European Parliament, Council and Commission. This strengthens Parliament's hand by obliging the Commission to respond to Parliament's amendments, and imposes strict time limits so that contentious issues cannot be subject to protracted and sterile negotiation. The Act also gave formal recognition to foreign policy cooperation between member states, and called for coordination of the 'political and economic aspects of security'.

The Single European Act undoubtedly revitalized a flagging community. The re-introduction of majority voting helped resolve the institutional difficulties, but the idea of the single internal market rapidly acquired a momentum of its own, and brought home to the citizen in the street the potential and the problems of European integration. It also gave both the Commission and Parliament an enhanced authority and confidence in their dealings with the previously dominant Council of

Ministers. By February 1991, after about four years of the programme, over 1000 individual measures either had been adopted, or were directly under discussion, or had been published by the Commission with the intention to submit for discussion. Of the nearly 300 measures referred to in general terms in the White Paper, 193 had been dealt with by the Council, amounting to about two-thirds of the programme.

5. EC Institutions in the 1990s

Having described the growth of the EC, we can conclude by describing briefly how the main institutions now operate.

5.1 The Commission

The Commission, sited in Brussels, consists of 17 members appointed by the governments of the member states. France, Germany, Italy, Spain and the UK appoint two members each, the remainder one each. Commissioners have responsibility to the Community, not to individual states. during their four-year term of office they cannot be sacked either by the governments which appointed them or by the Council of Ministers, though they can be dismissed en masse by the Parliament. The Commission has at its disposal the administrative apparatus of the Community, which means the approximately 12,000 staff employed to develop and implement policy or to provide services such as translation. Each commissioner is in charge of one or more Directorate-Generals dealing with individual policy sectors. The Commission has to

1) develop policies and legislative proposals for submission to the Council and to Parliament

2)   implement policies adopted by the Council, if
     necessary in consultation with committees of
     experts appointed by national governments
3)   implement the Community Budget, including the
     administration of the 'structural funds' (CAP, ESF,
     ERDF)
4)   carry out various tasks directly assigned to it by the
     treaties - for example, supervising prices in the coal
     and steel sector, monitoring the effectiveness of
     competition policy, controlling certain aspects of
     nuclear energy production.

In general, the role of the Commission is a
sometimes awkward mixture of the administrative and
the political. The Council relies on it for specific
proposals and cannot act without it, and the Commission
is the guardian of the community interest over and
above that of the individual states. But it also has
routine responsibility for the management of EC policy,
for which it needs the political and technical support of
member states.

5.2 The Council of Ministers

The Council consists of twelve representatives, one
from each of the member states. Its actual membership
varies depending on the matter in hand, though formally
it consists of the foreign ministers. It meets as often as
is necessary, and is the supreme decision-making body.
Its most important decisions have to be taken by
unanimous vote, but when majority voting is applicable
(for instance, on much of the single market legislation),
each country is allotted a specific weight in the voting
system. France, Germany, Italy and the UK have 10
votes each, Spain has 8, Belgium, Greece, the
Netherlands, and Portugal 5 each, Denmark and Ireland
3 each, and Luxembourg 2. The majority in the
qualified voting system is 54 votes, in some cases

including at least eight member states. The Presidency of the Council is held for six-month periods by individual member states in accordance with an agreed schedule.

The Council has a small secretariat to prepare its meetings. It also relies heavily on the Committee of Permanent Representatives, which is usually known by its French acronym COREPER. This consists of national officials of ambassador rank, who meet regularly to look at proposals before they come to the Council. COREPER acts as a filter for the Council, and if it is able to agree a proposal unanimously, the Council's agreement is usually a formality.

5.3 The European Parliament

The EP consists of 518 deputies, elected every five years. The four largest countries have 81 deputies (or MEPs) each, Spain 60, the Netherlands 25, Belgium Greece and Portugal 24 each, Denmark 16, Ireland 15, Luxembourg 6. The deputies are organised in party-political groupings, not by nationalities. The main sessions of the EP are held in Strasbourg (France), but its general secretariat is based in Luxembourg and its committees and party groups usually meet in Brussels.

The EP has a variety of functions, though in no area can it claim unconstrained authority. Its legislative function is limited to discussion and amendment - it cannot initiate legislation, though the SEA greatly enhanced its power to alter proposals from the Commission. Its power over the budget is greater, in that it can accept or reject the budget in toto, and can amend directly proposals on certain kinds of expenditure (known as non-obligatory, because not deriving directly from treaty provisions). The EP can require the Commission to answer written or oral questions relating to the implementation of policy. Though it cannot dismiss individual commissioners, it could dismiss the entire Commission, but this draconian weapon has never been used.

5.4 The European Court of Justice

This is an increasingly important body which constitutes the highest Court of Appeal on matters relating to the interpretation of Community Law. It consists of 13 judges, one from each country plus the President of the Court, who serve a six-year term. There are also five Advocates-General and a Registrar. All these are appointed by governments of member states after due consultation with one another. They are completely independent once appointed, and cannot be dismissed. Cases brought to the Court from national legal systems or directly by the other institutions are presented to the Court by an Advocate-General, who acts as an impartial counsel to the Court. It has no legal right to police staff of its own, and relies on the national judicial and police systems for implementation.

The court has two main functions: when requested by another Community institution, by a government or in some circumstances by an individual, it can directly annul any measures taken by the Commission, by the Council or by national governments which are incompatible with the treaties; and it passes judgement on the interpretation or validity of points of Community Law when requested to do so by a national court.

Finally, there are three other bodies with particular functions within the EC. The Economic and Social Committee (ESC) is a consultative organisation of 189 members representing employers, trade unions and other occupational and trade associations. Its opinion has to be sought for most proposals from the Commission before they can be adopted by the Council. The European Court of Auditors oversees the management of the Community's budget, and examines the legality and regularity of receipts and expenditure.

Its reports on the implementation of policy are sometimes very influential in redirecting programmes and changing procedures. The European Investment Bank was established by the Treaty of Rome to assist the balanced development of the Community by raising finance through normal commercial channels, which is then used to fund priority investment projects for the Community. Its funds go to support regional development, infrastructure, technological development, and EC projects in the Third World.

CHAPTER 2

COUNTRY STUDIES

1. BELGIUM

1.1 Key Indicators

Area	30,519 sq. km
Population	9.92 million
Head of State	HM King Baudouin
Languages	Dutch, German and French
Main Cities	Brussels 1,000,000
	Antwerp 480,000
	Ghent 235,000
	Charleroi 210,000
	Liège 200,000
	Bruges 120,000
Currency	100 centimes= 1 Belgian Franc
Average Exchange Rate 1989	39.40 Francs per dollar

1.2 Economy 1989

Total GDP(US$bn)	164.75
Real GDPGrowth	4.5%
Inflation	3.1%
Unemployment	8.5%
Exports (US$bn)	96.55
Imports (US$bn)	94.75

1.3 General Introduction

The Belgian economy has had to grapple in the post-war period with the fact that it has few natural resources (other than coal) and the major problem of having to end its over-reliance on those staple heavy manufacturing industries, such as steel, coal and textiles, which were the backbone of the economy. At the same time the Belgian economy is prey to international pressures because of its reliance on imports of most raw materials and foodstuffs and the need to export most industrial output even from staple industries. Belgium has also had the added difficulty of being politically, socially and geographically divided between the poorer Catholic French (Wallonia) and the wealthier Protestant Dutch (Flemish) and German speakers.

1.4 Post-War Economic Growth

Initial post-war prosperity in Belgium was based on the realization that it was not able to survive successfully as an independent economic entity. Similarly the USA, through its Marshall Aid programme, encouraged the Benelux countries to merge together to create a single integrated trading bloc. To this end the Belgian government created a customs union with Luxembourg and the Netherlands in January 1948 and was a founding member of the ECSC in 1951. This desire for collaborative union was eventually formalized into the Benelux Economic Union in November 1960, by which time the Benelux countries had become inaugural members of the EC in 1957. The result of these measures was that all trade between the three Benelux countries was tariff-free by the mid-1950s. Moreover the union also provided for the free movement of services, capital and peoples from each country and the harmonization of national economic policies. The main benefit to the Belgium economy was, of course, that this union immediately extended the size of the domestic market.

Given that Belgium was not primarily an agricultural country in 1945, it had, initially, to rely on the exports of traditional manufacturing industries. The major industrial sectors were heavy engineering and metal working (one-third of manufacturing output and the major export earner), steel (around Liege and Charleroi), coal, shipbuilding, Antwerp-based oil and chemicals (15% of manufacturing output), textiles, clothing and glass making. As a result in the 1950s its growth performance was not as successful as those EC countries which had the advantage of being able to shift the balance of their economy out of primary and heavy manufacturing products into consumer and service sector products. The performance of the Belgian economy picked up in the 1960s as it began to diversify into consumer, high technology and service (especially trade and distribution) industries - especially in the northern Flanders region - and growth rates were somewhat higher than the rest of Western Europe until 1973. The decision by a number of major US and European car manufacturers to locate assembly plants in the Ghent area of Flanders is symptomatic of this trend from the 1960s onwards.

The structure of Belgian industry is characterized by one or two large holding groups and a plethora of smaller and medium size firms below. One of the largest engineering groups is the industrial and financial holding company, Société Générale de Belgique. This is, like most major Belgian companies, privately rather than publicly owned. Other firms in this sector include Tractebel and Groupe Brussels Lambert. In chemicals the major firm is Solvay; though there is considerable German, French, Italian and US participation.

1.5 Post-War Recession

The initial response of the Belgian government to the first oil shock after 1973 was to retain existing economic policies in line with other West European economies. This involved maintaining high levels of public expenditure to counterbalance the fall in the level of demand and to mitigate, through social programmes, the worst consequences of rising unemployment. In particular the government pursued a policy of indexing wage rates to inflation levels. Not surprisingly this led to burgeoning public expenditure, rising inflation and escalating public sector deficits. After 1982 and the consequences of the second oil shock, which was accompanied by increased international competition from newly industrializing economies in the very staple industries which had been the basis of post-war prosperity, the Belgian government was forced into painful restructuring policies in staple industries and severe austerity in public expenditure commitments as it strove to shift the balance in the economy away from consumption and into investment. The main policy instruments after 1982 were increases in personal direct and indirect tax burdens (though corporation tax was lowered), cuts in public expenditure and welfare programmes and severe wage restraint policies in the public sector.

The central government initiated a programme of rationalizing and restructuring in the steel, coal, glass, textiles and shipbuilding industries. This led to the development of a ten-year programme in 1984 which aimed to merge and rationalize the Belgian and Luxembourg steel industries. Restructuring in the short term was to be aided by public subsidies to the major steel firms in Belgium (Cockerill-Sambre) and Luxembourg (ARBED). The coal industry also had to be rationalized despite the increase in energy prices associated with the oil crisis. This was because, while the Belgian economy was dependent on oil for much of its energy needs, the high cost of recovering increasingly inaccessible coal reserves made it uneconomic even with prices of oil rising. In order to offset oil import dependency the Belgian political parties appear to have arrived at a consensus on the need to encourage some nuclear power development rather than exploit coal reserves. Despite these efforts oil imports still account for up to 40% of energy consumption.

As a result of these and other public sector rationalization programmes unemployment rose to 14% of the workforce in the mid-1980s, declining to 10% thereafter and then remaining static at this level despite government attempts to reduce the total via job creation schemes. Growth rates also deteriorated until 1987 when they stood at a mere 1.5%, at a time when other EC countries were experiencing much higher performance. Since 1987, however, there has been considerable improvement in economic growth as the medicine of austerity has been digested.

One of the major problems with this recession was not just that it affected particular industries but that these traditional manufacturing industries tended to be located in French-speaking Wallonia. The relative prosperity of the Flanders and Dutch-speaking region, even through the early 1980s recession, has exacerbated linguistic, cultural and political tensions in Belgian society.

After 1984 there appears to have been some economic recovery, especially in the northern Flanders region and especially in the services sectors which now account for 70% of all economic activity. This had the unfortunate consequence that it further exacerbated the tensions between the different cultural and linguistic groups in the country. Nevertheless, the sensitiveness of the Belgian economy to the world market was generally rewarded from the mid-1980s onwards as the price of oil fell and the franc depreciated against a stronger US $. As a result growth rates averaged 4% in 1988 and 1989, inflation was contained within a fairly tight 1% to 3% band and unemployment fell from around 10% to 9%. There is little doubt that the decision to join the EMS in the early 1980s and pay the price in reduced wage levels (they generally fell in real terms between 1982 and 1985 while free collective bargaining was not allowed until 1986) and increased unemployment this necessitated, as inflation was squeezed out of the economy, was largely responsible for this improved competitive performance. As a result there has been a marked improvement in industrial investment and the stringency of public expenditure controls has assisted in sustaining a trade surplus over the last few years.

The resolve of political parties to maintain the commitment to reduce the public deficits run up during the late 1970s and early 1980s was also sustained. Even the election of a centre-left coalition in 1988 did not fundamentally undermine this commitment. The budget deficit was reduced from around 15% of GDP to 8% between 1983 and 1987 and the new government continued the all party consensus that has seen commitments to reducing the huge public sector debt (130% of GDP in 1988), tax reform, regional decentralization of political and economic structures and job creation schemes as the central planks of policy for the early 1990s. The centre-left coalition also maintained the privatization programme which had been formulated to assist in raising revenue and reducing public borrowing.

1.6 The Challenges of the 1990s

The Belgian economy is heavily reliant on trade with the EC. Well over 70% of trade is directed within the Community countries. This makes it a favourable location site for inward investment, especially for trade and distribution which is the major element of the service sector in the economy. It also has the added attraction of Brussels being the site of the major EC institutions. This has led to a boom in residential and commercial property development in the capital. While this may assist some sectors of the economy - especially services - it has also had the consequence of increasing the costs of living and increased inflationary pressures in the economy as too much money chases too few locational opportunities.

The Belgian state's political and social divisions provide acute problems for the continuation of the programme of reducing public sector debt. The political solution to the cultural divisions within the country has been to decentralize even greater power to the regions. Now the regions control 40% of all public expenditure and this makes it much more difficult for the government to control the huge public sector debts and spending programmes which have destabilised the economy since the 1970s. While there has been some success in reducing public expenditure nationally in 1989 and 1990 the overall level of public indebtedness (at 130% of GDP) remains the second highest in Western Europe. This will lead to higher levels of interest rates than might be desirable to stimulate economic activity in the 1990s and there is always the possibility that the interest on the debt could make public sector indebtedness self-perpetuating. This might cause horrendous problems for interest rate and public expenditure policy in the future. Even the government believes that it could take 15 years to sort the problem out.

Despite political, ideological and religious divisions which militate against unity and effectiveness Belgium is a highly unionized country. There was a history of successful competitive wage bargaining in the 1970s based on free collective bargaining. This was a major factor in explaining the lack of competitiveness of Belgian industry in the 1970s because wage rates were high relative to productivity and governments initially accepted the need to index wage rates to inflation. While the early 1980s recession has destroyed much of the power of the unions it is still too early to say whether this is a temporary or permanent phenomenon. There have continued to be major strikes organized by the unions to challenge government retrenchment and reconstruction policies in recent years.

Given its strategic location, the number of skilled workers and some of the highest personal tax rates (55% top rate) in the EC, it is likely that Belgium will remain primarily as a location site for distribution, assembly and trade rather than as a site for manufacturing industry in the future of the Community. Manufacturing now accounts only for around 20% of GDP with services taking the bulk of the share of output at 70%. Belgium, especially in the region around Brussels, is fast becoming a relatively expensive locational site - though it still has a long way to go to catch up with price levels in Britain. Belgium has since 1982 granted considerable tax benefits to expatriates and up to 1992 to foreign multinational companies setting up an office with at least 10 staff and this has obviously had a beneficial impact on inward investment. As the capital of the EC Brussels will also continue to enjoy increasing head office locational cache in the 1990s.

2. DENMARK

2.1 Key Indicators

Area	43,092 sq. km
Population	5.13 million
Head of State	Queen Margrethe II
Language	Danish
Main Cities	Copenhagen 1,344,500
	Aarhus 260,000
	Odense 175,000
	Aalborg 55,000
	Esbjerg 82,000
	Randers 62,000
Currency	Krone=100 Ore
Average Exchange	
Rate 1989	Dkr 7.31 per dollar

2.2 Economy 1989

Total GDP (US$bn)	104.5
Real GDP Growth	1.1%
Inflation	4.8%
Unemployment	9.4%
Exports (US$bn)	28.6
Imports (US$bn)	26.2

2.3 General Introduction

Although it is only a small country of 5 million people Denmark has one of the highest per capita incomes in the OECD countries. This post-war success was mainly caused by the shift out of agriculture and the creation of a manufacturing and service economy. Denmark has also become a significant trading nation, assisted by the close proximity of the strong Swedish and German markets. The US and the UK and the remaining EC countries are its other major trading partners.

Despite this Denmark retains a number of structural problems which may cause difficulties in the 1990s. The post-war growth resulted in a large public sector which accounts for over 20% of GDP, wage rates are high and industry is still relatively small in relation to the export earnings necessary to generate high living standards. As a result unemployment is relatively high and the level of wage rates undermines export competitiveness. This does not help an economy which has the highest per capita debt in the world.

2.4 Post-War Economic Growth

For the early post-war years Denmark was governed by the Social Democratic Party, often in coalition with smaller parties thrown up by the multi-party proportional representation system instituted in 1953. It was not until 1968 when a Conservative coalition came to power as a minority government that this social democratic consensus was challenged. Since then there has been very little political consensus and tremendous fragmentation of parties in Denmark.

The shift out of agriculture was the major feature of the post-war boom years. In 1950 21% of the population were employed in agriculture; by 1986 this figure was down to 4%. But it was the late, but rapid, shift into services which is the most startling development in this period. By the 1980s services accounted for almost 70% of GDP; while agriculture amounted to only 5% and primary commodity production was responsible for only around 7% of GDP. Despite this the traditional strength of intensive farming of bacon, beef and cheese has continued and up to 65% of agricultural produce is normally exported. Shipping however has historically been a major invisible earner and continues to be so.

Denmark's post-war prosperity also owed a great deal to the dramatic increase in manufacturing industry in the boom years between 1960 and 1973 when the economy grew at around 4.5% per annum. Although it is still small compared with the relative size of manufacturing in other EC economies the Danish have built up a diversified industrial structure which accounts for approximately 65% of total exports. Even so at only 20% of total GDP the relatively small size of the industrial base is one of the main reasons for import penetration and trade deficits.

The manufacturing base of the economy grew first out of its relationship with agricultural and fishing industry. Thus shipbuilding, food processing, tobacco and brewing are major industries. Agricultural machinery is also significant and there is a diversified iron and metal industry. Paper, printing, publishing and chemicals are also well established. The sector is however dominated by small and medium size firms and there is a lack of extremely large corporations. This makes Danish industry somewhat unique in the EC and helps to account for the relatively low export volume in production and low technology levels in products.

The political supremacy of the Social Democrats to 1968 and the protectionist traditions within the society and economy historically ensured that economic growth would be translated into a commitment to high levels of public welfare and expenditure. As a result up to 30% of the workforce have been employed in the public sector. Interestingly, apart from utilities, transport and telecommunications, there has been no history of public sector involvement in industry. The public role has primarily been a service and welfare one. This increase in public services was not a major problem in this period; it was however to become a significant problem after 1973 when the level of private investment failed to create sufficient export industries to offset the huge public debt which had been run up in the boom years and which was sustained initially after 1973. The current account deficit is primarily a function of debt service financing.

2.5 Post-War Recession

In 1973 Denmark was one of those countries which was almost totally dependent on imported oil for its energy needs. Around 95% of energy requirements came from oil imports and an aggressive policy of exploitation of off-shore oil and gas deposits in the North Sea has seen dependency decline to only 30% by the end of the 1980s. This has been a major success story but it also occasioned serious adjustment problems over the two decades as growth rates fell to 1.5% and unemployment rose.

Initially governments attempted to borrow and spend their way out of the stagflationary consequences of the crisis. In part this was inevitable given the past commitments to social democratic welfare and pay indexation policies. Unfortunately this was to create debt servicing problems in the late 1980s. The real crisis for the economy came after 1979 with the second oil shock when unemployment rose to 10%, trade deficits became endemic and government spending deficits accelerated.

The proper management of economic affairs was also not assisted by the fact that the Social Democratic Party lost office after 1968 and gradually lost popular support to more radical socialists on the left and a range of issue and populist parties in the centre. Political instability ensued for much of the 1970s with the Liberals in power between 1972 and 1975; the Social Democrats between 1975 and 1978 and a coalition of the two between 1978 and 1979. In all cases these were minority governments and this continued until 1982 when a four-party coalition was created under Poul Schluter. Schluter has dominated Danish governments throughout the 1980s.

Agriculture continued to decline in significance relative to other sectors, although the decision to join the EC in 1973 had a profound effect on the size of agricultural output and the efficiency of production. Denmark had always practised intensive farming techniques but the CAP subsidies stimulated even more land cultivation and output by encouraging smaller farms to set up and survive. Unfortunately after the second oil shock, when interest rates rose rapidly, many small farms went bankrupt and rural unemployment increased. The result has been a conscious attempt by governments to encourage agricultural investment and the formation of larger units via acquisition.

There was, as elsewhere, an initial attempt to mitigate the worst effects of the first and second oil shocks by state intervention and government subsidy. This was particularly marked in the hard hit shipbuilding sector which has been in decline since 1984. In recent years however the government has decided to reduce such blanket public subsidy and in practice has tried to limit public aid to high-tech pharmaceutical, medical equipment, electronics and information technology companies in an attempt to diversify the economic structure and encourage inward investment. In 1982 the Conservative-led government headed by Schluter also introduced a more financially orthodox policy regime involving a six-month wage freeze to combat the evils of the 1970s and early 1980s - budget deficits, inflation and unemployment. This required a policy of reducing both trade and public sector deficits and could only be achieved by holding tax rates and cutting wage rates and welfare programmes. This also involved sticking to a high exchange rate regime and accepting levels of unemployment which, at close to 10% of the workforce, were higher than had been the norm since 1945.

By 1986, assisted by the world recovery, these measures bore fruit and a budget surplus was recorded for the first time since 1974. Between 1983 and 1986 there was a strong growth performance at 3.5% per annum and by 1988 the trade deficits on current account was significantly reduced and exports improved. The financial services sector also improved its performance due to deregulation and liberalization measures at the same time. Despite this the country continued to run a small trade deficit and faced difficulties in financing the accumulated foreign debt incurred by high borrowing governments between 1973 and 1982. There was also a problem with relatively high wage rates and low productivity after 1987. Similarly the revaluation of the krone after the cumulative devaluations in the 1970s and early 1980s as a consequence of EMS membership created problems of international competitiveness for industry. This helps to explain the continuation of trade deficits into the 1990s despite the measures adopted by the Schluter governments.

2.6 The Challenges of the 1990s

Tax rates in Denmark are amongst the highest in the world because unemployment and welfare benefits are not paid for on a contributory basis; they are paid for solely out of income and other tax revenues. The Conservative government in 1990 announced the most radical cuts in tax rates this century. The top rate of personal tax was cut from 68% to 52%. Corporation tax was reduced to 40% from 50% and VAT was also reduced significantly although it is still high at 22%. This indicates a willingness by the government to take seriously the need to stimulate inward investment and reduce historically high welfare programmes in order to encourage market disciplines and harmonise with EC tax levels. Despite this, fragmentation of political alliances means that the government may fail to achieve these and other reforms - like structural changes in social welfare - fully.

There will continue to be relatively higher interest rates in Denmark than in other EC countries as it strives to reduce its public debts by 1992. This may attract short-term capital flows to the economy but it makes it more difficult to encourage investment in manufacturing. This is the pressing need for the future but it is not assisted by either interest rates or very high costs of living. Prices are extremely high by EC standards even for primary and agricultural products.

The prospects for the Danish economy in the future are not good even if one discounts the effects of the high levels of public debt and unemployment. Growth rates are likely to remain low and industry needs a fundamental restructuring for which there will be strong domestic opposition. There has been some merger activity increase since 1988 but in general large companies are few in number. The largest are the conglomerate groups, A.P.Moller and D/S Svenborg. The largest financial institution is the Den Danske Bank High; while the major industrial firms are Carlsberg, Danisco, FLS Industries, Novo Nordisk and ISS.

3. FRANCE

3.1 Key Indicators

Area	549,965 sq. km
Population	56.4 million
Head of State	President François Mitterrand
Language	French
Main Cities	Paris 2,200,000
	Marseilles 880,000
	Lyons 420,000
	Toulouse 355,000
	Nice 340,000
	Strasbourg 253,000
Currency	100 centimes = 1 Franc
Average Exchange Rate 1989	6.38 Francs per dollar

3.2 Economy

Total GDP ($bn)	961.7
Real GDP growth	3.9%
Unemployment	9.4%
Inflation	3.6%
Exports	23.0
Imports	-22.9

3.3 General Introduction

After the Second World War France was very much an undeveloped and protected agricultural economy. Since then it has been transformed into a modern economy and one of the top five exporting nations in the world. Much of this success came in the period between 1960 and

1973, when growth rates were only surpassed by Japan. Since 1973 there has been a gradual decline in economic performance with the worst of the recession being experienced in the period between 1979 and 1985. After 1985, growth performance has not matched that of the boom years and there was a relative stagnation in productivity and output growth. Since 1989 there has been a return to prosperity with growth rates rising to 4% and inflation being contained. Unemployment and trade imbalances remain the most worrying long-term problems.

The major problem for the French state has been twofold in the post-war period. First France was still a largely agrarian economy in the 1940s and 1950s and its ownership structures in agriculture and industry were highly fragmented and diversified. Thus the multiplicity of ownership and small scale of industry led to parochialism and a 'patronat' (or family owned) system which militated against economies of scale in investment and technology and left French industry relatively uncompetitive and prey to overseas competition.

The restructuring of the French economy traditionally has been through an active state interventionist role and the creation of highly diversified industrial groups or conglomerates. State planning has normally taken the form of five-year plans, a substantial state role in controlling finance through the nationalized banking system and through state owned industries and state financed infrastructure projects and contracts (especially for public procurement). The state also facilitated industrial mergers and acquisitions, particularly in the 1960s and 1970s, in order to aid concentration. Despite the obvious success of state policy in the boom years, in the more constrained environment of the 1980s the state's role has come under some criticism and the more draconian and statist solutions of the government, led by Mitterrand's Socialist Party, have been substantially scaled down in favour of a shift towards open markets, privatization, competitiveness and liberalization. The proper role for the French state in the economy remains a key issue for the 1990s.

3.5 Post-War Economic Growth

The single most important statistic which helps to explain France's shift into a high growth and industrially competitive economy by the 1960s is the decline in the number of agricultural workers. From 36% of the workforce in 1946, by the late 1980s agricultural workers amounted to less than 7% and contributed only around 4% of GDP. There is little doubt that part of the explanation for France's relatively high growth rates per annum of between 5-6% in the 1960s and 1970s was this belated shift which took place towards technological and industrial expansion.

It is perhaps no coincidence that this transformation took place under the aegis of De Gaulle's leadership, the foundation of the 5th Republic and the willing membership of the EC after 1957. Prior to the Algerian war and the reconstituted and more centrally and elite controlled political system which De Gaulle created, the French political system had been characterized by 'immobilisme'. This meant that the multi-party system failed to create enduring coalitions and economic policy was a constant battleground between short-term and parochial interests. After 1958 De Gaulle centralized power and provided the impetus for the French planning system, which had been struggling to modernize the economy, to force through radical state led reconstruction and infrastructure investment (especially for railways and telecommunications).

This contributed, along with the modernization of agriculture, to some of the highest growth rates in Western Europe and the world between 1960 and 1979. France became not only a major exporter of agricultural and vinicultural products, but also began to emerge as an exporter of high technological industrial products, as well as haute couture. The opening up of the EC market was also a major stimulus to French development in such diverse areas as aviation (Dessault and Matra), mechanical and electronic engineering (Thomson), textiles, chemicals (Rhône Poulenc) and food processing. France's major trading partners since the 1950s have been mainly European - in particular Germany, Italy and Belgium - although Britain and the USA have been of growing importance in recent years.

3.6 The Post-War Recession

The 1973 oil crisis hit the French economy hard because it was heavily reliant on oil imports. The apparently effortless ability of the French state to generate planned growth now came to an end abruptly. Between 1973 and 1979 growth rates were low at 3% on average; but this was respectable given growth rates in the rest of the world at this time. After 1979 however the French economy began to stagnate dramatically with growth rates of around 1.5% per annum. There was no effective turnaround until after 1988 by which time there had been something of a sea change in the attitude of the Socialist government about economic policy and the role of the state.

As a result after 1973 the French state appeared to be confused about what it ought to do. It tended to oscillate between ideological extremes until a consensus of sorts was arrived at after 1985. At first, along with many other countries, the French government, led by Giscard D'Estaing and Raymond Barre in the mid-1970s, came to appreciate that it was no longer possible to continue with past statist policies. The government therefore began to draw up plans to restructure the state's dominant role in industrial and financial affairs, which had seen 80% of the banking system in public hands and a substantial amount (between 30% and 40%) of all industrial investment being located in the public sector. It was the state in the 1970s which was responsible for the initiation of high profile investment projects in the railways (the TGV), France Telecom (telecommunications) and Electricité de France (the nuclear programme).

Many of these proposals for change were not however fully implemented because, in response to the crisis engendered by the second oil shock in 1979, France voted for a Socialist government which intended to expand rather than reduce the state's role in the economy. Mitterand's government was true to its word and nationalized further areas of the banking system, chemicals (Rhône Poulenc), electricity (Compagnie Generale d'Electricité), metals (Péchiney), computers (Honeywell-Bull), telecommunications (CGCT), defence and arms firms (Matra and Dassault), steel (Usinor and Sacilor) and glass and pipe manufacture (Saint Gobain). This brought the government's share of industry to 24%. The government also tried to spend its way out of the recession by high levels of subsidies to industry, welfare expenditure and unemployment relief. This policy mix could not be made to work in the fierce economic climate of the early 1980s and the development of huge trade deficits and a run on the Franc in 1981/82 quickly brought this experiment to a close.

Since 1982 the Mitterrand government has adopted many of the restructuring and rationalization programmes first initiated under D'Estaing. In particular there have been cuts in state spending and a major reduction in direct subsidies to state owned companies. This has forced those firms which have remained publicly owned - like Renault (cars), Aérospatiale and Snecma (aerospace and aero-engines),Charbonnages de France (coal) and Usinor Sacilor (steel) - to rationalize, restructure and end overmanning in order to become competitive in world markets. For other firms in the public sector the belated understanding of the need to become more profitable led eventually, under the political cohabitation of the Chirac and Socialist governments from 1986 onwards, to their eventual privatization at large profit to the state. This has been followed by the liberalization of the same banking system which had originally been nationalized in 1982. Even the ending of cohabitation in 1988, when the Socialists obtained an independent governing role again, did not see a return to nationalization.

By the end of the 1980s it was clear that the Mitterrand government had dropped a considerable amount of its ideological baggage and had come to adopt many of the rationalization and anti-statist policies of the liberal and rightwing opposition. This was not however totally at the expense of state led intervention. The French state continues to play an active planning role in such areas as nuclear energy - which at 70% of total consumption has seen the most extensive oil substitution policy of any of the OECD countries since 1973 - transport infrastructure (the TGV and Channel Tunnel) and tourism (a major foreign currency earner). Thus it would be true to say that the French state appears to have adopted a fairly pragmatic approach to managing the post-oil shock economy. After flirting with statism it has now accepted the need to rationalize French industry and end overmanning; but it continues to afford the state an active and important role in key areas of economic life.

3.7 The Challenges of the 1990s

Despite the success in dropping ideological policy the performance of the French economy at the end of the 1980s and into the 1990s still leaves something to be desired. Growth rates appear to have stagnated somewhat and there have been growing signs of deficits on industrial trade. In this light agricultural exports and tourism - both major foreign currency earners - are of crucial importance for the standard of living and well-being of the economy. Unfortunately the EC subsidies associated with the CAP, which have contributed mightily to the modernization and income support of French agriculture, are now under threat and even the French state is having to look at encouraging farmers to take land out of cultivation. This may be expected to pose serious problems for the balance of French trade if either subsidies are substantially reduced or GATT agreements expose French farming to a harsh competitive environment.

While tourism and arms manufacture have contributed significantly in recent years to trade performance there are fears that France's industrial structure is not as competitive as it needs to be to survive in an open trading world market. As a result, since 1982 there have been almost continuous trade deficits, especially in industrial products. The deficit was as high as £9.3 billion in 1982 and was still at £4.5 billion in 1989 despite severe retrenchment by the government and with unemployment rates apparently static at the 9% to 10% level. There had been a small surplus in 1986 but this was not sustained to the end of the decade as industrial competitiveness deteriorated. Perhaps one bright spot has been the government's ability to keep inflation within a narrow 2% to 4% band over recent years.

The French government appears to place great reliance on the trade imbalance on current and industrial account being solved by a major increase in service earnings in the 1990s. In particular the government expects tourism to continue to play an expanding role and that Paris will become a major financial centre. While the former expectation is likely to be achieved, it is probably over-optimistic to expect the small and under capitalized French Bourse to oust either London or Frankfurt as the main European financial centre in the near future. The government also appears to be hoping that the Single Market after 1992 will also provide major opportunities for French industry. This may be an illusion; however it is clear that France sees itself very much as a fully fledged and permanent member of the EC and is prepared to countenance high interest rate levels to sustain the French franc within the EMS.

The structure of French trade is also some cause for concern because it is substantially in deficit with most of the industrialized world and only in surplus with the Third World. The French success in former colonial markets has been built on the back of cheap government credit and export subsidies and this is now being restrained. Furthermore the increased problems facing developing countries in raising credit and the inroads that Far Eastern countries are making in those sectors (like electronics, textiles, cars and arms sales) which the French specialized in may well significantly affect France's traditional export markets. If this is the case the picture may be bleak in the short term. Ironically this export dependency may in part explain the somewhat muted and aberrant role played by the French in foreign policy - especially with African and Middle Eastern countries during the Gulf crisis. The plain fact of the matter is that France is heavily dependent on these overseas markets for its economic survival.

Perhaps the crucial question for the future of France is whether the relative stagnation of the late 1980s is merely evidence of a slow-down in its previous success as the industrial base restructures for the new competitive environment of the future or whether it is the beginning of a gradual decline in the economy. The risks may appear to be weighted on the pessimistic side as the guarantee of assured public procurement contracts and the lack of protection for industry in the Single Market may well see further rationalization of industry and the relatively high tax regime at close to 50% may undermine long-term inward investment. In 1990 however the government did begin to reduce the very high rates of VAT and has promised action to bring corporation tax in line with that prevailing elsewhere in Europe.

On the other hand France is a congenial environment to live and work in - as its tourist boom demonstrates - and it may be that the more relaxed attitude of the government to inward investment may presage a sustained increase in foreign investment. After all France is a large and still underpopulated country with relatively low land and property prices when compared with many other advanced EC countries. Furthermore, there has been evidence of renewed economic growth in 1989 and 1990 at the 3% to 4% per annum level. One explanation for this may be that the stagnation of the late 1980s and poor trade performance was primarily due to heavy capital investment by French firms as they geared up for the more competitive environment engendered by 1992. Indeed it would appear that both the public and private sector firms in France seem to have been adopting an aggressive EC and US wide strategy of acquisitions. This may augur well for French industrial performance in the public and private sectors after 1992. On the other hand there is evidence that in the last 18 months French companies may have been suffering from high indebtedness due to the borrowings incurred to finance the wave of acquisitions in Europe and the US. French companies have been some of the most active corporate raiders and, given the recession on the horizon, it may well be that some firms may find themselves over-exposed in the early 1990s.

4. GERMANY

4.1 Key Indicators

Area	138,000 sq.km
Population	79 million
Head of State	Richard von Weizsächer
Language	German
Main Cities	Berlin (3,300,000)
	Hamburg (1,600,000)
	Munich (1,200,000)
	Cologne (940,000)
	Frankfurt (630,000)
	Essen (620,000)
Currency	100 Pfennig = 1 D-Mark
Average Exchange	
Rate 1989	1.88 DM per dollar

4.2 Economy 1989

Total GDP (US$bn)	1,147.06
Real GDP Growth	4.0%
Inflation	3.9%
Unemployment	7.0%
Exports (US$bn)	406.0
Imports (US$bn)	314.0

4.3 General Introduction

The Federal Republic of Germany experienced something of an economic miracle after 1948 when it used Marshall Aid to reconstruct a war devastated economy. The first major downturn came in 1967 when the Social Democrats came into office for the first time since the war. Since then the German economy has weathered the storms of the oil crises and world recession remarkably successfully. This owes a great deal to the close relationship between financial institutions and leading industrial enterprises.

Germany, of course, is experiencing a rapid transformation as a consequence of the reunification with the territories of the former Democratic Republic of Germany in the East. This will impose severe burdens on the German economy in the 1990s and may undermine the relative economic miracle which has been experienced in the Federal Republic since the 1950s. This short survey will outline the main factors behind Germany's post-war economic growth and point to some of the major issues which will have to be addressed in the 1990s.

4.4 Post-War Economic Growth

The recovery of West Germany's economy began in 1948 when a central bank and national currency were created in the aftermath of the occupation after the Second World War. The period between then and the first post-war recession in 1967 was one of sustained economic growth characterized by low inflation, full employment and rising material living standards. In this initial period of growth the engine of recovery was the industrial and manufacturing sector of the economy which accounted for over 50% of GDP in the 1960s. Much of the increase in output was generated by initial reconstruction of the war devastated economy and then by the recovery of lost export markets. The economy was also characterized by high levels of investment and productivity. The West German State and concentrated Universal Banks were particularly active in creating long-term credit institutions - the KfW (Reconstruction and Development Loan Corporation) - to channel Marshall Aid into industrial investment. The initial recovery was also assisted by the fact that the FRG had substantial reserves of coal and lignite which provided a ready source of relatively cheap energy. By the 1960s this source of supply had been replaced by cheap oil imports resulting in something of a contraction in the coal-mining industry.

The Adenauer and Erhard governments adopted a policy of social market economics. This meant a privately owned economy supported by a close co-operative infrastructure of indirect collaboration between social and economic partners (business, finance and labour) backed by a limited state role in the economy. The state provided social infrastructure but only when the domestic economy was strong enough to allow for social consumption. The success of this policy was testified to by the reduction of unemployment from 2 million in 1950 to full employment and the need for guest workers in the 1960s, and by the continuing high growth rates until the 1970s recession. The highly organized and disciplined industrial relations and collective bargaining system has also contributed to this success. There are only 16 trade unions in Germany affiliated to the DGB. This has ensured relative labour discipline since the Second World War. Similarly the concentration of banking and finance into Universal Banks (the Big 3 are the Deutsche Bank, the Dresdner Bank and the Commerzbank) and their historic close ties with industrial firms has also limited the short-term speculative nature of investment in the FRG economy and the scope for equity or bond finance.

In agriculture there was a gradual decrease of people working on the land and a decline in the sector's overall importance to the performance of the economy. In the 1950s there was a large shift of labour out of agriculture into industry assisting in the growth performance of the economy. This is revealed by the fact that the overall number of farms was reduced by half between 1945 and 1986. The overall importance of the sector declined from 5.8 % of GDP in 1960 to 1.5% in 1986. Despite this the sector has been heavily subsidized through the Common Agriculture Policy of the EC and via government protection; as a result over-production has replaced former food shortages by the 1980s. Between 1950 and the mid-1980s agricultural output in the FRG doubled, enabling the domestic industry to meet 90% of German domestic food needs and to become a net export earner.

The German economy is heavily dependent on foreign trade of which close to 70% is with other European countries. The EC countries account for approximately 50% of all exports. The major industrial sectors in the Federal Republic are chemicals, electronics and mechanical and auto-engineering. In chemicals the main firms are Bayer, Veba, Degussa, Hoechst and BASF; in electronics Siemens and Bosch dominate; in mechanical engineering the top firms are MAN, Thyssen, Krupps and Mannesman; in auto-engineering BMW, VW-Audi, Adam-Opel and Daimler-Benz dominate. Industrial manufacturing produces approximately 35% of GNP and is a major export earner accounting for around 80% of exports. This industrial export performance is crucial because the FRG has experienced a deficit on invisible earnings throughout most of the period. This outflow has traditionally been accounted for by two phenomena: remittances home by guest workers and expenditure on holidays abroad.

In the field of political economy the FRG was administered by fairly conservative administrations until the 1967 recession. These Christian Democratic governments tended to limit public spending and keep federal deficits low in line with their desire to see a social market economy characterized by limited direct state economic involvement. It was only after 1967 when the SDP came into government that a more interventionist attitude was adopted but this was never taken so far as to undermine the essentially privately owned and controlled economic structure in the Federal Republic.

4.4 The Post-War Recession

Like the rest of the OECD countries the difficulties which began to be experienced in the late 1960s were sustained in the 1970s. The FRG experienced higher levels of inflation and unemployment and lower levels of growth than had been experienced in the 1950s and early 1960s. The Bundesbank was also forced to attack inflationary pressures actively through a policy of high interest rates between 1970 and 1980.

The oil crisis revealed a major structural problem facing the German economy. This was the dependence on imported oil supplies. The FRG has worked vigorously and perhaps more successfully than any other OECD country since then to remove oil dependency from its economy. It immediately commenced a programme of over-producing coal after the second oil shock in 1979 to create a strategic coal stockpile. Nuclear sources of supply have been increased and gas imports from the USSR were encouraged. The over-production of coal and lignite came to an end by the middle of the 1980s as oil prices fell. Coal mining has witness severe retrenchment along with steel and shipbuilding since then. This may create serious difficulties for the Ruhr, Saar and Aachen regions in the 1990s. Despite this coal and lignite are still likely to remain as major energy resources along with nuclear fuels rather than imported oil supplies which were down to 2% of consumption in 1986 from 15% in 1970.

Despite rising unemployment in the mid-1980s and historically high post-war inflation levels (7%) the FRG was able to improve its industrial and manufacturing output in the period. Between 1970 and 1986 it more than doubled manufacturing income. This was achieved however at the expense of jobs to the tune of almost 2 million. There has been an increase in information technology and service related industry but this has not counterbalanced the loss of jobs in manufacturing were capital intensive investment has replaced labour intensive production creating a guest worker and unskilled unemployment problem. The two major industries experiencing decline have been steel and construction.

Despite these adjustment problems the overall trade balance of the FRG has been extremely healthy when compared with most other OECD countries. The FRG had a trade deficit in the 1950s but has worked assiduously to remove this and by the mid-1980s had a healthy trade surplus, revealing the country's reliance on export markets for its overall economic performance. In 1988 import expenditure was DM 439,768 million and export earnings were running at DM 567,750 million. This improved performance in the mid-1980s came after a period of trade deficits between 1979 and 1983. There is little doubt that this turnaround came as a result of the depreciation of the D-mark against the US$ between 1981 and 1985 and the fall of the cost of oil after 1982 which had a major impact on the current account.

Other contributory factors are of course the continuing strength in the value of the currency supported by the independent Bundesbank and by the willingness of governments of all persuasions to limit government spending in line with overall economic performance. Despite this general tendency after 1967, and due to the oil crisis and recessions of the 1970s, the Federal governments led by the SPD and, later in the 1980s by the CDU, have had to accept larger budgetary deficits than in the 1950s and early 1960s. The SPD were brought down politically as a result of this in 1982 when their coalition partners, the FDP, joined the CDU over the issue of further reducing government spending at a time of rising unemployment. Chancellor Kohl after 1982 worked hard to reduce budget deficits to the DM 25 million level. This was achieved in 1986 but slippage occurred in the late 1980s and is likely again in the 1990s as a consequence of reunification.

4.6 The Challenges of the 1990s

The first major challenge of reunification will of course be the budget deficit which the CDU had hoped to contain at the DM 25 billion level prior to reunification. The influx, first, of refugees from the East and then the reunification in late 1990 have seriously impaired the government's ability to maintain this budgetary policy. The increase in expenditure that has seen the public sector deficit rise to DM 100 billion will either generate higher levels of inflation due to the printing of money or higher levels of interest rates which will affect investment and growth performance. The Federal government will also have the burden of financing the public sector in the Länder of the former East Germany, as well as the social costs of unemployment (which may reach 2 million in the East alone in 1991, pushing the combined total to 4 million) and retraining at a time when the competitive base of industry in the East is being undermined. There is also a huge environmental bill to be paid in the East due to the historic lack of controls over pollution by industry. It is likely that this will have to be paid for either by higher levels of tax or by earmarking German savings for the costs of reunification. The privatization of state assets is one alternative source of raising the necessary finance which the Bundesbank has recently proposed. In either case it is likely that the transition will have a short-term deleterious effect on German economic performance in which deflationary rather than inflationary tendencies appear the most likely consequence.

Despite these deflationary tendencies it is likely that the German state and business community will be prepared to pay the short-term economic price of reunification and protect its own as it has done in the past. The merger of Daimler-Benz and Messerschmitt-Bolkow-Blohm/AEG in November 1989 underscores the historical tendency to cartelization and concentration in the German economy. Over half of industrial output is derived from the top 50 industrial firms. It also indicates that the Federal Cartel Office and the German banking system can be expected to encourage defensive mergers and acquisitions to protect German industry from outside takeover whatever the competition policy of the EC. The German banking system has a long track record, going back to the 1970s rescue of VW through their opposition to the attempt by Kuwait to buy into Daimler-Benz and their rescue of AEG in the 1980s, of protecting the heart of German industry for Germany. This is derived from the historical fusion of industrial and financial capital in Germany. As a result the German state has provided subsidies to East German firms to allow them to weather the storm of increased competition from Western goods and a decline in orders for their products from Eastern European countries now buying the same Western goods.

A similar protectionist tendency can be seen in German agriculture which is unimportant to the overall performance of the economy but politically crucial to the survival of the CDU in office. As a result the government has tended to create new subsidies for farmers whenever the EC has reduced CAP subsidies since 1986. The political clout of the agricultural lobby is also partly responsible for the opposition to further reductions of the CAP which undermined the Uruguay Round of GATT talks in December 1990. The continuing need to accommodate these interests may well presage a higher level of budget deficit if the GATT talks are successful in 1991. At the same time reunification will bring into Germany the extensive agricultural lands of East Germany. This will create an additional political and economic adjustment problem as Germany already has the highest agricultural prices in

Europe and the East German agricultural system has apparently collapsed in the wake of reunification.

The German state will have to accommodate the social and political problems of reunification at the same time as it has to face increased levels of redundancy in the heavy industrial sectors of steel, coal and shipbuilding throughout the early 1990s. The formerly buoyant chemical industry is also suffering serious problems due to higher oil and raw material prices caused by the Gulf crisis. Unemployment has been rising as a result since 1988 with around 2 million unemployed in the FRG. This total has been massively increased since the reunification in 1990 posing a major policy dilemma for the government. The government has to counterbalance the demands from outside Germany for the country to adopt a more expansionary economic policy due to its strong currency and trade surplus against the internal desire to use its economic strength to mitigate the consequences of reunification. For instance it is expected that the former East German economy will actually contract by between 7% and 10% in 1990/91.

Despite all of this the German economy, with the Japanese, is one of the strongest in the world. In 1990 GNP was growing at around 4.5% (which is the highest level since 1976) with inflation at approximately 3% per annum. Industrial investment was very high at around 10% per annum in 1989 and approximately 12% in 1990. Construction investment was at 5% throughout 1989 and 1990, revealing the strength of domestic demand as an engine of growth in the new Germany over the last two years. Private consumption rose by 4.4% in 1990 after 1.7% in 1989, this boost coming from the 700,000 migrants from Eastern Europe and the Democratic Republic in the year. As a result the country experienced an increase in imports and a reduction in its trade surplus from DM 105 billion in 1989 to DM 75 billion in 1990. Nevertheless at a time of fears over global recession and the Gulf crisis the German economy continues to run a large trade surplus with the rest of the world and remains one of its strongest economic performers. An increase in oil prices due to a Gulf crisis would be serious but not as damaging as the two oil price shocks were in the 1970s. The price rises in 1990 associated with the Iraqi invasion of Kuwait led only to an increase of inflation to around 3%.

As a site for investment and productive location for outsiders Germany may well be too highly priced in terms of labour costs and rights, tax rates and regulation. As a potential market place for competitively priced goods the German economy is likely to remain the most lucrative in Europe for the foreseeable future. This raises the interesting question of whether the Länder representing the former territories of East Germany might, in the shortterm, be important locational sites for inward investment and infrastructure development. One of the key advantages - wage rates at one third of those in West Germany - has quickly been challenged however as the trade unions in the West have moved rapidly into the East negotiating between 20% and 50% wage increases at the end of 1990 and reducing the working week from 43 to 40 hours. This has led to wage rates at about 60% of those in West Germany in 1991 and moves to reduce the working week further to 35 hours. Some experts predict that there will be harmonization of working conditions and wage rates as early as 1993. These developments may militate against East Germany becoming a locational site for either European or foreign direct investment. Nevertheless even conservative forecasting bodies predict that East Germany will in the near future grow at around 7% per annum. This will provide an important vehicle for the further expansion of the whole German economy in the 1990s. If this comes about then Germany may provide the demand stimulus for the EC as a whole in the new decade.

5. GREECE

5.1 Key Indicators

Area	131,957 sq. km
Population	10,256,464
Head of State	Konstantinos Karamanlis
Language	Greek
Main Cities	Athens
	Thessalonika
Currency	Drachma
Average Exchange	
Rate 1989	139,980 Drachmas
	per 1000 dollars)

5.2 Economy 1986

Total GDP (US$bn)	1850.1
Real GDP Growth	1.3%
Inflation	9.3%
Unemployment	7.8%
Exports (US$ mn)	4539
Imports (US$ mn)	10,134

5.3 General Introduction

A long period of rapid growth in the Greek economy came to an end in 1979, and since then Greece has had almost a decade of stagnation, with virtually no growth in the period 1980-85, and an apparent process of 'de-industrialization'. After 1985, conditions showed some signs of improvement as inflation fell and profitability in industry began to pick up after several very difficult years. Greek standards of living rose steadily in the period 1950 to 1979. Though GDP per head (measured in purchasing power parity) was still only 53% of the EC average in 1987, other direct indicators such as life expectancy, infant mortality and literacy have shown spectacular improvements over the post-war period.

Greek post-war politics have been turbulent and disrupted, though in this sphere also the late 1980s gave some evidence of an increasing stability and the possible resolution of some long-standing divisions. The Civil War (1946-1949) resulted in the defeat and banning of the communists (KKE), and the establishment of a political system which added anti-communism to the traditional themes of Greek party politics - personalized factions, clientelism, direct involvement of foreign powers, and the influence of the military and the monarchy. The 1952 constitution declaring Greece a parliamentary democracy with a monarchy was followed by a decade of domination by the rightwing parties, particularly the National Radical Union (ERE) led by Constantine Karamanlis. A brief period of alternative government under the Centre Union (EK) led by George Papandreou resulted in a constitutional crisis over the role of the military in 1965. Political instability and mass political mobilization followed, but the elections scheduled for May 1967 were expected to resolve this at least temporarily with the forecast victory of the Centre Union. The military coup on 21 April 1967 pre-empted the elections, and closed down party politics and parliamentary democracy. The evident failure of the military to provide an alternative, together with the incompetence of their involvement in an abortive coup in the independent island of Cyprus, resulted in the collapse of the military regime in July 1974 and the recall of the veteran Karamanlis. The monarchy had already been dissolved by the military in June 1973. The new regime legalized the Communist Party and brought in a new constitution characterized by emphasis on civil rights together with an indirectly elected Presidency.

Since 1974, the new Greek Republic has seen alternation in power between the reformed rightwing party New Democracy (ND) under Karamanlis and a new Socialist party (PASOK) under Andreos Papandreou, son of the former leader of the Centre Union and himself an active politician in the post-war system. The strong elements of continuity with the 1952-67 regime (and indeed with the previous parliamentary tradition) have however operated within a broad consensual framework. Though bitter differences remain between the parties, erupting in occasional constitutional crises and manifested by vigorous rhetorical campaign pledges at elections, politics appears to have stabilized into a three-party system. Elections in June 1989 produced no overall majority and were followed by an unprecedented and temporary coalition between ND and the main communist party, the KKE-exterior. Elections held again in November 1989 resulted in a new government led by the ND Prime Minister Constantine Mitsotakis.

5.4 Post-war Economic Development

Between 1950 and 1979 the Greek economy grew at an average annual rate of over 6%. This was the result not only of international economic growth but also of favourable policy measures adopted particularly in the 1950s. Greek governments of the period concentrated on opening up the Greek economy to foreign trade and investment while at the same time putting public funds into the provision of infrastructure and into the modernization of the industrial and services sector. Exchange rate stability, removal of tariff and non-tariff barriers to trade, encouragement of inward investment, all contributed to a climate of confidence and growth. The share of agriculture in GDP declined relative to industry and services, though agriculture remains the largest single employment sector (27% of the active population in 1986). Two particularly striking features of the sustained growth were the very high investment ratio (consistently above 20% of GDP) and the persistence of emigration (mainly to the US) as a safety-valve in the labour market. Manufacturing and associated sectors increased, so that by 1979 basic manufactures and food processing accounted for about two-thirds of all exports of goods.

Greek foreign policy has traditionally emphasized its pivotal position between East and West, but this period of growth saw much closer links with the rest of Europe. Greece signed an association agreement with the EC in 1962, but its application for membership was delayed as a result of the military takeover. Greece became a full member of the EC in 1981. Greece's most important single trading partner is Germany, followed at some distance by Italy, and the majority of its trade is now with EC countries. Its persistent trade deficit with EC countries is partially redressed by net transfers to Greece from EC structural funds, from the Common Agricultural Policy and from direct aid and loans. Greece does have relatively small but diplomatically significant trading links with Middle East countries, particularly Saudi Arabia and Egypt.

Greece has generally run a substantial deficit on its trade balance, which has been covered to a greater or lesser extent by its surplus on invisibles (particularly shipping and tourism) and by the net inflow of private foreign capital. The 1979 oil shock reduced the flow from these sources considerably, and revealed in bleak terms the persisting structural weaknesses of the Greek economy: the weakness of its capital market, low productivity particularly in agriculture, the urgent need for further improvements to infrastructure to overcome the natural difficulties of the climate and the terrain, and the lack of competitiveness of its manufacturing base, now faced by the challenge of the newly industrializing economies outside Europe.

The response of the PASOK government which took over after the 1981 elections was expansion through fiscal and monetary measures designed to stimulate the private and public sector to raise their levels of economic activity. PASOK associated this with a more neutralist stance in foreign policy, opposition to NATO bases in Greece and cooler relations with Greece's EC partners. The PASOK government also attempted to contain inflation through price controls and a strong currency policy. The failure of these efforts was implicitly acknowledged in October 1985 with the adoption of the Stabilization Plan, which concentrated on a much tighter monetary policy and measures aimed at enhancing external competitiveness. Though these measures appeared to be successful in improving profitability and in establishing more realistic interest rate levels, problems of controlling the public sector deficit continued throughout the late 1980s. Partly because of the traditional fragility of the manufacturing base, a significant proportion of the non-agricultural economy is state-owned or state-controlled, and neither PASOK nor the post-1989 ND government showed themselves able to match the achievements of social objectives to the constraints of the domestic and international economic circumstances.

5.5 Prospects for the 1990s

The 1950s and 1960s were characterized by political instability and economic success; in the 1980s Greece appears to have achieved relative political stability, at least in the medium term, but has some major economic problems to resolve. The traditional equivocations over Greece's real place in international geopolitics appear to have been settled by the repeated victories of pragmatic views of national interest over anti-Western rhetoric in the 1981-1989 PASOK governments. Greece's membership of the EC is not questioned, though involvement in NATO is likely to remain an issue of symbolic importance certainly as long as the outstanding issues with Turkey (over Cyprus, and over levels of defence funding particularly) remain unresolved. The unfinished business of Greek economic development will however require continued support from the European Community. Greece has some natural resources which remain to be exploited, and has a strong comparative advantage in shipping and tourism. Areas which offer particular opportunities for expansion are agriculture, which is in urgent need of restructuring and infrastructural support, and the rail, road and telecommunications networks, which are continuing to be the target of EC support.

6. IRELAND

6.1 Key Indicators

Area	70,000 sq. km
Population	3.5 million
Head of State	President Mary Robinson
Language	Gaelic and English
Main Cities	Dublin 922,000
	Cork 175,000
	Limerick 77,000
	Galway 48,000
	Waterford 42,000
Currency	Irish Pound
Average Exchange	
Rate 1989	IR£0.61 per dollar

6.2 Economy 1989

Total GDP (US$bn)	34.0
Real GDP Growth	5.8%
Inflation	3.2%
Unemployment	17.0%
Exports (US$bn)	20.3
Imports (US$bn)	16.4

6.3 General Introduction

Ireland has struggled to overcome a primarily agricultural economic structure and to develop into a more diversified, less protectionist and more export based modern economy since 1945. While it experienced some economic success in the post-war boom years of the 1960s and through membership of the EC in 1973 it still has one of the lowest incomes per head at 65% of the GDP average for the EC as a whole and has a relatively high 10% of its economy in agriculture compared with the EC average of around 4%.

The country was seriously mismanaged economically in the 1970s and for part of the 1980s. This led to a huge debt burden which has only recently been contained and managed downwards. As a result the country is still characterized by high levels of unemployment, widespread emigration and low income and high poverty levels when compared with most other EC countries.

6.4 Post-War Economic Growth

The Irish state, led between 1951 and 1973 by the Fianna Fail (Republican) Party, attempted to undertake a pro-active role in industrial development. The creation of an Industrial Development Authority (IDA) in 1950 presaged the beginning of state led industrial diversification away from a primarily agricultural base. The IDA was active in stimulating foreign (multi-national subsidiaries, the EC, USA and Japan) and domestic investment in a relatively small number of high technology areas, particularly in the fields of services, chemicals/pharmaceuticals, electrical/electronic engineering and computer technology. This had a marked effect on economic performance and contributed to higher levels of economic growth in the two decades of the 1950s and 1960s. This had the ancillary benefit of reducing emigration and causing the population to grow for the first time in the 20th century.

Though the Irish state continued to play a major role directly and indirectly through its economic planning institutions in this period the reliance on protectionism which had characterized the inter-war economic policy of Ireland gave way gradually to a more laissez-faire approach in the 1960s and 1970s. A free trade agreement was signed with Britain (still today Ireland's premier trading partner with around a third of all trade) in 1966 and membership of the EC was achieved in 1973. The Irish were always more willing to join the EC when it was created in 1957 than the British. Ireland was, however, unable to join on practical grounds until Britain did in 1973. This was because the bulk of her trade until then was with the UK. Membership of the EC has been seen as a major advantage for Irish farmers whose produce had been uncompetitive but was, after 1973, increasingly protected by Community farm subsidies in the Common Agricultural Policy.

Ironically, the ending of protection and the shift to free trade for agriculture in the 1950s and 1960s was replaced after 1973 by Community-wide protection. For industry however the situation was less clear-cut. Traditional industries were now exposed to harsher competition in the Community than they had been outside and this would prove calamitous during the oil crises of the 1970s. Nevertheless by the 1970s the structure of Irish industry had become much more diversified than before. The traditional industries of foodstuffs, textiles, glass, crystals and beverages had been joined in the 1970s by chemicals, electronic data processing, engineering, transport equipment and pharmaceuticals. Furthermore economic growth had seen unemployment levels fall in these two decades to around 6% of the workforce. Membership of the EC also brought substantial transfer payments in the form of social, regional and structural funds with which to update infrastructure and society. In 1990 alone Ireland was contributing IR£1.6 billion while receiving IR£8.7 billion from the EC.

6.5 The Post-War Recession

The oil crises of the 1970s had an extreme effect on the energy dependent Irish economy. Lacking substantial indigenous supplies of oil or coal, and with only peat in any quantity, the Irish economy's expansion in the 1960s had been dependent on cheap oil imports. The quadrupling of oil prices after 1973 caused the two perennial problems of the Irish economy - unemployment and emigration - to reappear with alacrity. The major factor here was the increased cost of oil which generated inflationary pressures in Irish product prices at a time of increased international competition and falling world demand. The upshot was that the government found itself forced to pump money into Ireland's traditional and declining industries (steel, railways, textiles, fertilizers, sugar, energy and air transport) which were unable to deal successfully either with world-wide recession or the increased exposure to international and European competition engendered by membership of the EC in 1973. The result was burgeoning budget and financial deficits in the public sector and rising inflation. High public expenditure in the 1970s - which saw all parties committed to relatively high social spending to offset unemployment levels rising above 10% - could only be financed by foreign borrowing and high levels of domestic taxation.

Eventually this high borrowing, high spending and inflationary cycle had to be challenged and it was with the election of the Fianna Gael and Labour coalition led by Garret FitzGerald in November 1982 that a return to more financially orthodox budgetary management techniques was signalled. Between 1982 and the loss of office of this coalition government in 1987 public expenditure and borrowing was substantially reduced by high taxation and severe retrenchment in capital spending programmes. This shift to market forces has been continued under the Fianna Fail government led by Charles Haughey since 1987. This administration has maintained financial orthodoxy and pursued policies of privatization, tax reductions and increased trade and market liberalization. The most significant change has been the commitment not just to reduce capital spending but to tackle the high levels of current public sector spending as well. This has led to the public sector borrowing requirement being reduced from 20% of GNP in 1982 to around 5% in 1990. Despite this Ireland's public sector debt remains one of the highest as a percentage of GDP in the OECD countries.

In the attempt to contain this deficit there has been a high cost to be paid in terms of unemployment, poverty and industrial restructuring in this period. At between 17% and 19% of the labour force, unemployment in 1989/90 was the second highest in Europe. For this reason alone it is hardly surprising that emigration to the USA and England is at its highest since the 1950s. Tragically, while there was substantial capital investment in Ireland in the 1980s, it neither contributed to reducing unemployment levels nor to increasing income levels. In effect the investment in machinery in manufacturing led to greater unemployment and the benefits of higher economic growth were used primarily to pay for the interest on the huge foreign debts the country had run up after 1973 in mitigating the short-term effects of the recession. The finance necessary to pay off debt interest was normally paid for via high tax levels which further undermined economic growth and confidence. This vicious circle could only be tackled by reducing public spending and debts.

6.6 The Challenges of the 1990s

Early efforts by the government have seen a greater diversification of Irish industry than had been the case prior to 1945. Today services represent around 55% of GDP, manufacturing has 35% and agriculture a mere 10% of GDP. This has been a major achievement but much of the new development and investment (in particular the embryonic aviation maintenance and aerospace park around Shannon airport and its duty free zone) is likely to be capital rather than labour intensive in the future. This will create further problems for unemployment and emigration but it has to be noted that the capital intensive high technology sectors doubled their export volumes in the mid-1980s.

Perhaps more worrying for the future is the consequence for growth, income and employment of proposals to cut price supports to dairy and beef production in recent negotiations around the CAP of the EC. Any major changes to the price supports will have a serious effect on farm incomes which have been substantially subsidized by the EC since 1973. This will be calamitous for at least 10% of the Irish economy which is already reeling from the financial and political effects of the disclosure of debts of IR£500 million by the Goodman International food processing empire in 1990. Furthermore there is every likelihood that the substantial structural funds given to Ireland in the past from the EC will now be reduced in response to the demands emanating from Portugal, Greece and Eastern Europe. Ireland may no longer be the largest single recipient of EC aid as it has been in the 1980s.

The harsh economic measures inflicted on the economy in the 1980s appear to have had some beneficial effects. Growth rates have approached 4% and the balance of payments has been in current account surplus in each of the last four years. Inflation has also been kept in the 3% range since the end of the decade and government borrowing has been reduced. The real challenge however facing the government is whether inflationary pressures can be constrained once a fiscal or monetary stimulus is given to the economy in the 1990s. In the past governments tended to ignore economic in favour of political and social pressures and it will be interesting to see if similar problems appear if the 1990s see a return to recession after the relative boom years since the mid-1980s when the Irish economy prospered on the back of an export-led boom. This success in exports has allowed the government to meet the interest on its huge foreign debts. It will be interesting to see what happens to government financial resolve if a recession cuts exports to Britain, the EC and the USA and interest rates rise in the early 1990s on the back of a Gulf war, especially with unemployment levels at historically high levels of 17% for the post-war period. The Irish economy is one of the most highly taxed in the EC with marginal tax rates for average workers at around two-thirds of income. This may well be a major disincentive to people staying or investing in the country, especially with VAT and excise duties at some of the highest levels in Europe. On the other hand corporate tax rates are not as high as elsewhere in the EC and this may offset more punitive personal tax levels. It might also be assumed that wage rates in a relatively high unemployment and low income economy would be low by European standards. Unfortunately for inward investors the relatively well organized union coverage of 60% of the workforce (and as high as 80% to 90% in manufacturing) and ready access to the UK market for job seekers ensures that wage rates are higher than they might be given the other difficulties the economy faces. The continuing increase in public sector pay at 6% in 1990 is a further inflationary pressure in the economy. These difficulties are not aided by relatively high nominal interest rates at between 12% and 14%.

Despite this in recent years a number of major electronics firms (Intel, Maxtor and Fujitsu) as well as Swissair, Lufthansa, Wang, Analog Devices, Digital Equipment and Verbatim have located in the country. There is no doubt that the relative openness to free trade, the ready availability of well educated and skilled young people below the age of 28 and the relative cheapness of land have all played a major role in attracting inward investment of this type. Nevertheless Irish industry and firms located there face the problems that Irish firms tend to be small scale and, being a peripheral island, there are high logistical and transport costs in getting products to the internal market of the Community.

7.   ITALY

7.1 Key Indicators

Area	301,277 sq. km
Population	57.52 million
Head of State	Francesco Cossiga
Language	Italian
Main Cities	Rome 2,815,457
	Milan 1,495,260
	Naples 1,204,211
	Turin 1,035,665
Currency	Lira
Average Exchange Rate 1990	1,198.1 Lire(per dollar)

7.2 Economy 1986

Total GDP (bn Lire)	436,830
Real GDP growth	2.9%
Inflation	5.9%
Unemployment	12.2%
Exports (US$ mn)	97,606
Imports (US$ mn)	99,452

7.3 General Introduction

Italy has undergone an extraordinary transformation since 1945. Then, Italy was socially and economically underdeveloped, with heavy dependence on agriculture, and extremes of poverty in some southern regions. It is now the fifth largest economy in the West (measured in GNP), and has an international reputation for design and quality in clothing, fabrics and light manufacturing. The economy shows remarkable buoyancy even after serious recession, but is still heavily dependent on international trading conditions. Italy's most important trading partners are almost all in the EC, with Germany its largest single partner counting for about 15% of all Italy's exports. Outside Europe, only the US is of comparable commercial importance to Italy. Italy is frequently described as a country of startling contrasts, and one of the most startling is that between the dynamic modern economy and its byzantine political system. The 1987 Parliamentary elections sent 13 political parties to Parliament, the largest among them the Christian Democrats, who have been in every post-war Cabinet, the second largest being the Communists, who have been in no Cabinet since 1947. By the end of 1990, Italy had had 49 governments in 45 years, but the government instability masks the stability and resilience of the overall political system. This has withstood not only the repeated governmental crises but also the terrorism and high inflation of the 1970s, followed by a serious recession in the early 1980s.

Participation in the European Monetary System has brought a relative coherence and discipline to external economic policy, but major problems remain internally - in particular, high interest rates exacerbate a very large public sector deficit, and Italy has had one of the worst unemployment rates in Western Europe for most of the 1980s. Also, Southern Italy is still a relatively poor and underdeveloped region, which requires considerable the support from public and private sector before it can achieve self-sustaining growth. Continuing disagreement between and within the governing parties make these problems difficult to resolve, and there is every indication that the contrast between Italy's economic and social transformation and its political stagnation will continue into the 1990s.

7.4 Post-War Growth

Italy's 'economic miracle', as it was dubbed at the time, was a period of sustained high growth rates beginning in 1950 and ending around 1963. The economy grew at an average rate of 5.5% per year in the first part of the 1950s, and then by a rate of over 6% on average until the early 1960s. This growth was stimulated by a happy convergence of domestic and international economic conditions and policies, and was in effect stimulated initially by the US-funded Marshall Plan together with a rapid introduction of free trade policies in all areas except capital markets. The costs of this, particularly in a country with a tradition of intermittent tariff protection, were considerable: social and commercial dislocation, immediate high inflation, and supply difficulties of essential products including food. The government responded to these problems with the introduction of a massive programme of public works aimed particularly at improving the infrastructure in the South, which was associated paradoxically with a switch of labour out of agricultural under-employment into the rapidly growing industrial cities of the North. Italy's relatively cheap labour costs, the introduction of new technologies, the stability of the Lira and the expansion of the public sector industries combined with the buoyancy of international trade to allow Italy a period of unprecedented (and unrepeated) export led growth in the late 1950s.

But structural imbalances remained. The downturn in international economic activity in 1963 occurred as Italy began to face labour bottle-necks and a slowing down in the technological innovation of the previous period. Increasing labour unrest culminated in 1969 in the famous hot 'autumn'. The triennial renewal of the labour contracts throughout Italy's largest companies was the occasion for an outburst of mass political unrest, in protest not only against the worsening employment conditions but also against the general failure of public infrastructure to keep pace with the economic development. The long-term effects of this were not so much on labour costs directly, though the political pressure did lead to the introduction of the 'Workers' Charter' in 1970, which gave much improved job security and welfare benefits to employees in manufacturing. A greater effect was felt in the impact on the confidence of domestic and foreign investors. The resultant drop in investment over the following four years was only partially compensated by the counter-cyclical measures adopted by Italy's extensive public sector.

The public sector in Italy was established in the inter-war period under the Fascist regime as a response to the financial and industrial collapse during the depression. It consists now of several large holding companies, of which the most important are the Institute for Industrial Reconstruction (IRI) and the National Hydrocarbons Agency (ENI). IRI controls separate sectoral holding companies, which in turn own and direct the multitude of active trading companies. IRI's activities cover a very wide range: it is responsible for most of Italy's steel production, owns three of the five national banks, controls the national TV and Radio network and has interests in shipping, road building, telecommunications and food processing. As well as being a major instrument of national economic policy, the public sector conglomerates are important levers of patronage for the governing parties, which they have not hesitated to use for overt political purposes. It is not surprising then that the public sector plays a large and active role in attempting to compensate for Italy's structural imbalances.

As they emerged particularly in the 1970s, these came to be seen as directly linked with Italy's rapid uncontrolled growth, leading to what one commentator described as 'precocious maturity'. A notable feature of

Italy's economic structure is its lack if home energy resources, a lack which made it particularly vulnerable to the oil crises of 1973 and 1979. The 1970s were a period of great difficulty for the Italian economy as it struggled to come to terms with increased energy costs on top of the fall-out from the 'hot autumn' of 1969. Though employment in industry remained high, growth was limited by domestic inflation and balance of payments difficulties, including a major exchange rate crisis in 1976 from which Italy was extricated with the help of the IMF.

After a brief period of adjustment, the exchange rate mechanism of the EMS began to exert deflationary effects on the economy, with high interest rates and pressures for international competitiveness which depressed wage costs and investment. As a result, Italy went through a deep trough in economic activity from 1981 to 1984, signalled most notably by an unprecedented shake-out of labour from the big private sector companies of the North such as FIAT and Olivetti. Since then, Italy has once again shown its remarkable capacity for recovery with several years of relatively high growth rates, helped by a period of unusual governmental stability from 1983 to 1986, which saw Italy's longest-running government led by the Socialist Bettino Craxi last just a few days short of three years.

7.5 Prospects for the 1990s

Italy's future growth prospects depend to a large extent on its capacity to tap the potential of its undoubted strengths, hitherto often constrained by the structural weaknesses. The difficulties relate particularly to agriculture and energy. Employment in agriculture fell from 46% of the active population in 1946 to just over 10% in 1987, but agricultural productivity remains low - gross market production per worker is estimated at about

64% of the European average. Italy is a net importer of food, and the weakness of the agricultural sector contributes to Italy's recurrent import bill. Italy is not generally thought to have taken full advantage of the restructuring funds available through the European Community's Common Agricultural Policy, which might be used to increase the size of farms and to encourage capital investment. Also, much of Italy's agricultural produce is 'Mediterranean', which is less favoured by the CAP and of which there is a consistent surplus of supply in Western Europe. The predominance of under-developed agriculture in the South contributes to that area's difficulties in fostering stable employment and stimulating trading links outside Italy. Economies of scale and technological improvement remain to be exploited, though it is not clear that the single internal market will necessarily have a beneficial effect in this context.

Perhaps less obvious but no less serious is Italy's reliance on imported energy. Italy has few domestic fossil fuel reserves, and has generally adopted a policy of enhanced political and economic links with neighbouring oil producers so as to provide stability and relative independence of supply. A nuclear energy programme was approved in 1981, but this met with vigorous local opposition and has not been implemented sufficiently to reduce the external dependency. Italy will continue to be sensitive to international oil prices and will find the balance of payments constraints an obstacle to sustained economic growth.

Italy has also suffered in the past from the automatic connection between inflation and wage rates, bound together in a system known as the *scala mobile*, literally the 'escalator'. This provided automatic increases in wage rates in the public sector and in most of the large private sector companies in accordance with increases in the cost of living index produced by the Central Statistical Institute ISTAT. The *scala mobile* was originally intended to help reduce conflict in labour relations by removing the wages issue from contractual dispute. It was however widely if sometimes misleadingly blamed for persistently high inflation and declining competitiveness during the late 1970s and after protracted negotiations was reformed in 1983 and 1984. Though this problem has been partially resolved, labour relations in the big multi nationals remain subject to intermittent conflict particularly over restructuring issues. But Italy's industrial performance is increasingly seen as dependent on the flexibility and innovative capacity of its small and medium sized firms, which for a variety of reasons are often free of the formal restrictions on employment practice which govern the larger companies.

The continuing high public sector deficit constitutes a major brake on Italian economic performance. At over 10% of GDP in 1989, the public sector borrowing requirement clearly imposes great strain both on monetary policy and on the supply of credit to potential industrial investors. In the run-up to 1992 Italy has been required to open up its previously regulated financial markets, and will undoubtedly go through a difficult period of adjustment, particularly as finance houses accustomed to more competitive regimes are seeking to expand into the Italian market.

None of the above should be read to mean that Italy is about to go through major economic crises. On the contrary, the problems referred to should be understood as a counterpoint to Italy's continued capacity to adapt to new conditions and to thrive despite its evident and much rehearsed structural weaknesses. It is a widespread and not unreasonable belief among Italian policy makers that further integration with the rest of Europe may provide the stimulus to resolve the problems which its own domestic arrangements appear unable to deal with.

8. LUXEMBOURG

8.1 Key Indicators

Area	2.586 sq. km
Population	380,000
Head of State	Grand Duke Jean
Language	French, German and English
Main Cities	Luxembourg-Ville 79,000
	Esch-sur-Alzette 25,500
	Differdange 16,800
	Dudelange 14,200
	Petange 12,000
Currency	Luxembourg Franc tied to
	Belgian Franc
Average Exchange	
Rate 1989	LFr 39.40 per dollar

8.2 Economy 1989

Total GDP (US$bn)	7.5
Real GDP Growth	4.0%
Inflation	3.4%
Unemployment	1.8%
Exports (US$bn)	6.8
Imports (US$bn)	6.7

8.3 General Introduction

Luxembourg suffered severe damage during the Second World War and had to find most of the resources to rebuild its society and economy domestically. Given this, and its relatively small size and lack of natural resources, it is to the Grand Duchy's credit that by the end of the 1980s it had the fifth highest per capita income in the world and had created an economy with zero inflation, relatively non-existent unemployment and healthy growth rates of 4% per annum.

Much of the reason for this success can be attributed to the relatively easy social and political cohesion which exists in the Grand Duchy. Immediately after the War a government of National Unity was formed and the collectively organized economic reconstruction was achieved in the early 1950s; after which a relative 'economic miracle' was achieved until the onset of the post-war recession.

In recent years the Grand Duchy has diversified its economic structure further and by the 1980s had well over 50% of its workforce in services and is now second only to London as a financial centre in Europe. It also has the benefit of being an international and EC administrative centre. Once again there is little doubt that the dominance of coalition politics by the Christian Social Party in virtually all governments since 1945 has provided a degree of political continuity and stability which has been extremely beneficial for economic management.

8.4 Post-War Economic Growth

After 1945 Luxembourg consciously directed Marshall Aid into the diversification of its traditional economic structure which had been dominated by the steel industry. The steel industry's share of industrial production fell from 60% to 50% by the early 1970s and, in the relatively benign world conditions of the period, new industries flourished in textiles and related metal engineering as the economy was opened to the rest of the world and multinational investment flowed in. Goodyear Tyres and General Motors were major investors in this period. In the 1960s then, led by a competitive steel sector, the economy grew at around 4% per annum.

In achieving this growth success and diversification Luxembourg was assisted by the formation of the Benelux Economic Union which came into full operation in 1960, but followed earlier treaties with Belgium and the Netherlands as early as 1944. The early participation in the EC as a founder member in 1957 further contributed to this diversification of economic activity and the closer involvement in both the European and world economies. Luxembourg has, therefore, taken a much more open and active role in economic affairs since 1945 but its major trading partners remain those which had dominated before the Second World War. These are the four neighbouring economies of Germany, France, the Netherlands and Belgium. Of these Belgium has been by far the most important trading partner contributing up to 40% of all imports and receiving up to 20% of Luxembourg exports up until the 1980s when Germany started to take over as lead partner. To a large extent Belgium and Luxembourg operate in an economically synergistic way. This relationship going back to the Belgo-Luxembourg Economic Union of 1921 which fused the financial and monetary instruments of the two countries.

8.5 The Post-War Recession

Ironically the onset of the post-war recession coincided with the loss of office by the Christian Socialists and their replacement up until 1979 by a Socialist and Liberal/Democratic coalition. While the new government introduced some long overdue social reforms (abortion, death penalty and divorce) and was more willing to indulge in corporatist style bargaining with labour and industry, there was no radical departure from previous policies. A recovery plan was negotiated for the uncompetitive steel industry, but this was continued by the Christian Socialists when they returned to office in 1979.

If the Luxembourg state had taken advantage of the boom years to diversify some of its manufacturing and industrial base, after 1973, when industry came under increased demand and competitive pressure, the Luxembourg economy was re-invigorated by a shift into services and by a diversification of industry into aluminium, chemicals, and glass making in the 1970s and 1980s. This was achieved using government incentives and subsidies. The state also provided employment retraining schemes for those losing employment in the steel sector. By the late 1980s banking had also become a, if not the, major contributor to the performance of the economy. The success of banking was based on the rise of the Eurocurrency markets and negligible taxation on dividends, interests and capital gains for holding companies - of which there are more than 8000 including Renault and Banco Ambrosiano located in the Grand Duchy - and for investment funds. This helped to compensate for the further radical surgery which was necessary in the steel industry in the early 1980s. The major private employer, ARBED, with 90% of the industry, saw its capacity reduced by 30% between 1980 and 1984 as it was merged successfully with the big Belgian steel firm, Cockerill-Sambre. The government providing public subsidies up to 1986 to assist in the rationalization process.

There was also an intensification of agricultural production with particular emphasis on bringing more land into cultivation and increasing the size of farms - especially for livestock and dairy farming. The oil dependency which followed from the decline of coal mining in the Grand Duchy has also resulted in tremendous investment in hydro-electric power. Despite this Luxembourg still relies for about 10% of its energy from imported oil supplies.

All of these developments were important after 1973 because the recessionary conditions of the time had a deleterious effect even on formerly historic relationships like the Belgo-Luxembourg Economic Union. In the difficult times being experienced in Belgium during 1982 that government chose to devalue its currency without discussing the issue with its historic partner. The result was that, although the Union persists, Luxembourg took the precaution of creating its own monetary institute and asserting its right to create its own currency if it felt it necessary. In 1990 agreement was eventually reached on the need to allow a return to totally free capital movements between the two countries once again. So although harmony has been restored the Luxembourg government has been given a warning of what can happen when economic circumstances become difficult. The need for further economic diversification in the context of the development of the Single Market was thereby reinforced.

Since 1982 growth rates have recovered and began to return to the 4% figures of the boom years towards the end of the decade.

8.6 The Challenges of the 1990s

Luxembourg has one of the highest per capita incomes in the world and is in the top five for standards of living. It also has the highest par capita income in the EC. This has been achieved with a very small budget deficit, low inflation rates at between zero and 4% and, after 1986, growth rates between 2% and 5% and negligible unemployment.

Clearly the Grand Duchy intends to make sure of the continuation of this recent success. The Banking Law of March 1989 allows banks to withhold all information on their clients' accounts from all tax authorities (bar for inheritance cases) and clearly demonstrates that the Luxembourg authorities are positioning themselves to challenge Switzerland's banking role in the integrated

EC after 1992. It also demonstrates the importance that is attached to keeping the largely foreign banking groups which are located in the Grand Duchy. However, new laws in November 1989 somewhat undercut this by insisting on extremely tough rules and penalties for those not properly checking on money laundering in their banking transactions. On the other hand the Duchy was successful in resisting EC-wide moves to impose a withholding tax on investment profits. Despite this there have also been worries about the loss of Eurocurrency and Eurobond business to London and other centres since 1986 and renewed fears that the EC might impose disclosure of information to tax authorities on her secretive non-disclosure banking rules. Given that the trade surplus is largely dependent on invisible earnings from banking and services, it is crucially important to the Luxembourg economy that it remains as a major financial centre in face of the increased competition from many other EC capitals in the 1990s.

Luxembourg may suffer from restructuring and rationalization of the EC institutional presence. The Secretariat is set to move from Luxembourg taking with it over 1500 staff and many more ancillary jobs and there is a steady trickle of staff back to Brussels from the European Parliament. This would be a major blow to the Grand Duchy even if other EC institutions remained because the total population is a mere 380,000. The Grand Duchy is therefore fighting very hard to obtain the Eurofed or Trademark office when they are set up in the future.

Political cohesion and stability appears assured in this small country. All the political parties have managed to work in coalition with one another since 1945. Trade unionism is also quite quiescent, with only two strikes since 1942. The population is also highly skilled and educated, although there are labour shortages which push up wage costs. On the down side it is an extremely expensive place to live and their are problems of housing and infrastructure. Despite this its financial and physical locational advantages may make it an ideal site for high technology and service investment for the future, especially as investment in infrastructure is set to rise by a staggering 45% in 1991.

If, however, the EC drive to harmonize tax and business laws continues, the advantages for private individuals from withholding and secrecy rules and the tax holidays for holding companies may quickly disappear. On the plus side the government is planning to further reduce income tax in 1991. Whatever happens Luxembourg's talent for invention is not likely to disappear. A country without a coastline is about to offer a shipping register and broking service!

9. THE NETHERLANDS

9.1 Key Indicators

Area	37,291 sq. km
Population	15 million
Head of State	Queen Beatrix Wilhelmina Armgaard
Language	Dutch (English/German widely understood)
Main Cities	Amsterdam 692,000
	Rotterdam 574,000
	The Hague 444,000
	Utrecht 230,000
	Eindhoven 191,000
	Groningen 168,000
Currency	100 cents=1 Guilder(Fl)
Average Exchange Rate 1989	Fl=2.12 per dollar

9.2 Economy 1989

Total GDP (Fl bn)	474.11
Real GDP Growth	4.3%
Inflation	1.1%
Unemployment	9.3%
Exports (US$ bn)	111.7
Imports (US$ bn)	93.7

9.3 General Introduction

The material standard of living in the Netherlands has improved considerably since 1945 so that it has experienced one of the highest per capita incomes in the world. This is due to the strength of trade, agriculture and energy sectors and also owes a great deal to the practical interdependence between the Dutch economy and its larger German, and now European, neighbours. In many respects The Netherlands acts as a trading entrepôt for Germany and Europe; but has always been a trading nation with the world. The post-war success of the country has been achieved despite that fact that its politics is perhaps the most fragmented in the EC. There is a plethora of political parties and the society itself is riven with religious, ideological and functional divisions. In the past - and certainly through the immediate post-war period of high growth rates - these centrifugal tendencies were accommodated by an acceptance of the need for power sharing and harmony. Higher living standards and the recession appear to have combined to reinforce divisions and made the task of economic management more difficult in the 1980s.

In recent years there has been a renewed willingness to return to consensus and in 1989 the two major parties of the right and the left (the CDA and PvdA) agreed to form a coalition government. This may herald a period of greater political harmony at a time when recession confronts an economy which still has some way to go before it has resolved the economic difficulties created by the high consumption created in the 1960s.

9.4 Post-War Economic Growth

The post-war period saw substantial economic growth and almost non-existent inflation rates under the *verzuiling* system. This is the expression for the creation of pillars or segmentation in society along religious or ideological lines which extends into all aspects of social, economic and political life. Thus most of the period up to the late 1960s was characterized by tremendous consensus and power sharing. First Social Democratic and Catholic coalitions (1948-1958) and then the centre-right and all the major religious parties

(1958-1965) formed governments. The consensual system began to break down and be replaced by a fragmentation into multi-party politics after 1965 when the growth performance of the post-war period began to decline. Immediate post-war governments used Marshall Aid wisely after 1945 and growth rates averaged an unparalleled 5% per annum in the 1950s. Given the massive war devastation - much of it occasioned by the retreating German army - immediate post-war governments used positive state intervention to drain the water-logged land and rebuild industrial infrastructure. In 1959 natural gas was discovered at Groningen and this enabled the economy to grow throughout the 1960s. At the same time the political effect of Christian and Social Democracy and the need to buy off a vast array of groups and interest in the community saw the development of an extensive publicly financed social welfare system. Relatively high wage rates were also awarded in both the public and private sectors. All of these developments in the 1960s sowed the seeds of the rampant inflation, decline and unemployment of the 1970s. Strongly unionized Dutch workers and the government conspired between them to create a high wage and high social consumption economy.

Due to its relatively small size of around 15 million people the Dutch economy has historically been trade and export related and this explains the early willingness to tie its economy more closely to Belgium and Luxembourg between 1948 and 1960 and to become a founding member of the EC in 1957. Since the country has historically lived by trade it is not surprising that it has a large number of domestic multinational companies consolidating their global role in these years. The most important of these were Philips, Royal Dutch Shell, Unilever, DAF, KLM and Heineken. By the end of the period over 45% of GDP and over 50% of the workforce normally came from trade and services. Manufacturing,

construction and energy industries contributed around
25% of GDP and 30% of the workforce, with
agriculture at a significant 4% of GDP and 5% of the
workforce.

The shift out of agriculture and its increased
mechanization, which took place after 1945 when 20%
of the workforce were employed in this sector, was
clearly a major factor in post-war growth. Agricultural
products - especially dairy, food processing, brewing
and horticulture - are produced extremely efficiently and
are substantial export earners. Chemicals (around
Rotterdam and Amsterdam) and electronics are also key
export earners which were the fastest growing industrial
sectors in the boom years. Related industries like oil
refining, tobacco, metal engineering and natural gas
were also of crucial importance at this time. Even
traditional industries like textiles, steel and shipbuilding
prospered in the easy trading conditions before 1973. As
in the past Dutch transport firms continued to dominate
the EC market for road haulage and maritime freight.
But, as a result of a lack of indigenous raw materials,
Dutch industry has been a major importer of raw
materials and exporter of semi and fully manufactured
products.

The EC continued to be the major trading arena for
the economy. Germany (30%), Belgium and
Luxembourg (15%) and France and Britain (10% each)
are the major export markets for Dutch products.
Imports are similarly distributed, although the US plays
an important role in this regard too.

9.5 Post-War Recession

The recession was characterized not only by economic
decline but also political turmoil, with over 14 political
parties vying for power. The old pillars of social
consensus were broken and new political parties formed.
Democrats 66 (centre-left) had formed with immense

electoral success in the 1967 elections. The old Labour party (PvdA) suffered from internal divisions in the early 1970s and a breakaway party - the Democratic Socialists '70 was formed until it was dissolved in 1983. Similarly the centre-right suffered change, with a new party - the Christian Democratic Appeal (CDA) - forming in 1977. This led to considerable political instability throughout most of the 1970s and 1980s as power oscillated between centre-left and centre-right coalitions and destabilized economic management. It was not until 1982, when the centre-right took power and was able to cling on to office until 1989, that the management of the economy was put on a more financially orthodox basis. By the end of the 1980s growth rates had returned above the 2% per annum level after stagnating below 1% for much of the decade.

The country might have gas reserves but oil imports were substantial in 1973. Indeed, with Rotterdam as the leading entrepôt in the world and the key port for oil trading, the downturn in oil imports and recessionary tendencies were bound to provide an immense short-term shock to a highly paid and increasingly uncompetitive economy. As a result growth rates for the 1970s were below 2% per annum and the need to maintain diverse political coalitions ensured economic mismanagement. Public expenditure and social welfare payments were maintained to offset rising unemployment (which at over 12% for much of the 1980s were some of the highest in the EC) and this led to burgeoning borrowing requirements. This problem of rising public debts as a percentage of annual GDP (over 40% by 1980) was exacerbated by the unwillingness to countenance increasing income tax rates.

The possession of natural gas was a major benefit to the economy but it also has had its deleterious side effects. The reduction in oil imports and the export of gas along with other exports contributed to a huge trade surplus and a rising guilder value on world currency markets. The effect of this rise in currency values was to undermine the export competitiveness of industry and cause high levels of unemployment - especially in the least competitive traditional labour intensive industries. In industry itself oil substitution was quickly adopted and since the mid-1970s over half of the country's energy needs have come from indigenous gas supplies. This was not sufficient to save redundancy and closure in traditional industries like steel, shipbuilding and textiles, however. The government has also worked to diversify industrial structures and has provided subsidies and tax incentives for developments in microelectronics, aerospace and biotechnology. But the real problem of the Dutch economy was that wage rates were far higher than productivity and products were increasingly uncompetitive in the fierce market conditions of the 1980s as a result.

The realization of this problem and the recognition that state protection of industry and employment subsidy could not be maintained ensured that subsidies would not be given to traditional industries when a centre-right government led by Ruud Lubbers took power after 1982 and began to impose austerity measures on the high borrowing and high deficit economy. In the 1970s centre-left governments had attempted to deal with wage problems by neo-corporatist wage bargaining in industry or by imposing wage freezes. Neither of these policies was wholly successful in cutting wage levels and after 1982 the new government withdrew from wage bargaining altogether and allowed free collective bargaining to operate. This meant that the government was signalling its intention not to bail out the non-market consequences of wage settlements.

It appears that this and unemployment imposed some needed discipline on wage based inflation in the economy. The government also moved to liberalize the Amsterdam stock exchange and adopted a policy of severe public expenditure cuts (especially in education,

public pay and welfare benefits). These measures, plus
the upturn in the world economy, clearly had some
effect. By the late 1980s public pay had actually been
cut by 3% in real terms and the PSBR was down to
around 5% of GDP from the 12% and 15% levels
achieved during the 1970s. Furthermore growth rates
were back to 2% per annum and unemployment had
begun to fall a little to 11% from its 18% level of 1984.
Inflation was also almost at zero levels between 1985
and 1987.

9.6 The Challenges of the 1990s

The centre-right (CDA) and centre-left (PvdA) coalition
which took office in November 1989 has adopted a less
austerity based budgetary stance. This involved
corporation, direct and indirect tax cuts and only limited
public spending reductions in order to ease the high
level of unemployment. It is debatable therefore whether
the lessons of the 1980s have been fully learnt. The
Dutch economy is still prone to short-term politically
misguided policies (like the linkage of public pay with
private rates agreed by the coalition in 1989). The need
to keep this coalition together in a recessionary
environment might see further high spending problems,
given the past legacy of the highest OECD welfare
system. There tends to be a consensus about maintaining
historically high welfare expenditure levels; the real
political question is how to pay for it. This is borne out
by the experience of the disability scheme (WAO) -
which allows people to claim permanent disability
benefit for stress and nervous disorders - which is
subject to gross abuse by young people who do not want
to work.

Despite the PvdA and CDA coalition after 1989 the
instability of multi-party politics is likely to continue in
the 1990s and affect consistent economic management.
Not only has there been a history of the largest vote

winners (PvdA) being kept out of office by multi-party coalitions; but there is also a tendency to even greater party fragmentation. In The Netherlands any new idea appears to be able to instigate the formation of either a significant pressure group and/or a political party, the recent creation of a Green Party and Green Left being particular cases in point.

The Dutch economy will continue to face wage related problems. While it has a highly educated and skilled workforce it is a high wage economy relative to productivity and this may adversely affect inward and domestic manufacturing investment. The relatively high personal and corporate tax rates when compared with other EC centres may also be a disincentive for inward investment.

The severe medicine being meeted out at Philips in the wake of its appalling results at the end of the 1980s was symptomatic of an apparent Dutch dilemma in the 1990s. Philips had been a major paternalistic firm which diversified in its attempt to expand in the 1970s and 1980s. In expanding out of its core business it was unable to achieve success in new sectors and failed spectacularly to meet Japanese competition in new consumer markets. The consequence is that unless Philips cuts back on paternalism it will not be able to compete and there is every likelihood that it may well be dismembered in the 1990s. This will become easier if, as expected, under pressure from the US the EC brings pressure on the Dutch government to end the defensive laws which make it extremely difficult for contested takeovers to be achieved. In the past companies have been expected to have supervisory boards which administer companies on behalf on workers as well as shareholders. If this change happens then the Netherlands will become an easier market for acquisitions in the 1990s.

Environmental and pollution issues are extremely important in the Netherlands. Its pollution levels are high and the cost of financing clean-up programmes was one major reason for the collapse of the Lubbers government in 1989. Inward investors are likely to have to ensure that they meet stringent environmental standards in the future. The economy as a whole is very much dependent on the free flow of world trade. It is likely to suffer if world trade shifts towards protectionism in the 1990s. On the other hand this might be off-set somewhat if oil prices rise and drag gas prices along with them. This would increase government revenue while at the same time cause problems through a high exchange rate for exports.

Recent moves to bolster the competitive position of the Amsterdam financial centre in the EC have come up against only limited reforms and a tendency to stick to parochial working practices. London appears to be stealing a considerable share of Dutch government bond business and futures markets are also under intense competitive pressure. This poses severe problems for a sector which has historically been a major invisible export earner. The recent merger of the two largest banks AMRO/ABN and the defensive merger boom amongst other Dutch financial institutions in the last two years presages, perhaps, a more aggressive response by some market players.

Physically almost half the country is below sea level and only exists because of sea defences which are a major strain on public finances. The consequence of even some of the less chilling conclusions about global warming may cause considerable financial difficulties for the government in the future.

As a trading nation the Dutch have consistently striven to reduce barriers to trade and earn substantial income from transporting and distributing goods through Europe. It is also expected that the Dutch economy will benefit tremendously from German reunification as German demand increases and as direct and indirect trade with Eastern Europe as a whole increases. For firms looking for distributional centres there is little doubt that the Netherlands offers significant advantages. The chemical industry is also of crucial importance as the continuing high level of US investment in the Dutch industry demonstrates. There is also considerable Japanese and Korean investment in the Amsterdam financial market. The chemical, services and transport/distribution sectors appear to be the most likely growth and locational centres for future investment.

10. PORTUGAL

10.1 Key Indicators

Area	92,072 sq. km
Population	10,291,000
Head of State	Mario Soares
Language	Portuguese
Main Cities	Lisbon 2,119,600
	Porto 1,644,400
Currency	Escudo
Average Exchange Rate 1986	149.6 (per dollar)

10.2 Economy 1986

Total GDP (bn escudos)	1319.6
Real GDP Growth	3.3%
Inflation	11.7%
Unemployment	10.2%
Exports (US$ bn)	7,242
Imports (US$ bn)	9,650

10.3 General Introduction

Portugal stayed aloof from the rapid industrialization and economic growth which characterized almost all other Western European countries in the 1950s. The opening up of its economy from the mid-1960s on gave Portugal a late start, but its progress was rudely halted by the economic disruption which followed the collapse of the Salazar dictatorship in 1974. The international economic consequences of the oil shock of 1979 found Portugal in a particularly vulnerable position. It was only after 1985 that the Portuguese economy began to expand again after a period of austerity. With large proportions of its active population employed in traditional agriculture and in an unmodernized public sector, Portugal suffers from low productivity in many sectors, and has the lowest GDP per head in the European Community (about 48% of the EC average in 1987).

The authoritarian regime usually known as the Salazar dictatorship lasted from 1926 to 1974. Salazar ruled the country as Prime Minister without effective democratic restraint from 1932, when his *Estado Novo* (New State) constitution was promulgated, until 1968, when ill-health forced him to relinquish control. The regime came to power with explicitly conservative objectives drawn from a particular Iberian reading of Catholic social policy together with an almost obsessive concern for fiscal prudence. His control of the security services was used to repress formal opposition movements, though the hard-line Communist Party (PCP) managed to survive underground. The regime was supported by the Armed Forces, the Catholic Church and the large landowners, and by the traditional bureaucracy. In foreign policy, Salazar's neutralism won him allied friends during the Second World War, and Portugal was never subject to the same overt isolation treatment meted out to the neighbouring Franco regime in Spain. Portugal was a founder member of NATO in 1949, though Salazar formally and explicitly dissociated Portugal from the democratic principles contained in its founding declaration.

Portugal's domestic and foreign policy in the 1950s and 1960s were dominated by the priority given to defence of its colonies against independence movements. This required extensive and unpopular conscription, and drained resources from the government budget. The immediate cause of the downfall of the regime in 1974 was the revolt of junior and middle-ranking officers, who formed the Armed Forces Movement (MFA) with the explicit aim of seeking an end to the costly and futile colonial campaigns through peaceful decolonisation. The collapse of the authoritarian regime was rapid, but it was followed by a long period of political and social instability. Initially the transition was dominated by the PCP together with the newly radicalized MFA, who were able to push through radical land reforms and nationalizations of the banks in 1975. The elections of April 1975 weakened the formal position of the PCP considerably, though they continued to use mass mobilization and the support of the MFA to press for revolutionary change. The PCP was eventually ousted and a semblance of legitimate authority established in November 1975 by a cross-party coalition headed by the Socialist leader Mário Soares. The constitution promulgated in February 1976 established a parliamentary democracy with a powerful directly elected President, and gave an influential role to the 'Council of the Revolution', one of whose functions was to protect the reforms of the 1974-75 period.

Partly because of party-political fragmentation, and partly because of the enduring bitterness engendered by the way the transition to democracy took place, government instability continued to bedevil efforts to build up the Portuguese economy until 1985. The minority government of the Social Democrat (PSD) leader Aníbal Cavaco Silva, installed in that year, survived until the elections of July 1987, when the PSD won an unprecedented outright majority of votes. Cavaco Silva returned to power committed to a policy of deregulation, denationalization and expansion. The underlying problems of the Portuguese economy, particularly its trade deficit, international indebtedness and large public sector deficit, constrain the policy options available.

10.4 Economic Development

The strategy of self-sufficiency pursued by Salazar entailed protectionism and controlled prices, and resulted in relatively low growth, with very little of the shake-out of labour from traditional agriculture which occurred elsewhere. From the early 1960s, within the budgetary constraints imposed by the colonial wars, the dictatorship began to seek to attract foreign investment both to modernize industry and to improve the infrastructure. The new strategy did succeed in stimulating growth at over 6% per year from the mid-1960s until 1974. The oil shock of 1973 together with the unsuitable economic climate following the collapse of the Salazar regime led to a loss of confidence on the part of domestic and foreign investors. Nationalization of large parts of the banking system, land collectivization and a prodigal expansion of public expenditure all in different ways contributed to a dramatic and unpleasant economic crisis with high inflation followed by negative growth in the year 1975-76. Governments had to impose and continue painful austerity measures, particularly following the IMF loans in 1978 and 1983, which included devaluation, increased prices for public goods and services, and downward pressure on real wages in the effort to achieve greater competitiveness. Agriculture stagnated, and the emerging industrial base found itself operating in conditions of severe financial stringency.

The 1985 Cavaco Silva government took advantage of improved international economic conditions (particularly the falling oil prices) to relax the austerity measures, and a renewed climate of optimism followed Portugal's accession to the EC in 1986. This has been followed by very rapid increases in foreign investment as multinationals seek to take advantage of Portugal's relatively low labour costs, and its more relaxed planning and factory inspectorate regime, together with the large-scale transitional support being provided through the EC structural funds. The EC has allowed Portugal lengthy periods of adjustment as it removes its tariff barriers, and considerable compensatory funds. One area which has yet to be modernized to any great extent is agriculture, which is still divided between the small-scale peasant farmers of the north-west and the extensively farmed *latifundia* (great estates) of the South. Though over 20% of the active population was engaged in agriculture in the mid-1980s, it accounts for less than 10% of GDP and until recently has been predominantly traditional in methods, with productivity at about one-third of the EC average for some products. Portugal is self-sufficient in fruit and vegetables, but has to import most of its cereal requirement. Unlike Spain, Portugal has not yet successfully tapped the export market through intensive cultivation of vegetables under glass. Probably the strongest sector in this context is still forestry, where the main markets are furniture and construction, together with the demand for paper-pulp.

Portugal's manufacturing base has seen significant changes in the wake of the rush of foreign investment after 1985. While it is difficult to anticipate the specific consequences, quite clearly there has been a shift away from traditional activities (processing indigenous raw materials such as textiles and cork) towards modern manufacturing by foreign multinationals whose main interest in Portugal is in its low labour costs, pleasant working environment and suitability as a platform for exports.

The public sector was built up in the 1960s to support an indigenous heavy industrial base, particularly in petrochemicals and steel, but this has had difficulty competing and continues to contribute to the public sector deficit, a problem unresolved as yet by the otherwise activist Cavaco Silva government.

10.5   Challenges for the 1990s

Like other Southern European countries, Portugal has tended to look to the Single European Market to impose solutions which it is unable or unwilling to apply itself. This suggests that its main problems from the 1992 project will not come as a threat to new industries or to increased foreign investment. Portugal continues to have much to offer the foreign investor, and if the Common External Tariff is applied fully will be attractive to investors from outside the EC particularly. The threat is to its traditional manufacturing base in textiles and wood, and to its inefficient agriculture, neither of which has undergone significant restructuring despite the pressures of recent years. Coupled with this is the programme of denationalization and deregulation of its financial system, which has proceeded only slowly, and the reform of its public administration, which does not appear to have proceeded at all. Portugal is likely to continue to need special EC funds to support infrastructural development and to assist the move out of agriculture, as well as help with training the emerging labour force. The assurance of an attentive acknowledgement of its special position from the EC is a not insignificant factor in maintaining Portuguese economic stability and rates of growth.

11. SPAIN

11.1 Key Indicators

Area	504,782 sq. km
Population	39.4m (1990 estimate)
Head of State	King Juan Carlos
Language	Spanish
Main Cities	Madrid
	Barcelona
Currency	Peseta
Average Exchange Rate 1990	102.0 (pesetas per $1)

11.2 Economy 1986

Total GDP (bn pesetas, 1980 prices)	16,845
Real GDP Growth	4.5%
Inflation	8.8%
Unemployment	21.5%
Exports (US$ mn)	27,206
Imports (US$ mn)	35,057

11.3 General Introduction

Spain acceded to the European Community in 1986 after a long period of dictatorship followed by a relatively smooth transition to liberal democracy. In 1974, few observers would have been willing to predict that the Franco regime, marked at first by international isolation, autarky and stagnation, and later by uneasy attempts at modernization, would be succeeded by such enthusiasm and consensus around the process of European integration. However, Spain has already made a series of surprising changes, and it continues to do so. The political elites are virtually united in their support for

105

further integration in Europe, and reserve their radical objections for Spanish involvement in NATO, a much more controversial and difficult association.

The transition was aided by a convergence of the most influential parties and interest groups around an implicit agreement to put aside the bitter conflicts of the past. There were two obvious indications of the convergence. Firstly, by the end of 1976 the Communist Party (PCE) accepted the monarchy and parliamentary democracy, and secondly in the agreement known as the Moncloa Pacts (October 1978) the PCE and the Socialists (PSOE) accepted wage restraint and public expenditure reductions in return for pledges of future reforms. Since 1981, Spain has been governed by the PSOE, which after initial radical campaign pledges has pursued policies based on fiscal prudence, combating inflation, and industrial restructuring. The success of this strategy however was balanced by a steady growth in unemployment, which has led to increasingly bitter conflict between the government and the trade unions.

11.4   Post-war economic development

The dictator Franco continued the traditional Spanish strategy of seeking to protect domestic employment and profits behind high tariff walls both for manufactured goods and for agriculture. In industrial relations, the regime tried at first to pursue a corporatist strategy, organizing the workforce in compulsory hierarchical unions, imposing an extensive battery of regulations on conditions of work, and reducing job mobility. Even prior to Franco, protectionism had reduced the impact of the international depression in the 1930s, but the cost of these policies together with a stifling corporatist framework and the disruption of the Civil War was a lengthy period of stagnation. During the 1940s and 1950s the Spanish economy grew only fitfully, and suffered from the constraints of shortage of raw materials, a lack of technological innovation, and the persistence of a large unmodernized agricultural sector. From 1951 on, Spain's importance for American military strategy in Europe led to gradual improvement in its international relations, and US aid also stimulated a growth in consumer demand. But development was restricted by the weakness of Spain's trading position, by lack of capital for investment and by the tendency for relatively rapid periods of growth to be followed by balance of payments and inflation difficulties.

Domestic economic strategy altered radically in 1959 with the adoption of the Stabilization Plan supported by the IMF and the US. The Plan reflected not only renewed international interest, but also the emergence of a compact and ambitious new political and economic elite centred on the Catholic lay organization Opus Dei, which supported and implemented a programme of economic liberalization backed by continuing conservative social and political policies. The Stabilization Plan prioritized economic growth through encouragement for foreign investors, a limited deregulation of capital markets and a steady increase in the import of raw materials. The Plan was followed by an almost relentless growth from 1961 to 1973, which averaged 7.3% per year for the whole period. Critics of the Plan argued that it encouraged unbalanced growth, did little to resolve Spain's agricultural problems, and left a legacy of environmental damage. It was also argued that the Plan coincided with an increase in foreign earnings from tourism and from emigrants' remittances, and that it was these rather than the partial liberalization which were primarily responsible for the undoubted rapid growth of the period. The development enhanced the regional predominance of the traditional concentrations of industrial employment in the Basque country, around Barcelona and around Madrid.

The political transition of the 1970s coincided with more difficult international conditions to which Spain was particularly vulnerable because of its dependence on imported fuels. From 1974 to 1981 growth was limited to under 2% per year on average, including a period of stagnation in 1979 and 1980. This resulted partly from government austerity policies adopted against the high inflation and balance of payments problems of the mid-1970s. The period also saw a wave of banking collapses or serious crises affecting banks with about 20% of all deposits, to which the banking system responded with a quickening process of consolidation and further encouragement for foreign entry. Since 1982, growth rates have increased steadily, aided by the prospect and then the reality of EC membership after 1986.

Spain had originally had an association agreement with the European Community dating from 1970. Its membership application of 1979 had political as well as economic implications, since the existing members, who had refused to consider membership for Franco's regime, believed that economic integration could be used to give support to the new liberal-democratic system. Despite the favourable political wind, negotiations were delayed over transitional arrangements, over agriculture, over fisheries and over emigration (particularly for Spanish workers seeking jobs in West Germany).

Spain finally joined the EC on 1 January 1986, the same day as Portugal, with an agreed transitional period of seven years, during which Spain was to phase out its extensive system of quotas and tariffs on industrial imports.

Spain has identified the priority of using the EC to help it modernize its industrial base, to stimulate technological innovation and to build up its transport and telecommunications infrastructure, which is still some way behind EC standards. Some regions of Spain (for example Almeria) have modernised their agriculture by introducing intensive cultivation of crops for Northern markets under plastic, but there remain great disparities between the rich and the poor areas (Catalonia and Estremadura, for example). Undoubtedly some of the problems of agriculture relate to climate and terrain, with severe difficulties of irrigation and land erosion in many of the poorer areas. But there are also problems of fragmentation of land, of low capital investment and limited adoption of modern technical aids.

Spain's industrial base is particularly strong in traditional manufacturing areas such as wood and textiles, and there is a sizeable heavy industrial sector dominated by the state-owned conglomerate INI (founded by Franco in 1942 on the Italian IRI model). Its diverse industrial holdings include interests in shipbuilding, defence, steel, electronics and financial services. One of the largest sectors overall is chemicals, which make up 9.9% of total Spanish GDP and about 10% of total EC production in the sector. Spain's indigenous private sector is dominated by a very large number of very small firms, many of them family enterprises suffering from low productivity and underinvestment, which are finding it difficult to adjust to the international competition engendered by EC membership and the single internal market. But Spain's fastest areas of growth since the end of the Franco regime have been, on the one hand, tourism and associated sectors, and on the other, direct investment by foreign multinationals seeking to take advantage of Spain's relatively low labour costs and of the locational incentives provided by some of the entrepreneurially minded regional governments. This has been particularly striking in the automobile sector. Among the recent entrants have been Ford, GM, Renault and Peugeot, with differing results. The former state-owned car company SEAT is now part-owned by VW.

11.5   Challenges for the 1990s

Spain's integration into Western Europe has been far from painless, imposing costs in employment and requiring political and business elites to translate the ready rhetoric of European cultural identity into major restructuring of traditional institutions. In some areas, such as banking and financial services, this is clearly proceeding apace; in others, such as agriculture, the success has been spectacular but regionally limited; and in others, such as education and transport infrastructure, the results of reforms adopted are yet to be fully felt.

Spain has proved well able to fight its own corner within the EC, and it is likely that Spanish governments will continue to pursue the dual strategy adopted from the outset: selective use of European integration to push through important changes against domestic opposition, and vigorous defence of Spanish interests in Brussels (e.g. in fishing policy) in cases where removal of tariff and non-tariff barriers conflicts with governmental objectives for development. Areas which have not yet been radically altered by integration are public procurement and employment in the public sector, which still tend to be used for directly political objectives in a way which may bring the Spanish government into conflict with the European Commission. Nevertheless, there is clearly considerable potential for growth remaining.

12. UNITED KINGDOM

12.1 Key Indicators

Area	244,800 sq. km
Population	57.52 million
Head of State	HM Queen Elizabeth II
Language	English
Main Cities	London 6,850,000
	Birmingham 1,010,000
	Glasgow 732,000
	Leeds 712,000
	Sheffield 535,000
	Liverpool 485,000
Currency	100 pence= £ pound
Average Exchange	
Rate 1989	£0.53 per dollar

12.2 Economy 1989

Total GDP (US$bn)	831.6
Real GDP Growth	1.9%
Inflation	0.0%
Unemployment	8.5%
Exports (US$bn)	194.1
Imports (US$bn)	213.2

12.3 General Introduction

Britain's post-war economic performance has not been very successful when taken in comparative perspective. There is little doubt that Britain has experienced much higher levels of material growth than ever before; but this absolute increase in living standards has gone hand in hand with a relative decline in her position vis-à-vis other countries in Europe.

The gradual decline in Britain's world economic position led to a breaking with the post-war consensus when the Conservative party was returned to office under Mrs Thatcher in 1979. This coincided with the discovery and coming on stream of oil reserves in the early 1980s. The Thatcher government's approach of privatization and liberalization led, first, in the early 1980s to massive recession and, then, to historically high economic growth rates from 1983 onwards. This came to an end after the 1987 stock market crash when government economic mismanagement in pursuit of electoral expediency appears to have predominated.

The upshot is that Britain finds itself in the early 1990s facing a massive balance of trade deficit, a high interest rate regime, rising unemployment, deepening economic recession and steeply rising inflationary pressures. This has led to a heated debate in the UK about the Thatcher legacy. For some the government was responsible for turning the economy around; for others the government was always criminally negligent because it first engineered an unnecessary recession and then used oil revenues to create an artificial consumer boom which created an import dependency after the government's policies had destroyed much of manufacturing industry. While this debate is likely to run and run there is little doubt that the British economy in the early 1990s looks very much like the sick man of Europe once again. It is hardly surprising that the Conservative party decided, in these circumstances, to jettison its leader in late 1990.

12.4   Post-War Economic Growth

During the benign years of the 1950s and 1960s the British economy oscillated between limited state intervention and a relatively hands-off Keynesian economic policy approach. While there was some nationalization of old, declining staple industries (coal, railways) and more profitable firms (road transport, steel and utilities), the bulk of the manufacturing and the financial sectors remained in private hands.

Approximately 20% of industry was in public hands and these nationalised industries did not operate along strictly commercial lines. All too often these industries were used as macro economic instruments: either they were used to restrain unemployment levels or they were refused permission to invest or raise prices on commercial lines in order to control either inflation or the public sector borrowing requirement. It is hardly surprising that they were inefficient and suffered from both over-capacity and under-investment in capital equipment. As a result public sector industry in Britain was relatively unproductive despite being a major employer in the boom years.

It would be wrong however to lay the relative decline of British industry and export performance in these years solely at the door of the public sector. In truth Britain's decline in world manufacturing export markets and poor productivity levels owes a great deal to two phenomena which were apparent in the period to 1973. These were respectively the poor quality of private management and its fusion with anarchic (almost feudal) industrial relations practices by trades unions and, perhaps more importantly, the way in which the structure of employment and investment was quietly and inexorably transforming the balance of the British economy.

There is little doubt that the conflictual and competitive system of wage bargaining, based on the principles of voluntarism and free collective bargaining, which has spawned a weak central hierarchical structure for unions with a well organized and effective plant and local level structure and a plethora (over 100) of individual unions, was a key factor in the relatively poor productivity performance of industry. This defensive and disruptive union structure militated against capital intensive investment and modernisation. It was not aided by the generally poor quality of managers in British industry, itself partially a function of the low esteem given to engineers in the UK. Historically the education system has displayed an anti-industrial and anti-technical bias, with the best minds opting for the higher status occupations of the City, the professions, the media, teaching and politics rather than industry.

This is hardly surprising in a society in which the highest rewards appeared to go to those outside industry rather than those within it. Thus individuals appear to have acted rationally in their own short-term interest even though the overall societal consequence of these apparently inconsequential individual choices was extremely damaging taken as a whole. In the short term the trade unionist was merely defending his job against the fear of unemployment; the professional was merely voting logically for high rewards in a society in which the whole structure of the economy was shifting away from industry and agriculture towards service based employment.

Some basic statistics emphasize this point. As early as the middle of the 19th century Britain had shifted away from an agricultural/primary economy towards an industrial and service based one. Although British agriculture has been subsidized and protected since the 1930s' by the late 1980s only 2% of the labour force and 1.5% of GDP was accounted for by agriculture. In the public sector industries - especially railways, coal mining and the utilities - which had once been major employers accounting for up to 25% of GDP, were continuously under pressure as closures and rationalization reduced their importance in the economy. By the late 1980s these sectors employed only around 1% of the labour force and provided only 5% to 6% of GDP. Manufacturing as a whole also witnessed a serious and rapid decline over the period, leading some to talk of de-industrialization. From accounting for 25%

of world manufacturing trade in 1945 and employing over 50% of the workforce and supplying over 50% of GDP, by the 1980s Britain's manufacturing share of world trade had fallen into single figures; it employed only 20% of the domestic workforce and contributed only about 24% of GDP. It was the financial and services sectors of the economy which were the backbone of Britain's post-war economic performance. The services sector in the late 1980s accounted for around 60% of the workforce and 60% of GDP.

The fact that union members vigorously defended their jobs and wage rates in a manufacturing sector that was in decline and in which relative earnings were falling is therefore intelligible. The fact that the best and the brightest opted for the City, the professions and the media is similarly explicable. What is perhaps more damning is not this behaviour but the complete lack of understanding by those in government of what was going on. All too often governments, whether Labour or Conservative, used economic policy as a means of reducing unemployment levels or to massage short-term economic indicators to bolster electoral advantage. Britain in the 1950s and into the 1960s therefore experienced a continuous stop-go cycle of relative economic decline even though the individual standard of living of the people in general was continuously rising in absolute terms. What was also criminally negligent was the apparent belief in all parties that it was possible to increase consumption (often in the form of social welfarism) even though underlying economic performance was weak.

It is true that governments in the 1960s - first under Macmillan and later under Wilson - did attempt to address these questions. Both governments flirted with a more positive state interventionist or corporatist role - similar to that in many Continental European countries - without ever implementing this policy effectively. The major problem facing the British economy was that the short-term interest of the financial sector (which was now the dominant income earner in the economy) did not coincide with the need by the government to reduce interest rates, devalue sterling and force investment into manufacturing industry. As a result, every time governments attempted to manage the economy along corporatist lines there was a short-term financial crisis which forced the government to change course in defence of sterling. This made it impossible to aid manufacturing industry. Governments of all persuasions were of course not helped by the fact that the population as a whole had come to expect high levels of personal consumption, whether in the form of tax cuts or social welfare handouts. It is hardly surprising that the British economy did not perform well relatively even in the boom years after the war.

12.5   The Post-War Recession

The post-war recession brought these problems home with some force. The oil crisis exacerbated the problems facing manufacturing industry because it penalized the inefficient and uncompetitive. This was the bulk of British manufacturing industry. At the same time the entry into the EC in 1973 exposed British industry to the competitive disciplines of the European market. There is little doubt that, without the stagflationary consequences of the two oil price increases in the 1970s, British manufacturing industry would have suffered. The oil crises simply made the problem more acute because they necessitated substantial short-term reductions in private consumption as import prices rose and Britain had to devalue its currency to maintain export competitiveness.

The need for austerity was palpable in the early 1970s but, unfortunately, this problem was further exacerbated by the misguided economic policy of the Conservative government led by Ted Heath between 1970 and 1972. Rejecting the stop-go and corporatist logics of the past the Heath administration chose to further liberalize the financial markets in the expectation that lower interest rates and an increased supply of capital would channel into domestic manufacturing industry and generate an export led boom. This did not happen. Pursuing short-term rather than long-term economic logic the City lent the increased supply of credit to property speculators. This led to an unsustainable and inflationary boom in property prices which further reduced manufacturing investment, exacerbated manufacturing uncompetitiveness and led, technically, to the financial collapse of the City of London in 1973. The City was only saved from collapse by a lifeboat operation organized by the Bank of England which provided a moratorium on property debts and used taxpayers' money to bale out bankrupt financial institutions.

Tragically, although the Heath government learned the lesson of these mistakes and shifted back to corporatist policies' the inflationary crisis generated by property speculation and the oil crisis led, through union militancy in the form of a miners' strike, to the loss of office for the government. It was not surprising in these circumstances that the Labour governments between 1974 and 1979 completely failed to resolve the problems facing the economy. Faced with uncontrollable inflationary pressures, rising public expenditure commitments and the imminent collapse of manufacturing industry and the City of London, the government was forced into a policy of severe retrenchment and austerity. It was the Labour governments after 1975 which, after asking for short-term financial aid from the IMF, were forced to begin pruning public expenditure, raising taxes and imposing fairly stringent wage controls.

Not surprisingly the government alienated its traditional trade union and working class supporters who were forced to experience a reduction in their material expectations unseen since the Second World War.

Unfortunately for Labour, even though it managed to rescue the City of London from its own financial profligacy and was willing to limit its nationalization programmes to bailing out inefficient industries like shipbuilding, the business and financial community was not impressed. It feared that future Labour governments might intervene even more than they had. In these circumstances, even though by 1979 Labour had managed to reduce inflation significantly, cut public expenditure and get trade and exports back into surplus, both its own traditional supporters and those in the business and financial community wanted a return to the gratification of their own short-term self-interest.

The Thatcher led Conservative party offered the possibility of both these historically opposed interests being able to achieve their self-interest at the same time. On the one hand the City and business were offered the chance to have more laissez-fairism, reduced government expenditure and less state intervention. On the other hand, the working class was promised an end to wage controls and curbs on taxation levels. These promises were sufficient to fuse together a previously unholy alliance of traditional Labour-voting skilled and semi-skilled working class people with the traditional Conservative-voting business and financial community. Only the public sector middle class and the poor appear to have remained loyal to the Labour party in 1979 and throughout the 1980s.

This alliance, which persisted for three general elections in the 1980s, was sufficient, in the face of the divisions within the old Labour party (which led to the breakaway of less socialist inclined social democrats under Roy Jenkins and David Owen) to keep the Thatcher governments in office. Of course the coming on stream of North Sea oil reserves after 1979 was also crucially important, as was the US led expansionary policy of Ronald Reagan after 1982, which generated a world boom until 1987.

Between 1983 and 1987 Britain appeared to have gone through an economic miracle. Britain's productivity levels and growth rates were the envy of Europe and of the rest of the world. Trade union militancy was curbed and inflation had fallen into single figures and was as low as 4% to 5% by the mid-1980s. There was also an apparent turnaround in export performance in manufacturing industry and public expenditure cuts had led, by 1988 and 1989, to a public sector surplus. This revenue surplus was used to pay off historic debts. The current account of the balance of payments was also moving into surplus by 1987. It appeared that the Thatcher medicine of the most severe government induced recession - via historically high interest rates and severe retrenchment in public expenditure programmes between 1979 and 1982 - had been the sort of short sharp shock the economy needed to set it back on course.

This has been a popular view of the Thatcher years but it is now becoming apparent to the majority what was only naggingly warned of by a small academic minority at the time. It is probably a tragedy for the British economy that the Thatcher government was ever elected. With hindsight it would appear that the Thatcher government's and its advisers' reading of the failures of the Heath and Wilson eras was completely misguided. It would appear that the government continuously mistook cause and effect. Since the state was dragged into bailing out collapsing private sector industries and into wage bargaining in the 1960s and 1970s the New Right appear to have come to the wrong-headed conclusion that it was the state's intervention, rather than the inefficiency of private industry itself, which was the root of the problem. In this way they appear to have mistaken cause and effect.

This is not to argue that the state's role was always benign; rather it is to argue that it was the private sector's failure to tackle the problems of low investment, technical backwardness, overmanning and low productivity which caused uncompetitiveness, not the state's role per se. If the state was culpable it was in providing more social consumption - whether via public expenditure or tax cuts - than the economy could afford over the long term. The Thatcher government decisions to reduce public expenditure, cut back investment in industrial infrastructure and provide tax cuts for the consumer were in reality just more of the same under different ideological labels. The Thatcher governments merely reinforced the propensity for the British economy to increase its consumption of imported manufactured goods and to invest in wasteful property speculation which, in pushing up asset prices, generated the very wage spiral which creates the relatively high pay to output and,therefore, low productivity ratios which are the basic cause of Britain's poor export performance and de-industrialization..

12.6   The Challenges of the 1990s

The short to medium term offers a bleak prospect for the British economy. The country has a huge trade deficit of between £15-£20 billion. It has one of the highest inflation rates in the OECD at around 9.5% and unemployment fast approaching the 10%+ levels of the early 1980s. The corporate sector is struggling to export with historically high debts of £20 billion and crippling interest rates of around 14-17%. Growth rates were only just at 1% in 1990 and may be negative in 1991 on some predictions. Despite the severe recession which the government has imposed on the economy to squeeze out inflationary and import tendencies the trade deficit shows little sign of abating quickly. Added to this the government appears to have tied its hands by taking the country into the ERM at a relatively high exchange rate level. This will make it more difficult to improve export performance and will also ensure that unemployment levels are extremely high over the next two years at least. The prospect of the worst recession since the 1930s, whatever the consequences of the Gulf conflict for the world economy as a whole, appear inevitable in 1991/1992.

It is not surprising in this climate that the Conservative government dropped Mrs Thatcher and replaced her with the less ideologically blinkered John Major. The Thatcher experiment appears increasingly to have been a failure because it failed miserably to address the key issues facing British trade relationships with the rest of the world. Basically Britain has historically been a net importer of food, raw materials and semi-manufactured goods. This deficit on current account has historically been paid for by manufactured exports and, when these have fallen short, by invisible earnings from the City of London and other service industries. This situation persisted until the late 1970s when the Thatcher government came to office.

Unfortunately, under this misguided government, the manufacturing base of the economy was decimated by a self-inflicted government high interest rate policy which destroyed manufacturing exports. The result was that the deficit on current account (raw materials, food and manufactured goods) could only be paid for by earnings from service industries. Thankfully, in the mid-1980s, these service industries experienced a boom and the gap between their earnings and imports was made up by revenue from North Sea oil export earnings. Indeed in the mid-1980s these oil receipts were so large as to allow the government to mask the structural effects of its wrong-headed policy and also provide large tax cuts for consumers. Unfortunately these tax cuts were used either to buy imported manufactured goods or speculate in property assets. In this sense the Thatcher government appears to have used British oil to make its own industry even more uncompetitive (through exacerbating wage inflation relative to productivity and by providing demand for foreign manufactured products). In a real sense the government used British oil revenue to stimulate Japanese and German production at the expense of domestic industry.

The challenge of the 1990s is clearly to try to resolve this calamity. This will not be an easy task because Conservative governments have done little to invest in the infrastructure of industry or of education for the future. In fact the 1980s have been a decade of severe retrenchment in education and public sector construction. Furthermore, the size of manufacturing industry was reduced by one third in the 1930s and it will not be easy to reconstruct industry in the more competitive environment of the 1990s. This is especially true given the macro economic policy forced on the government after the collapse of its policy approach after 1989.

Thus while Britain may have a number of locational advantages for inward investment - the language, openness of trade and profit repatriation, the low corporate tax regime, the history of multinational investment - it has a number of macro and micro problems. Interest rates will have to remain high for the foreseeable future. Membership of the ERM is likely to occasion a severe labour shake-out and a rapid and sharp decline in asset prices. These falls in value are likely to be at their most extreme in the South East where the highest property price increases were recorded in the 1980s. This is also a function of the shake-out which is beginning to occur in the over manned and over priced financial and service sector of the economy.

On all fronts then there are severe difficulties facing the British economy in the 1990s. It is not yet clear whether these macro economic and corporate difficulties will be sufficient to overcome the historic willingness of investors to locate in this country. In the absence of inward investors it is probable, however, that the relative standard of living will decline throughout the 1990s.

CHAPTER 3

EC CENTRAL ADDRESSES AND INFORMATION SOURCES

1. CENTRAL ADDRESSES OF EC INSTITUTIONS

Consumer Policy Service
200 Rue de la Loi
B1049 Brussels
Tel.235-1111 telex 218-77 Comeu B

Court of Auditors
12 Rue Alcide de Gasperi
L1615 Luxembourg.
Tel.43981 telex 3512 Euraud Lu

Court of Justice of the European Communities
Palais de la Coeur de Justice
L-2925 Luxembourg
Tel.43031 telex. (Registry) 2510 CURIA LU
Telex (Press and Information) 2771 CJINFO LU

D.G.I (External Relations)
200 Rue de la Loi
B1049 Brussels.
Tel.235-1111 telex 218-77 Comeu B

D.G.II (Economic and Financial Affairs)
200 Rue de la Loi,
B1049 Brussels
Tel.235-1111 telex 218-77 Comeu B

D.G.III (Internal Market and Industrial Affairs)
200 Rue de la Loi
B1049 Brussels
Tel.235-1111 telex 218-77 Comeu B

D.G.IV (Competition)
200 Rue de la Loi
B1049 Brussels
Tel.235-1111 telex 218-77 Comeu B

D.G.V (Employment, Industrial Relations & Social Affairs)
200 Rue de la Loi,
B1049 Brussels
Tel.235-1111 telex 218-77 Comeu B

Bâtiment Jean Monnet
Rue Alcide de Gasperi
2920 Luxembourg
Tel.43011
Telex 3423/3446/3476 Comeur Lu

D.G.VI (Agriculture)
200 Rue de la Loi
B1049 Brussels
Tel.235-1111 telex 22037

D.G.VII (Transport)
200 Rue de la Loi
B1049 Brussels
Tel.235-1111 telex 218-77 Comeu B

D.G.VIII (Development)
200 Rue de la Loi
B1049 Brussels
Tel.235-1111 telex 218-77 Comeu B

D.G.IX (Personnel and Administration)
200 Rue de la Loi
B1049 Brussels
Tel.235-1111 Wetsraat 200 1049 Brussels
Telex: 21877 Comeu B

Bâtiment Jean Monnet
Rue Alcide de Gasperi
2920 Luxembourg
Tel.43011 telex 3423/3446/3476 comeu B

D.G.X (Information, Communication and Culture)
200 Rue de la Loi
B1049 Brussels
Tel.235-1111 telex 218-77 Comeu B

D.G.XI (Environment, Consumer Protection and Nuclear Safety)
200 Rue de la Loi
B1049 Brussels
Tel. 235-1111 telex 218-77 Comeu B

Bâtiment Jean Monnet
Rue Alcide de Gasperi
2920 Luxembourg.
Tel.43011 telex 3423/3446/3476 Comeur Lu

D.G.XII (Science, Research and Development)
200 Rue de la Loi
B1049 Brussels.
Tel.235-1111 telex 218-77 Comeu B

D.G.XIII (Telecommunications, Information Industries and Innovation)
200 Rue de la Loi
B1049 Brussels
Tel.235-1111 telex 218-77 Comeu B
Fax 235-0148

Bâtiment Jean Monnet
Rue Alcide de Gasperi
2920 Luxembourg
Tel.43011 telex 2752 Eurodoc Lu
Fax 43012165

D.G.XIV (Fisheries)
200 Rue de la Loi
B1049 Brussels
Tel.235-1111 telex 218-77 Comeu B

D.G.XV (Financial Institutions and Company Law)
200 Rue de la Loi
B1049 Brussels
Tel.235-1111 telex 218-77 Comeu B

D.G.XVI (Regional Policies)
200 Rue de la Loi
B1049 Brussels
Tel.235-1111 telex 218-77 Comeu B

D.G.XVII (Energy)
200 Rue de la Loi
B1049 Brussels
Tel.235-1111 telex 218-77 Comeu B

D.G.XVIII (Credit and Investments)
Centre A Wagner Rue Alcide de Gasperi,
2920 Luxembourg
Tel.43011 telex 3366 Eurfin Lu
Fax 436322

D.G.XIX (Budgets)
200 Rue de la Loi
B1049 Brussels
Tel.235-1111 telex 218-77 Comeu B

Bâtiment Jean Monnet
Rue Alcide de Gasperi
2920 Luxembourg
Tel.43011 telex 3423/3446/3476 Comeur Lu

D.G.XX (Financial Control)
200 Rue de la Loi
B1049 Brussels
Tel.235-1111 telex 218-77 Comeu B

D.G.XXI (Customs Union and Indirect Taxation)
200 Rue de la Loi
B1049 Brussels
Tel.235-1111 telex 218-77 Comeu B

D.G.XXII (Co-ordination of Structural Policies)
200 Rue de la Loi
B1049 Brussels
Tel.235-1111 telex 218-77 Comeu B

D.G.XXIII (Enterprise Policy, Commerce, Tourism and Social Economy)
200 Rue de la Loi
B1049 Brussels
Tel.235-1111 telex 616-55 Burap/B

Economic and Social Committee
2 Rue Ravenstein
B-1000 Brussels
Tel.519-9011 telex 25983 Ceseur
Fax 5134893

Euratom Supply Agency
200 Rue de la Loi
B1049 Brussels
Tel.235-1111 telex 218-77 Comeu B

European Centre for the Developement of Vocational Training(CEDEFOP)
22 Bundesallee
D-1000 Berlin 15
Tel.88-4120 telex 184163 Eucen D

European Commission
200 Rue de la Loi
B1049 Brussels
Tel.235-1111 telex 218-77 Comeu B

London Office
8 Storey's Gate
London SW1P 3AT
Tel.071-222-8122

European Foundation for Improvement of Living & Working Conditions
Loughlinstown House
Shankill
County Dublin
Republic of Ireland
Tel.82-6888 telex 30726 Eurf

European Investment Bank
100 Bud. Konrad Adenauer
L2950 Luxembourg
Tel.43791 telex 3530 Bnkeu Lu

U.K. Office
68 Pall Mall
London SW1Y 5ES
Tel.071-839-3351 telex 919159 Bankeu G

European Parliament
L-2929 Luxembourg
Tel. 43001 telex 3494/2894 Euparl Lu

Palais de l'Europe
647006 Strasbourg Cedex
France
Tel. 88 374001

U.K. office
2 Queen Anne's Gate
London SW1H 9AA
Tel.071-222-0411

Financial Control
Bâtiment Jean Monnet
Rue Alcide de Gasperi
2920 Luxembourg
Tel. 43011 telex 3423/3446/3476 Comeur Lu

Joint Interpreting and Conference Service
200 Rue de la Loi B1049 Brussels.
Tel.235-1111 telex 218-77 Comeu B
Fax 2359584

Legal Service
200 Rue de la Loi
B1049 Brussels
Tel.235-1111 telex 218-77 Comeu B

Office for Official Publications of the EC
2 Rue Mercier
L-2985 Luxembourg.
Tel.49928-1 telex 1324 Pubof Lu
Fax 495719

Political Information on European Parliament Parties
European Centre Plateau du Kirchberg,
L2929 Luxembourg
Tel.43001 telex 2894 Euparl Lu

Security Office
200 Rue de la Loi
B1049 Brussels
Tel.235-1111 telex 218-77 Comeu B

Spokesman's Service
200 Rue de la Loi
B1049 Brussels
Tel.235-1111 telex 218-77 Comeu B

Statistical Office (EUROSTAT)
Bâtiment Jean Monnet
Rue Alcide de Gasperi
2920 Luxembourg
Tel.43011 telex 3423/3446/3476 Comeur Lu

Task Force for Human Resources, Education, Training and Youth
200 Rue de la Loi
B1049 Brussels
Tel.235-1111 telex 218-77 Comeu B

Translation Service
200 Rue de la Loi
B1049 Brussels
Tel.235-1111 telex 218-77 Comeu B

Bâtiment Jean Monnet
Rue Alcide de Gasperi
2920 Luxembourg
Tel.43011 telex 3423/3446/3476 Comeur Lu

2. E.C. INFORMATION SOURCES

2.1 E.C. Information Offices

N.B. If dialling from within the country concerned then the S.T.D. prefix (0) must be added to all the numbers given below

BELGIUM
73 Rue Archimède
B-1040 Brussels
Tel.0235-1111 telex 26657 Cominf B
Fax 0235-0166

DENMARK
Hojbrohus 61 Ostergade Postbox 144
DK-1004 Kobenhavn K
Tel.3314-4140 telex 16402 Comeur K
Fax 3311-1203

FRANCE
61 Rue des Belles-Feuilles
F-75782 Paris Cedex 16
Tel.4501-5885 telex 611019 F Comeur
Fax 4727-2607

GERMANY
22 Zitelmannstrasse
D-5300 Bonn
Tel.023-8041 telex 88-6648 Europ D
Fax 023-8048

102 Kurfurstendamm
D-1000 Berlin 31
Tel.892-4028 telex 184015 Europ D
Fax 892-2059

27 Erhardstrasse
D-8000 Munchen.
Tel.202-1011 telex 521-8135
Fax 202-1015

GREECE
2 Vassilissis Sofias PO Box 11002
Athens 10674
Tel.724-3982 telex 219324 Ecat Gr
Fax.722-3715

IRISH REPUBLIC
29 Molesworth Street Dublin 2.
Tel.71-2244 Telex.93827 Euco Ei
Fax 71-2657

ITALY
29 Via Poli
I-00187 Roma
Tel.678-9722 Telex.610184 Euroma I
Fax.679-1658

61 Corso Magenta I-20123 Milano.
Tel.80-1505/6/7/8 telex316002 Eurmil I
Fax 481-8543

LUXEMBOURG
Bâtiment Jean Monnet
Rue Alcide de Gasperi
L-2920 Luxembourg.
Tel.43011 telex 3423/3446/3476 Comeur Lu
Fax.4301-4433

NETHERLANDS
29 Lange Voorhout
Den Haag
Tel.46-9326 telex 31094 Eurco Nl
Fax 64-6619

PORTUGAL
Centre Européen Jean Monnet
56 Rua do Salitre
D-1200 Lisbon.
Tel.154-1144 telex 0404/18810 Comeur P
Fax 155-4397

SPAIN
41 Calle de Serrano 5A Planta
Madrid 1
Tel.435-1700/435-1528 telex.46818 Oipe E
Fax 276-0387

UNITED KINGDOM
8 Storey's Gate
London SW1P 3AT
Tel.71-222-8122 telex 23208 Euruk G
Fax 71-222-0900

Windsor House 9-15 Bedford Street
Belfast BT2 7EG
Tel.232-24-0708 telex 74117 Cecbel G
Fax 232-24-8241

4 Cathedral Road
Cardiff CF1 9SG
Tel.222-37-1631 telex 497727 Europa G
Fax 222-39-5489

7 Alva Street
Edinburgh EH2 4PH
Tel.31-225-2058 telex 727420 Euedin G
Fax 31-26-4105

2.2 European Information Centres

BELGIUM
Bureau Economique de la Province de Namur
2 Avenue Sergent Vrithoff
B-5000 Namur
Tel.3281-73-5209

Kamervan Koophandel en Nijverheid
12 Markgravestraat
B-2000 Antwerpen
Tel.32-3-233-6732

DENMARK
Arhus Amtskommune 18-20 Haslegardvaenget
DK 8210 Arhus
Tel.45 615-0318

Odensen Erhvervsrad 51 Norregade
DK-5000 Odense C
Tel.45-912-6121

FRANCE
Chambre de Commerce et d'Industrie de Comité
d'Expansion Aquitaine
2 Place de la Bourse
F-33076 Bordeaux
Tel.5652-6547-9894

Région Lorraine
1 Place St Clément BP.1004
F-57036 Metz Cedex 1
Tel.8733-6000

Chambre de Commerce et d'Industrie de Nantes
Centre des Salorges BP.718
F-44027 Nantes Cedex 04
Tel. 4044-6008

Chambre de Commerce et d'Industrie de
Strasbourg et du Bas-Rhin
10 Place Gutenberg
F-67081 Strasbourg
Tel.8832-1255

Chambre de Commerce et de l'Industrie
de Lyon
16 Rue de la République
F-69289 Lyon Cedex 02
Tel.7838-1010

GERMANY
ZENIT. 54 Dohne
D-4330 Molheim
Tel.2083-0004

RKW. 33 Heilwigstrasse
D-2000 Hamburg 20
Tel.40460-2087

DIHT. 148 Adenauer Allee Postfach 1446
D-5300 Bonn 1
Tel.228-1040

Industrie und Handelskammer
12 Martin Luther Strasse
D-8400 Regensburg
Tel.9415-6941

Handwerkskammer
43 Heilbronner Strasse
Postfach 2621
D7000 Stuttgart 1
Tel.7112-5941

DHKT
1 Johanniterstrasse
Haus des Deutschen Handwerks
D-5300 Bonn 1
Tel.228-5451

GREECE
Association of Industries of Northern Greece
Chamber of Commerce of Northern Greece
1 Place Morihovo
GR-54653 Thessaloniki
Tel.31-53-9817 /31-53-9682

Eommex
16 Rue Xenias
Gr-11528 Athens
Tel.1-362-5630

IRELAND
Irish Export Board Merrion Hall PO Box 203
Strand Road
Sandymount
Dublin 4
Tel.1-69-5011

One Stop Shop
The Granary
Michael Street
Limerick
Tel.61-40777

ITALY
Camera di Commercio Industria Artigianato
e Agricultura di Napoli.
58 Corso Meridionale
I-80143 Napoli
Tel.81 28-5322

Camera di Commercio Industria Artigianato
e Agricultura di Milano
9b Via Merivigli
I-20123 Milano
Tel.2-85151

Confartigianatoic NA/CLAAI/CASA
18 Via Milano
I-25126 Brescia
Tel.30-28-9051

Confindustria
30 Viale dell'Astronomia
I-00144 Rome
Tel.6-59031

Ass. della Provincia di Bologna
4 Via San Domenico
I-40124 Bologna
Tel.51-52-9611

LUXEMBOURG
Chambre de Commerce/Chambre des Métiers/
Fédération des Industriels
7 Rue Alcide de Gasperi
BP 1503
L-1981 Luxembourg
Tel.43-5853

NETHERLANDS
CIMK-RIMK Dalsteindreef BP 112
NL-1112 XC Dimen-Suid
Tel.20-90-1071

INDUMA/BOM/LIOF
21a Prins Hendriklann
PO Box 995
NL-5700 AZ Helmond
Tel.49-203-4035

PORTUGAL
Associação Industrial Portuguesa
Exponsor
P-4100 Porto
Tel.2-68-4814 / 2-67-3220

Banco de Fomento Nacional
59 Avenida Casal Ribeiro
P-1000 Lisboa
Tel.1-56-1071 / 1-56/2021

SPAIN
CIDEM 4031 Avenida Diagonal
E-08008 Barcelona
Tel.3-217-2008

Camera Oficial de Comercio Industria y
Navegacion 50 Avenida de Recalde
E-48008 Bilbao Vizcaya
Tel.4-444-5054

Confederacion de Empresarios de Andalucia
Avenida San Francisco Javier s/n
1-9 Edificio Sevilla
E-41005 Sevilla
Tel.54-64-2013

Confederacion Espanola de Organizaciones
Empresariales 50 Diego de Leon
E-28006 Madrid
Tel.1-450-8048

IMPI-INFE 141-2 Paseo de la Castellana
E-28046 Madrid
Tel.1-450-8048

UNITED KINGDOM
Strathclyde Euro Info Centre
25 Bothwell Street
Glasgow G2 6NR
Tel.41-221-0999

North of England Euro Info Centre
The Library
Newcastle-upon-Tyne Polytechnic
Ellison Place
Newcastle-upon-Tyne
NE1 8ST
Tel.91-261-5131
Fax. 091-261 6911

Birmingham European Business Centre
Chamber of Commerce House PO Box 360
75 Harborne Road
Birmingham B15 3DH
Tel.21-455-0268

Centre for European Business Information
Small Firms Centre Ebury Bridge House
2-18 Ebury Bridge Road
London SW1W 8QD
Tel.71-730-8115

2.3 European Library Locations and European Documentation Centres

* Denotes that the library only receives basic information from the EC. In other cases the supply is comprehensive.

BELGIUM

Antwerp	Universiteit Antwerpen (UFSIA).*
Bruges	College of Europe.
Brussels	Université Libre de Bruxelles. Centre for European Policy Studies.* Royal Institute of International Relations.* Vrije Universiteit.*
Ghent	Rijksuniversiteit Gent.
Liége	Université de Liegé, Faculté de Droit.*
Louvain	Université Catholique de Louvain, Institut d'Etudes Européennes. Katholieke Universiteit Leuven, Universiteitsbibliotheek.* Institut de Recherches (IRES).*
Namur	Bilbiothèque Universitaire Moretus Plantin.*

DENMARK

Aalborg	Aalborg Universiteitsbibliotek.
Aarhus	Handelshojskolen i Aarhus Statsbibliotek. Frederiksberg Handelshojskolens Bibliotek.

Copenhagen for International Odense	Koebenhavns Universiteit- Institut Ret og Europaret. Odense Universitetsbibliotek.

FRANCE

Aix-en-Provence	Faculté de Droit et de Science Politique d'Aix-Marseille.
Amiens	Université d'Amiens.*
Angers	Université d'Angers.
Besançon	Universite de Besancon.
Brest	Université de Bretagne Occidentale.*
Caen	Université de Caen.*
Clermont	Université de Clermont.
Dijon	Université de Dijon.*
Ecully	Groupe Ecole Supérieure de Commerce de Lyon.*
Fontainebleau	Institut Européen d'Administration des Affairs.*
Grenoble	Centre Universitaire de Recherche Européen et Internationale.
Lille	Université de Lille Villeneuve.
Limoges	Université de Limoges.*
Lyons	Université Jean Moulin. Université de Lyon.*
Le Mans	Bibliothèque Universitaire du Maine.*
Malakoff	Bilbiothèque de l'Université René Descartes.*
Montigny	le Brx.Manistel Management Info ServiceTélématique.
Montpellier	Université de Montpellier.
Mont-St-Aignan	Faculté de Droit et Sciences Economiques et de Gestion.*
Nancy	Université de Nancy.
Nanterre	Université de Paris Nanterre.*

Nantes	Université de Nantes.*
Nice	Université de Nice.*
Orleans	Université d'Orléans.*
Paris	Université de Paris.
	Université de Paris, Centre Universitaire d'Etudes Communautés Européennes.
	Université de Paris-Nord, Villetaneuse.*
	Livres Hebdo/Livres de France.
	Ecole Nationale d'Administration.*
	Université de Paris XII, La Varenne St Hilaire.
	Palais de Justice.
Pau	Université de Pau et des Pays l'Audour.*
Perpignan	CDRE Université.*
Pessac	Université de Bordeaux.*
Poitiers	Université de Poitiers.
Rheims	EUR Faculté de Droit et Sciences Economiques de Rheims.
Rennes	Facultés des Sciences Juridiques.
Sceaux	Université de Paris.
Strasbourg	Université des Sciences Juridiques, Politiques et Sociales de Strasbourg.*
St. Martin d'Heres	Université des Sciences Sociales de Grenoble.*
Toulon	Université de Toulon.*
Toulouse	Université des Sciences Sociales.
Tours	Université Francois Rabelais.*

GERMANY	
Aachen	Aachener Zentrum für Europäische Studien.
Augsburg	Universitätsbibliothek Augsburg.*
Bayreuth	Universitätsbibliothek Bayreuth.*
Berlin	Freie Universität Berlin, Universitätsbibliothek. Europäische Akademie - Bibliothek.
Bielefeld	Universitätsbibliothek.*
Bochum	Universitätsbibliothek.*
Bonn	Dokumentationsstelle der Deutschen Gesellschaft für Auswärtige Politik EV.*
Bremen	Universität Bremen.*
Cologne	Universität Köln. Universität Köln - Institut für das Recht der Europäische Gemeinschaften.*
Darmstadt	TH Darmstadt - Fachbereich Gesellschafts.*
Duisberg	Universitätsbibliothek Duisberg.
Ebenhausen	Stiftung Wissenschaft und Politik.*
Frankfurt	Universitat Frankfurt.*
Freiburg	Universität Freiberg.*
Giessen	Justus Liebig Universität.
Gottingen	Universität Gottingen.*
Hamburg	HWWA - Institut für Wirtschafts- forschung, Hamburg. Universität Hamburg.
Hanover	Fachbereichsbibliotek.*
Heidelberg	Max-Planck Institut.

Kiel	Institut für Weltwirtschaft an der Universität Kiel.
Konstanz	Universität Konstanz Bibliothek.
Main	Gutenburg Universität Institut für Politikwissenschaft.
Mannheim	Universität Mannheim.*
Marburg	Philipps-Universität Marburg.*
Munich	Universität München.*
Munster	Westfälische Wilhelms Universität.
Nuremberg	Universität Erlangen-Nürnberg - Gruppenbibliothek.*
Osnabruck	Universität Osnabruck.
Passau	Universität Passau - Lehrstuhl für Staats und Verwaltungsrecht, Volkerrecht und Europarecht.*
Regensburg	Universitätsbibliothek Regensberg.*
Saarbrucken	Universität des Saarlandes.
Siegen	Universitätsbibliothek.*
Speyer	Hochschule für Verwaltungswissenchaften.
Stuttgart	Universität Hohenheim.*
Trier	Universität Trier.
Tubingen	Universität Tubingen.
Wurzburg	Universität Wurzburg.

GREECE

Athens	Spoudastirio Domioisio v Dikaio, Kentro Europaikis.
Komotini	Universite Demokritos de Thrace.
Thessaloniki	Centre de Droit Economique International et Européen.

IRELAND

Cork	University College.
Dublin	University College.
	Trinity College
Galway	University College.*
Limerick	National Institute for Higher Education.

ITALY

Ancona	Universita di Ancona.*
Bari	Universita di Bari.
Bologna	Universita degli Studi di Bologna.
Cagliari	Universita di Cagliari.
Catania	Universita di Catania.
Ferrara	Universita di Ferrara.*
Florence	Dipartimento di Scienza Politica e Sociologia Politica.
	Instituto Universitario Europeo, Biblioteca and Archivi.
Genoa	Universita di Genova.
Milan	Universita degli Studi di Milano.
	Centro Internazionale di Studi e Documentaziome sulle Comunita Europee.
	Universita Commerciale Luigi Bocconi - Biblioteca.
Modena	Centro di Documentazione e Richerche sulle Comunita Europee della Universite degli Studi.*
Naples	Societa Italiana per l'Organizzazione Internazionale.
	Universita di Napoli - Dipartimento de Economia Politica Agraria.*
	Universita di Napoli - Instituto Sociologico Giuridico.*

Padua	Universita degli Studi di Padova.
Palermo	Universita di Palermo.*
Parma	Universita di Parma.
Pavia	Universita degli Studi di Pavia.*
Perugia	Universita di Perugia.*
Pescara	Universita 'G.D'Annunzio'.*
Pisa	Universita di Pisa.*
Reggio Calabria	ISESP Insituto Superiore Europeo di Studi Politici.*
Rome	Societa Italiana per l'Organazzione Internazionale (SIOI). Universita di Roma. Centro Studi di Diritto Comunitario.*
Sassari	Universita degli Studi di Sassari.
Siena	Universita degli Studi di Siena.
Turin	Universita di Torino.
Trieste	Universita degli Studi.*
Urbino	Centro Alti Studi Europei.*
Verona	Universita di Verona.*

LUXEMBOURG

| Luxembourg | Centre International d'Etudes et de Recherches Européennes Institut Universitaire International. |

THE NETHERLANDS

Amsterdam	Universiteit van Amsterdam. Vrije Universiteit.*
Delft	Technische Hogeschool.
The Hague	TMC Asser Instituut.
Enschede	Technische Hogeschool.
Groningen	Rijksuniversiteit Bibliothek.
Leiden	Rijksuniversiteit te Lieden.*

Maastricht	Raad der Europese Gemeenten en Regio's.
Nijmegen	Katholieke Universiteit.*
Rotterdam	Erasmus Universiteit.*
Tilburg	Katholieke Hogeschool.*
Utrecht	Rijks Universiteit.*
Wageningen	Agricultural University Library.*

PORTUGAL

Braga	Universidade do Minho.
Coimbra	Universidade de Coimbra.
Lisboa	Universidade Técnica de Lisboa.
	Universidade de Lisboa - Faculdade de Economia.*
	Universidade de Lisboa - Faculdade de Direito.
	Universidade Católica Portuguesa.
	Oeiras Instituto Nacional de Administração.
Ponta Delgada	Universidade dos Acores.
Porto	Universidade do Porto.

SPAIN

Alicante	Camera de Comercio.
Badajoz	Universidad de Extremadura.
Barcelona	Escuela Superior de Administracio de Empresas.
Bilbao	Universidad de Deusto.
	Universidad de Bilbao.*
Cordoba	Universidad de Cordoba.
Granada	Universidad de Granada Economicas.
Madrid	Universidad Politecnica de Madrid.

	Universidad Autonoma de Madrid.
	Universidad Complutense.
	Universidad de Alcala.*
Murcia	Universidad de Murcia.
Oviedo	Universidad de Oviedo
Palma de Mallorca	Les Islas Balearas Centros de Documentacion Europea.
Pamplona	Universidad de Navarra.
Salamanca	Universidad de Salamanca.
San Sebastian	Empressariales (ESTE)
Santander	Universidad de Cantabria.
Santiago de Compostela	Universidad de Santiago.
Seville	Universidad de Sevilla.
Tenerife	Universidad San Fernando de la Laguna.
Toledo	Camera de Comercio y Industria.
Valencia	Universidad de Valencia.
Valladolid	Universidad de Valladolid.
Zaragoza	Universidad de Zaragoza.

UNITED KINGDOM

Aberdeen	Aberdeen University.*
Ashford	Wye College.*
Bath	University of Bath.
Belfast	Queen's University.
Birmingham	City of Birmingham Polytechnic.* Birmingham University.*
Bradford	University of Bradford.
Brighton	University of Sussex.
Bristol	University of Bristol.*
Cambridge	Cambridge University.
Canterbury	University of Kent.

Cardiff	University of Wales, College of Cardiff.
Colchester	University of Essex.*
Coleraine	University of Ulster.
Coventry	University of Warwick.
Lanchester	Polytechnic.*
Dundee	University of Dundee.
Durham	University of Durham.*
Edinburgh	University of Edinburgh.
Exeter	Exeter University.
Glasgow	University of Glasgow.
Guildford	University of Surrey.*
Hull	University of Hull.
Keele	University of Keele.*
Lancaster	University of Lancaster.
Leeds	Leeds Polytechnic.*
	University of Leeds.*
Leicester	Leicester University.
London	Queen Mary College.
	Polytechnic of North London.
	Royal Institute of International Affairs.*
Loughborough	Loughborough University.
Manchester	University of Manchester.*
Newcastle-u-Tyne	Newcastle Polytechnic.
Norwich	University of East Anglia.*
Nottingham	University of Nottingham.
Oxford	Bodleian Library.
Portsmouth	Portsmouth Polytechnic.
Reading	University of Reading.
Salford	University of Salford.*
Sheffield	Sheffield Polytechnic.
Southampton	University of Southampton.*
Wolverhampton	Wolverhampton Polytechnic.*

2.4   European Library Locations: EC Depository Libraries

BELGIUM
Brussels   Royal Library.

DENMARK
Copenhagen   Det Kongelige Bibliothek
                             Kontoret for Internationale
                             Publikationer.

FRANCE
Paris   Bibliothèque Nationale.

GERMANY
Berlin   Staatsbibliothek.
Bonn   Deutscher Bundestag - Bibliothek.
Frankfurt   Deutsche Bibliothek.
Munich   Bayerische Staatsbibliothek.

GREECE
None.

IRELAND

ITALY
Florence   Biblioteca Nazionale Centrale.
Naples   Biblioteca Nazionale.

LUXEMBOURG
Luxembourg   Bibliothèque Naionale.

THE NETHERLANDS
None.

PORTUGAL
None.

SPAIN
Madrid   Biblioteca Nacional.

UNITED KINGDOM
Boston Spa   British Library.
Liverpool   City of Liverpool Central Library.
London   British Library.
                        City of Westminster Library.
                        British Library of Political and
                        Economic Science.

2.5 European Library Locations: European Reference Centres

BELGIUM
Antwerp   Europees Studie en
                        Informatiecentrum.
Arlon   La Maison de l'Europe du
Luxembourg   (CIFEL).
Mons   Université de l'Etat.
Saint-Ghislain   Centre International de Formation
                        Européenne   (CIFE).

DENMARK
None.

FRANCE
Paris   Universit de Paris XII, 94210 La
                        Varenne-St-Hilaire
                        Faculté Droit
                        Sciences Politiques et
                        Economiques.

Strasbourg	Chambre de Commerce et d'Industrie de Strasbourg et du Bas-Rhin.

GERMANY

Bamberg	Universitätsbibliothek Bamberg.
Bonn	Interdisziplinares Zentrum für Europäische Fragen und Lehrerausbildung.
Dortmund	Universität Dortmund.
Emden	Fachhochschule Ostfriesland.
Essen	Universitätsbibliothek.
Flensburg	Pedagogische Hochschule Flensburg.
Fulda	Fachhochschule.
Hamburg	Universität de Bundeswehr Hamburg.
Heidelberg	Institut für Ausländisches und Internationales.
Kassel	Gesamthochschulbibliothek.
Koblenz	Fachhochschule des Landes Rheinland-Pfalz Bibliothek.
Mainz	Universitätsbibliothek.
Munich	Universität der Bundeswehr München.
Oldenburg	Universität Oldenburg.
Osnabruck	Fachhochschule.
Pforzheim	Fachhochschule, Wirtschaft Pforzheim.
Reutlingen	Hochschulbibliothek Reutlingen.
Stuttgart	Württembergische Landesbibliothek Zeitschriftenstelle.
Worms	Fachhochschule des Landes Rheinland - Pfalz.

GREECE
None.

IRELAND
None.

ITALY

Bergamo	Instituto Universitario di Bergamo Biblioteca Economia e
Commercio.	
Brindisi	Centro Informazioni e Studi sulle Comunita Europee. CampobassoASCOM Associazone dei Comuni Molisani.
Castiglione	Scalo Universita degli Studi della Calabria.
Cuneo	Biblioteca Civica.
Macerata	Universita di Macerata.
Messina	Universita di Messina.
Milan	Universita Cattolica del Sacro Cuore.
Nuoro	Biblioteca 'Sebastiano Satta'.
Parma	Collegio Europea di Parma.
Ragusa	Camera di Commercio, Industria Artigianato e Agricultura.
Rome	Centro Studi di Dirito
Comunitario.	
Scuola	Superiore della Pubblica Amministrazione.
Salerno	Universita di Salerno.
Sassari	Centro Studi e Informazione Europea.
Trento	Libera Universita degli Studi. Ufficio Studi della Regione.
Trentino	Alto Adige.

LUXEMBOURG
None.

THE NETHERLANDS
None.

PORTUGAL
Lisbon   Colegio Universitario Pio XII.

SPAIN
Gijon   Universidad de Oviedo.
Madrid   Escuela Diplomatica Cursos sobre
                          las Comunidades Europeas.

UNITED KINGDOM
Aberystwyth   University College of
                          Wales, Aberystwyth.
Chalfont St Giles   Buckinghamshire College of
                          Higher Education.
Chelmsford   Chelmsford Institute of Higher
                          Education.
Middlesbrough   Teeside Polytechnic.
Edinburgh   National Library of Scotland.
Exmouth   Rolle College.
Halifax   Percival Whitley College of
                          Further Education.
Hatfield   Hatfield Polytechnic.
Inverness   Highlands Regional Council
                          Library Service.
Ipswich   Suffolk County Library.
London   Ealing College of Higher
                          Education.
Northampton   Nene College.
Plymouth   College of St Mark and St John
                          Foundation.

Preston	Preston Public Library. Lancashire Polytechnic.
Reading	Bulmershe College.
Sheffield	University of Sheffield.
Stirling	Stirling University.
Swansea	University College of Swansea.
Wrexham	North East Wales Institute of Higher Education.

CHAPTER 4

GLOSSARY

GLOSSARY

AAM Association of the Maize Starch Industries of the EEC. *Avenue de la Joyeuse Entrée 1-5, Boîte 10,B - 1000 Brussels, Belgium.*

AASM Associated African States and Malagasy. Participants in the Yaoundé Convention.

ABEL Provides subscribers with access to legislation information once it is published in the Official Journal. Available via OOPEC. Host EUR-OP. OOPEC, European Communities, *OP/4-7, 2 Rue Mercier, L - 2985 Luxembourg.*

ABEX Expert system for the automatic calculation and presentation of FMEA and Fault Tree Analysis. EUREKA approved December 1986.

Accession Treaty (Treaty of Brussels) Signed on 22 January 1972 by the original six Member States of the EC plus the UK, Denmark, Norway and the Republic of Ireland; came into force in January 1973. Provided detailed arrangements for the accession of the four new members. Norway did not join following an unfavourable national referendum.

ACE Action by the Community relating to the Environment (1984), One of the groups set up under EYE but still being supported by the Commission, engaged in the promotion of clean technology and recycling techniques.

ACICAFE Association for the Coffee Trade and Industry in the EEC. *Markgravestraat 12, B - 2000 Antwerpen, Belgium.*

ACMDP Advisory Committees on the Management of Demonstration Projects.

ACOR Advisory Committee on Communities' Own Resources.

ACP States The 66 African, Caribbean and Pacific countries party to the Lomé Convention. *Secretariat: Ave nue G Henri 451, B - 1200 Brussels, Belgium.* DG VIII

ACPM Advisory Committee on Programme Management.

Acquis Communautaire Literally 'Community acquisition', refers to secondary Community legislation, that is, the measures giving effect to the primary legislation (the Treaties establishing the Communities).

ACSTT Advisory Committee on Scientific and Technical Training.

Action Committee for United States of Europe known as the Monnet Committee after its founder, Jean Monnet. Established in 1955 by the main political parties and non-Communist trade unions of France, Germay, Italy, Luxembourg, Belgium and the Netherlands. Aim was, 'to ensure the unity of action of those organizations which are its members and on the basis of those concrete achievements, progress towards the United States of Europe'. Took a central role in the formation and ratification of the Treaties of Rome. Disbanded in 1975.

ACTU Abbreviation of actualites. A database of SII, it contains information on any document by the Secretariat-General to the Commission, and is updated daily.

ADECO Dismantling workshop for Orgel fuels (JRC - safety of nuclear materials programme).

Adenauer, Konrad (1876-1967) First Chancellor of the Federal Republic of Germany, 1949-1963; and Foreign Minister 1951-1955. A founder member of the Christian Democratic Union in West Germany, in 1945. He proposed a Franco-German union in 1950 as a first step towards a united Europe. In 1963, he signed the Franco-German Treaty of Cooperation.

ADKMS Advanced Data and Knowledge Management Systems. (ESPRIT Project approved 1984.)

ADP Agricultural Development Programme. Generic term for programmes under Regional Policy targeting particular areas for rural regeneration (e.g. Scottish Islands ADP 1987-).

ADR European Agreement on the International Carriage of Dangerous Goods by Road. Began in 1968 and had 14 countries as signatories including all the EC countries except Denmark and Eire. The Agreement enabled some dangerous goods conveyed by road to pass through international borders without further checks as long as the goods were labelled according to the Agreement's rules.

Advisory Committee on Banking. Set up in 1977 as part of the First Council Directive on banking. Composed of three representatives from each of the bodies responsible for bank supervision in the Member States.

Advisory Committee on Foodstuffs. Set up in 1975 to advise the Commission on all difficulties relating to the harmonization of laws on foodstuffs. Comprises consumer representatives, workers and other representatives from agriculture, industry and trade. DG III and DG XI.

AEA Association of European Airlines. Represents over 20 airlines accounting for around 90 % of Europe's air traffic. *Avenue Louise 350, Boîte 4, B-1050 Brussels, Belgium.*

AEDCL Association of EDC librarians in the UK. *Hon. Sec: Mr I .Thomson, University College Library, PO Box 78, Cardiff 1XL, United Kingdom.*

AEFA European Association for Animated Films. *Rue Frans Merjay 127, B - 100 Brussels, Belgium.*

AEIH European Association of Clothing Industries. Body formed in 1948 to represent and futher the interests of the international clothing industry. *Rue Montoyer 47, 1040 Brussels, Belgium.*

AEPPC Association of European Insolvency Administrators. Founded in 1981 to exchange experience of insolvency procedures. *Shelley House, 3 Noble Street, London, EC2V 7DQ, United Kingdom.*

AFG Association of the Glucose Producers in the EEC. *Avenue de la Joyeuse Entrée 1-5, Boîte 10, B - 1040 Brussels, Belgium.*

AGEE Association of European Students. *Rue de Washington 40, B - 1050, Brussels, Belgium.*

AGEFT On-line database transmitting data from the disbursing agencies to the EAGGF. Provides daily updates on activities of EAGGF.

.

AGINFO Database providing trade figures from the CAP. Access through 'Telecom Gold'.

Agreement of Association Provides for special relationships between EC and non-EC countries having particular requirements in regard to the CCT (e.g. AA with Morocco, Tunisia, etc.) Came into force in 1969, and allowed almost all Moroccan and Tunisian products to receive EC treatment. In return, Morocco and Tunisia agreed among other things not to discriminate between Member States of the EC.

AGREP Agricultural Research Projects. A database on SII. Access via ECHO and DATACENTRALEN.

AGREX Mechanism for overseeing expenditure under the Guarantee Section of the EAGGF.

AGRIS International Information System for the Agricultural Sciences and Technology. Access via ESA-IRS and DIMDI.

AGROMET Meteorological database in conjunction with the CADDIA Programme.

AIDA Advanced Integrated Circuit Design Aids. ESPRIT approved 1985.

AIME Advanced informatics for medicine in Europe. A project, not yet operational, designed to develop and improve the use of IT and telecommunications through cooperation between users and manufacturers in the field of biotechnology and biomedicine.

AIPCEE Association of Fish Industries of the EC. *Pathoekeweg 48, B - 8000 Brugge, Belgium.* Also at *1 Green Street, Grosvenor Square, London, W1Y 3RG, United Kingdom.*

Airbus Industrie European aircraft consortium.

AMADEUS Multi-method Approach for Developing Universal Specifications. ESPRIT project approved 1985.

AMFEP Association of Microbial Food Enzyme Producers within Western Europe. *Avenue de Cortenberg 172, B - 1040 Brussels, Belgium.*

AMICE European Computer Integrated Manufacturing Architecture. ESPRIT project approved 1984.

AMIS Agricultural Market Intelligence System. A database within CADDIA.

AMPES Advanced Logical Programming Environments. ESPRIT project approved 1985.

AMPI National accounts database. Access via CRONOS.

AMS Aggregate Measure of Support. Under the CAP, calculated on the basis of the costs to the taxpayers and consumers of both domestic farm support and export subsidies.

AMUE Association for a Monetary Union of Europe. *Rue de la Paix 4, F - 75002, Paris, France.*

AMUFOC Association of Fodder Seed Producer Houses in the EC. *Rue de la Science 25, Boite 10, B - 1040 Brussels, Belgium.*

ANGO Association for the Oilseeds, Animal and Vegetable Oils and Fats and Derivatives Trade in the EEC. *Avenue de la Joyeuse Entrée 12, Boîte 9, B - 1040 Brussels, Belgium.*

Ankara Agreement 1963   Between the EC and Turkey, it envisaged the accession of Turkey to the EC in the fullness of time.

ANNIE Application of Neutral Networks for Industry in Europe. ESPRIT approved project 1988.

Annual Report A General Report on the activities of the EC states as laid down by Article 18 of the Merger Treaty. It appears annually in all the EC languages, and is placed before the European Parliament at the beginning of February. DG III.

ANTICI Group Informal group of the personal assistants to the Permanent Representatives of COREPER.

Anti-Dumping Policy Established initially with Regulation. Enables anti-dumping measures to be enforced if the whole, or a major part, of an EC industry has suffered from foreign competition. See also Dumping.

AOC Associated Overseas Countries. The generic name for countries having Agreements of Association with the EC.

AORS Abnormal Occurrences Reporting System. A database in ERDS. Set up to exchange information on potentially dangerous incidents at nuclear power stations.

AORSA Abnormal Occurrences Reporting System Association. *Commission of the European Communities, Joint Research Centre, 21020 Ispra, Italy.*

APEX Advanced Project for European Information Exchange: concerned with the aerospace industry. EUREKA approved June 1986.

API Association of Producers of Isoglucose of the EC. *Avenue de la Joyeuse Entrée 1-5, Boîte 10, B - 1040 Brussels, Belgium.*

APM Action Plan for the Mediterranean.

APOLLO A joint project of the European Space Agency (ESA) and the Commission for satellite document delivery (1985).

APPE Association of Petro Chemical Producers in Europe *250 Avenue Louise, Boîte 71, B-1 1050 Brussels, Belgium.*

APRYCLEE Network grouping the national information centres specializing in new information technologies (NITs).

APSIS Application software prototype implementation scheme. ESPRIT project.

AQUARIUS Project engaged in the protection of the oceans, under the EYE programme. Launched in 1987.

Architects' Directive Council Directive 85/384/EEC that concerns the general acceptance and recognition of formal qualifications in architecture throughout Member States.

ARCHON Architecture for Cooperative Heterogenous On-Line Systems. ESPRIT approved 1988.

ARCOME Database for organization, researchers and publications, regarding communications technology. Free access via ECHO.

ARGOSI Application Related Graphics and OSI Standards Integration. ESPRIT approved 1988.

ARI Appraisal of the Regional Impact.

ARION Exchange scheme for education policy makers and experts. *Arion Assistance Team, Pedagogischer, Austauschdienst, Nasse Strabe 8, D - S 300 Bonn.*

Article XXXV The article in the General Agreement on Tariffs and Trade which allows a state, at the time of its accession, not to apply the General Agreement in its dealings with any other contracting party. The article may also be invoked by any contracting party against a state on its accession.

Article 6 Committee Commission committee to be established to implement Financial Protocols in Mediterranean countries (proposal in COM(86) 528).

Arusha Agreements A series of Agreements of Association established between the EC and the three East African countries: Kenya, Uganda and Tanzania. The first signed in 1968, but expired before it could be ratified. The second Agreement came into force in 1971. It enabled the industrial products of these three African states to enter the EC free of tariffs, and accorded favourable terms to their agricultural products.

ASCOT Assessment of Systems and Components for Optical Telecommunications. RACE approved February 1986.

ASEAN Association of South-East Asian Nations. *Jalan Sisingamangaraja, POB 2072, Jakarta, Indonesia.*

ASFALEC Association of Concentrated and Powdered Milk Manufacturers of the EC. *Bd Haussman 140, F - 75008 Paris, France.*

ASMODEE Database of SII, describing progress of directives, and to demonstrate their application within the Member States.

ASPEC Association of Sorbitol Producers within the EC. *Rue de l'Orme 19, B - 1040 Brussels, Belgium.*

ASPIS Application Software Prototype Implementation System. ESPRIT approved 1984.

ASSET Automated Support for Software Engineering Technology. ESPRIT approved 1984.

ASSIFONTE Association of the Processed Cheese Industry of the EC. *Schedestrasse 11, D - 5300 Bonn, Germany.*

ASSILEC Association of Dairy Industries of the EC. *Bd Haussman 140, F - 75008 Paris, France.*

Association Agreements See Agreements of Association.

ASSOPOMAC Association of EC Potato Breeders. *Kaufmannstrasse 71, D - 5300 Bonn, Germany.*

ASTRA Advanced integrated office systems prototypes for use with European public administration. ESPRIT project.

ATA Carnet An international customs temporary importation document that can be used in all EC countries and some other European countries. It covers exhibits for international trade fairs, and samples, for example.

ATC Agreement between the Community and Finland, Norway, Sweden, Switzerland and Yugoslavia on international combined road and rail transport.

ATOMS Research into High Densities Mass Storage Memory Systems. ESPRIT project.

Audiovisual Eureka Programme launched in Paris in October 1989 to support European television production against competition from American and Japanese inputs. To promote high technology research and development, a £5 million budget was awarded from the EC Commission. *53 Avenue Victor Hugo, 75116 Paris, France.*

AVAIT Tourist Information System. EUREKA approved project December 1986.

AVEC Association of Poultry Processors and Poultry Import and Export Trade in the EC countries. *Vester Farimagsgade 1, DK - 16C6 Kobenhavn V, Denmark.*

AWG Permanent Working Group 'Information on Agriculture'.

BABEL European Foundation for Multilingual Audio Visual *European Broadcasting Union. Case Postale 67, 1218 Grand Saconnex, Geneva, Switzerland.*

Bank for International Settlements See BIS.

BAP Biotechnology Action Programme (1985). Concentrates on research in information technology and risk assessment.

Balfe Report (1985) Written by the Socialist Group in the European Parliament. Proposed that in view of the absence of safeguards for human rights in Turkey, the E.P. delegation to the joint. Turkey Committee should not be reconstituted.

Bangemann's Proposals (May 1990) Proposals by Martin Bangemann, EC Commissioner on internal trade and industry, to reduce barriers to company takeovers in the EC. Include asserting the rights of individual shareholders, particularly in relation to powers to dismiss non-performing directors; limiting the possibility of 'poison pill' defences; and restricting the issue of non-voting shares.

Banking Federation of the EC Composed of the National banking Federations of the 12 Member States along with those of Austria, Norway, Sweden, Finland and Switzerland to look after the interests of international banking. *Rue Montoyer 10, B1040 Brussels.*

Barre Plan Proposals for the encouragement of monetary union. 1969-1970, by Raymond Barre, then vice-president of the EC Commission. The substance of the plan was that each Member State should allot some of its reserves for use by other members in case of economic difficulties. A Member State would be entitled to request financial assistance from its partners and following this, medium-term aid would either be granted or the loan would have to be repaid within three months. The plan sought closer alignment of EC Members' economic policies (published in Bulletin of the EC Supplements 3/69; 2/70).

Barre, Raymond (1924) French politician who became Prime Minister of France 1976. Vice-president of the EC Commission, 1967-1972; author of the Barre Plan.

Basic Price   Equivalent to the target price, or cost of production price under the CAP when applied to pigmeat, fruit and vegetables. If the average market price drops below the basic price, then intervention may occur to prop up the market by buying in surplus produce.

Basket of Currencies   System for calculating the value of the **ECU**, taking into account all the national currencies of the EC. The weighting accorded to each currency in the 'basket' is dependent on its current international value.

Basle Credits   As the location of the BIS, Basle provides a regular rendez-vous for central bankers. The term Basle credits has come to mean the transactions engaged in by the central banks when giving each other foreign exchange assistance.

BC-NET   Business Cooperation Network. Development of BCC in 1988. A computerized network of some 250 business advisors set up to further cooperation between firms. DG XXIII.

BCC   Business Cooperation Centre. Set up in 1972 with the aim of assisting small and medium sized enterprises (SMEs) to enter into cooperation agreements in accordance with European competition rules. DG XXIII. *Rue Froissart 89, Boîte 1, B - 1040 Brussels, Belgium.*

BCR   Community Bureau of References. A programme to improve the reliability of physical measurements covering foodstuffs, agriculture, environment and health. *C/o Dr H. Marchandise Rue de la Loi 200, B - 1040 Brussels, Belgium.*

BD II Development of a database for distribution of expert systems on low-level computers. EUREKA approved project June 1986.

BEC Bulletin of the EC; issued to inform the public comprehensively and concisely of **EC** developments.

Bech Prize (Federal Republic of Germany) Awarded yearly since 1977 in recognition of special services and personal engagements carried out in the European cause. It commemorates Dr Joseph Bech of Luxembourg. Awarded by the Freiherr von Stein Foundation in Hamburg.

Bech, Joseph (1887-1975) Luxembourg politician. Prime Minister and Minister of Foreign Affairs 1953-1958. One of the signatories to the Statute establishing the Council of Europe in 1949; member of the Council of Ministers of the EC, 1958.

BEDA Bureau of European Designers Associations. *C/o STAD, 12, Carlton House Terrace, London SW1 5AH.*

BEEP Bureau Européen de l'Education Populaire. European Bureau of Adult Education.

BENELUX Benelux Economic Union (Belgium, the Netherlands and Luxembourg)

BEP Biomolecular Engineering Programme (1982-86).

Bentinck Prize (France) Awarded yearly since 1973 to commemorate Adolphe Bentick, formerly French ambassador to the Netherlands, for his efforts in encouraging European cooperation; enhancing European institutions; and promoting closer European ties with the remainder of the world.

Berne Union International Convention established in Berne in 1886. The terms of the Convention state that any artistic and literary works of a member nation are subject to copyright in all other member countries.

BEUC European Bureau of Consumer Unions. A consumer organisation based in Brussels, made up of consumer groups from member countries. *Rue Royale 29, Boîte 3, B - 1000 Brussels, Belgium.*

BICs Business and Innovation Centres. Begun in 1984 to encourage the establishment of new and innovative small firms and to help existing ones to diversify. DG XXIII.

BICEPS Bioformatics Collaborative European Programme and Strategy (not yet operational).

BIFI Financial accounts domain on the CRONOS database.

BIO COMAC Biology Concerted Action Committee.

Birkelback Report Published in January 1962, written by M. Birkelback. First official document to address directly the question of association with the EC. Stipulated that full membership should be restricted to those democratic countries militarily and politically aligned with the West. Agreements of Association could be made with European countries less developed economically, with a recommendation that certain overseas states with strong ties with a particular EC state might also be considered.

BIS Bank for International Settlements, in Basle, founded in 1930. See also Basle Credits.

BIS Budget Information System.

BISE Energy and industry domain on the CRONOS database.

Black List (Lists most harmful substances discharged into rivers and seas) Council Directive 76/464/EEC (updates); (OJ L129/76 for original on control of water pollution; also, following OJ C176/82; OJ L181/86 - List 1).

BLIC Rubber Industries Liaison Bureau of the EC. *Avenue des Arts 2, Boîte 12, B - 1040 Brussels, Belgium.*

Block Exemptions Those categories of agreement with non-EC countries stipulated by the EC Commission, which enjoy exemption from the ban on restrictive trade agreements.

BME COMAC Bio-medical Engineering Concerted Action Committee.

BRAIN Basic Research in Adaptive Intelligence and Neurocomputing (not yet operational).

Brandt, Willy (1913-) West German politician. Chancellor of the Federal Republic of Germany, 1969-1974. In 1968, proposed extending EC membership to include the countries that were currently applying for entry, and submitted two plans for enhanced cooperation between the original Six and the prospective members in order to facilitate smoother entry into full membership.

Briand Plan proposed by the French politician, Aristide Briand, in 1930, for the creation of a united states of Europe, with a federal government in control of economic affairs.

BRIDGE Biotechnology Research for Innovation, Development and Growth in Europe. Programme adopted by the Council in 1989 as part of EC research and technological development policy (1990-1994).

BRITE Basic Research in Industrial Technology for Europe Programme. A four-year Programme (1985-1988 inclusive), aimed at furthering the spread of new technologies to the traditional industries. DG XII.

BRITE/EURAM Programme involving manufacturing technologies, advanced materials, design methodology and quality assurances. 1989-1992: a sequel to the original BRITE and EURAM programmes. OJ C 228 3/9/88.

Brittan, Leon (1939-) British barrister and politician; Conservative MP 1974-1988. Home Secretary 1983-1985, and Secretary of State for Trade and Industry 1985-1986. Britain's Senior Commissioner to the EC, succeeding Lord Cockfield in 1989, with responsibility for competition and financial services.

Brokersguide An on-line directory of current information for brokers within the EC. Access via ECHO.

Bruges Group Campaign group for a Europe of sovereign states. Formed after Mrs Thatcher's speech in Bruges, September 1988. *C/o Lord Harris of Highcross, House of Lords, London, SW1A 0PW, United Kingdom.*

Budget The amount that Member States pay towards the EC funds through Own Resources. Comprises around 1% of the EC's GDP, and around 3% of the total budgetary expenditure of Member States. The budget runs from 1 January to 31 December.

BUILDING 2000 Solar energy pilot project.

Bulletin of the European Communities Periodical published monthly in the official languages of the EC. Formally a supplement to the Annual Report.

Butter Mountain In EC parlance a glut of butter arising from over-production followed by EC intervention to buy surplus amounts which are then kept in storage or disposed of cheaply outside the EC. Also known are Beef and Grain mountains. See CAP and EAGGF.

BWG Permanent Working Group 'Information on Biomedicine and Health Care'.

CECG Consumers in the European Community Group. *24 Tufton Street, London SW1P 3RB, United Kingdom.*

CECOP European Committee of Workers' Co-operative Societies. *Rue Vilain XIV 38, B - 1050 Brussels, Belgium.*

CEDB Component Event Data Bank, part of ERDS.

CEDEFOP European Centre for the Development of Vocational Training. Established to promote standardization of national vocational qualifications within the EC. DG V *Bundesallee 22, D - 1000 Berlin 15, Germany.*

CEDI European Confederation for Independent Workers. *Oberbexbacher Strasse 7, D - 6652 Bexbach, Germany.*

CEDIC European Committee of the Consulting Engineers of the EC. *Bd de Waterloo 103, B - 1000 Brussels, Belgium.*

CEE Centre for European Education. A series of 5 national centres in Western Europe linked together, engaged in information, activities, and curriculum developments. *Seymour Mews House, Seymour Mews, London, W1H 9PE, United Kingdom.*

CEEA Confederation of European Economic Associations. *Rue Richepanse 8, 75001 Paris, France.*

CEEP European Centre for Public Enterprises. *Rue de la Charité 15, B - 1040 Brussels, Belgium.*

CEFIC European Council of Chemical Industry Federations. *Avenue Louise 250, Boîte 71, B - 1050 Brussels, Belgium.*

CEFS European Committee of Sugar Manufacturers. *Ave de Tervveren 182, B - 1150 Brussels, Belgium.*

CEJA European Council of Young Farmers. *Rue de la Science 23-25, Boîte 3, B - 1040 Brussels, Belgium.*

CELAD Coordinators' Group on Drugs. Approved by the Council in December 1988 to coordinate proposals and measures adopted by the different EC bodies in all areas, in the fight against drugs.

CELEX Database of the Legal Service of the Commission established 1971, provides an information service on matters such as Treaties; legal acts resulting from the external relations of the European Communities; secondary legislation; judgements of the Court of Justice; and questions and answers in the European Parliament. Access via Eurobases.

CEMR Council of European Municipalities and Regions. *Quai d'Orsay 41, F - 75007 Paris, France* and at *35 Great Smith Street, London SW1P 3BJ, United Kingdom.*

CEN   Comité Européen de Normalisation.   EC standard-making body, based in Brussels, set up to promote common safety standards and to protect the consumer within the EC. Now covers over 2100 subjects. Weighted voting used. DG III. *Rue de Brederode 2, Boiîe 5, B - 1000 Brussels, Belgium.*

CENCER   CEN's Certification Body.

CENELEC   Comité Européen de Normalisation Electrotechnique.   Based in Brussels, a standard-making body set up to promote safety and to protect the consumer within the EC, with particular reference to the electrical and electronic industries.   It is the electrotechnical counterpart of CEN, and has replaced CENEL and CENELCOM. DG III. *Rue de Brederode 2, Boîte 5, B - 1000 Brussels, Belgium.*

CEPAC   European Confederation of Pulp, Paper and Board Industry.   *Rue Washington 40, Boîte 17, B - 1050 Brussels, Belgium.*

CEPCEO   Association of the Coal Producers of the European Community.   *Avenue de Tervueren 168, Boîte 11, B - 1150 Brussels, Belgium.*

CEPFAR   European Training and Development Centre for Farming and Rural Life.   *Rue de la Science 23-25, Boîte 10, B - 1040 Brussels, Belgium.*

CEPREM   Centre for the Advancement and Study of the European Currency.   *Avenue Berthelot 16, F - 69007, Lyon, France.*

CEPS Centre for European Policy Studies. A European policy making body financially independent from the EC. *Rue Ducale 33, B - 1000 Brussels, Belgium.*

CEPT European Conference of Postal and Telecommunications Administrations. A standardization body set up as the result of guidelines laid down by the Council in May 1984. *Liaison Office, PO.Sox, CH-3001 Berne, Switzerland.*

CERAMIE-UNIE Liaison Bureau of Ceramic Industries of the EC. *Rue des Colonies 18-24, Boite 17, B - 1000 Brussels, Belgium.*

CERD European Research and Development Committee. Established in 1973, comprises 21 independent scientific advisers whose duty is to decide research and development aims and priorities in science and technology, bearing in mind the socio-economic needs of the EC. DG XII.

CERISE European centre for image synthesis: to improve and market computer imaging technology. EUREKA approved June 1986.

CERN European Nuclear Research Organization based in Geneva. *CH1211, Geneva 23, Switzerland.*

CERT European Parliament Committee on Energy, Research and Technology.

CERTICO The ISO's Certification Committee.

CES Document Working Document of the Economic and Social Committee.

CET Common external tariff.

CETIL   Committee of Experts for the Transfer of Information between European Languages.

CFI See Court of First Instance.

CFP Common Fisheries Policy. First proposed 1970, aims are to prevent the depletion of fish stocks while protecting the interests of the fishermen, using quotas and controls; to encourage Member States to adjust their fleet sizes, by providing adjustment support funds; to preserve employment; to eliminate unfair competition; and to ensure regulated marketing, by means of a Community marketing policy.

CGC Management and Coordination Consultative Committee.

CGD Waste Management Committee.

Charlemagne Prize (Federal Republic Germany) Originated in 1949 to be awarded yearly by the city of Aachen for exceptional efforts in the cause of European unity and in the promotion of international understanding.

Charzat Report 1986 Produced by the Socialist Group in the EP, proposed ways of achieving a just, peaceful and comprehensive negotiated settlement to Middle East problems.

Chasse gardée Literally 'protected competition', refers to the argument that the EC is engaged in a battle for survival with two economic giants: the United States and Japan, and can only win the contest by providing a protected home market for EC firms.

Cheysson, Claude (1920). French Socialist politician. Foreign Minister, 1981-1984; French ambassador to Indonesia, 1966-1970. EC commissioner, 1973-1981, with special responsibiity for aid and development. Negotiated the first two Lomé Conventions.

Cheysson Facility   A financial scheme to provide capital backing for firms wishing to establish links with Asia and Latin America.

CHIEF   Customs Handling of Import and Export Freight. Introduced to accommodate changes introduced by the Single Administration Document (SAD).

Christian Democratic Parties, Federation of West European.   'European People's Party - Federation of Christian Democratic Parties of the EC' established in 1976, comprises 13 Christian Democrat and Centrist parties in the EP.

CIAA   European Food Industry Association. A private body which is responsible to the Commission for drawing up standards for the food industry with respect to areas such as consumer information, fair market practices, protection of public health and public inspection. *Rue de Loxum 6, B - 1000 Brussels, Belgium.*

CICI   Confederation of Information Communication Industries.

CID   Centre for Industrial Development. Set up in 1977 under the Second Lomé Convention, with the objective of helping the industrial development of ACP states. DG VIII.

CIDIE   Committee of International Development Institutions on the Environment.

CIDST   The Committee for Information and Documentation in Science and Technology. Advisory Committee to DG XIII, it comprises two delegates from each member country with a neutral chairman of one of the countries. The Committee has played a central role in the development of EURONET. A sub-committee of CREST.

CIMCEE Committee of the Mustard Industries of the EC. *Avenue de Cortenberg 172, B - 1040 Brussels, Belgium.*

CIMEC Committee for the Electrical and Electronic Measuring Instrument Industries of the Community. *Rue Hamelin 20, F - 75116 Paris, France.*

CIMSCEE   Committee of the Mayonnaise and Condiment Sauce Industries of the EEC. *Avenue de Cortenberg 172, B - 1040 Brussels, Belgium.*

CIRCCE International Confederation of Commercial Representation in the EC. *Bd Bonne Nouvelle 30, F - 75480 Paris Cedex 10, France.*

CIRCE European Communities Information and Documentary Research Centre. (May occasionally be referred to in EC documents but is no longer in use - replaced by SII).

CIRD   Interservice Committee for Research and Development. Established in 1975, CIRD comprises representatives of the different Directorates-General and Services of the Commission, and the JRC. Its task is to ensure that the scientific and technical research work of the different departments of the Commission is efficiently coordinated. DG XII.

CIRRs Commercial interest reference rates. Refers to minimum interest rates available for the principal currencies with regard to Export Credits.

CIT Advisory Committee for Innovation and Technology Transfer.

CITES Convention on International Trade in Endangered Species of Wild Fauna and Flora.

Citizens Europe Advisory Service Launched by the Commission in January 1990; has the task of advising individuals within the EC on their rights, and to give assistance with special problems, in areas such as medical treatment, benefits, housing and pensions. *8 Storey's Gate, London, SW1, United Kingdom.*

CJUS A database of case law providing details of the judgements reached by the European Court of Justice; part of the CELEX.

Classical System of Taxation Company taxation principle applied in the Netherlands, Luxembourg and the United States, in which corporate profits are taxed twice: dividends paid to shareholders are subject to tax without any credit against corporate tax. See Imputation System of Taxation, Split-Rate System of Taxation.

CLCA Liaison Committee for the Motor Industry in the EC countries. *Square de Meeus 5, Boîte 8, B - 1040 Brussels, Belgium.*

CLECAT European Liaison Committee of EC Forwarders. *Centre International Rogier, Passage International 14, Res Pallas Boîte 10, B - 1000 Brussels, Belgium.*

CLITRAVI Liaison Centre of the Meat Processing Industries of the EC. *Avenue de Cortenberg 172, Boîte 6, B - 1040 Brussels, Belgium.*

CMC EC Group of Ceramic Tile Producers. *Rue des Colonies 18-24, Boîte 17, B - 1000 Brussels, Belgium.* See also CERAMIE-UNIE.

CMC-ENGRAIS EC Committee of the Nitrogenous and Phosphatic Fertilizers Industry. *Avenue Louise 259, Boîte 54, B - 1050 Brussels, Belgium.*

CMEA (Comecon) Council for Mutual Economic Assistance. *56 Kalinin Avenue, Moscow G - 205, USSR.*

CMGM Committee on the Monitoring of the Seriously Ill.

CN Combined Nomenclature. Adopted by the Commission, 1989; became operational 1990. Set up to ensure the correct classification of commodities and to improve the effectiveness of customs services at external frontiers. OJ L 256 7/9/1987.

CNMB Central Nuclear Measurements Bureau at GEEL (JRC establishment).

Co-responsibility Levy Tax levied on farmers as a contribution towards the cost of storing farm surpluses. DG VI.

COBCCEE Committee of Butchery Organizations of the EC. *Rue Joseph II 95, B - 1040 Brussels, Belgium.*

COCERAL Grain and Feed Trade Committee of the EC. *Avenue de la Joyeuse Entrée 12, Boîte 9, B - 1040 Brussels, Belgium.*

COCIR Coordination Committee of the Radiological and Electromedical Supplies Associations.

Cockfield, Lord Francis (1916-) British barrister and politician; Minister of State, UK Treasury, 1979-1982; Secretary of State for Trade, 1982-1983. British EC Commissioner from 1984. From 1985 to 1989, Britain's Senior Commissioner, and Vice-President of the Commission, being responsible for the Internal Market, Tax Law and Customs. Largely responsible for the EC Commission's White Paper on the Single European Market, entitled, 'Completing the Internal Market', which detailed over 300 measures necessary to complete the Single Internal Market by 31 December, 1992.

COCOM The Coordinating Committee for Multilateral Export Controls, based in Paris. Handles export of security-related high technology. A NATO committee, crucially important in blocking exports of sensitive equipment to the Warsaw Pact countries and elsewhere.

COCOR Iron and Steel Nomenclature Coordination Committee.

COCOS Components for Future Computing Systems. ESPRIT approved 1985.

CODEST Committee for the European Development of Science and Technology. Advises the Commission on the funding of EC R&D to stimulate European scientific and technical cooperation.

CODING   Colour desktop publishing.   ESPRIT approved 1988.

CoE   Council of Europe.   Set up in 1949 as an inter-governmental body of European states, the Council now has 21 members including all Member States of the EC. It comprises two institutions: an inter-governmental Committee of Foreign Ministers and a Consultative Assembly, which share a Secretariat in Strasbourg. Provides an important forum for wider European cooperation. DG I. *67006, Strasbourg, France.*

COFACE   Committee of Family Organizations in the European Communities. *Rue de Londres 17, B - 1050 Brussels, Belgium.*

COFALEC   Committee of the Bakers Yeast Manufacturers of the EC. *Rue du Louvre 15, F - 75001 Paris, France.*

COFENAF Committee of the National Ferrous Scrap Federations and Associations of the EC. *Place du Samedi 13, Boîte 5-6, B - 1000 Brussels, Belgium.*

COGECA   General Committee of Agricultural Co-operatives. *Rue de la Science 23-25, Boîte 3, B - 1040 Brussels, Belgium.*

Cohesion   A 'shorthand' term in EC documents meaning reduction in disparities between EC regions.

College of Europe   A body founded in 1949, offering 1-year courses on European integration to international students.   Courses are taught in English and/or French. *DDyver 11, B-8000 Bruges, Belgium.*

COLIPA Liaison Committee of European Associations of the Perfume, Cosmetic Products and Toiletries

Industries. *Rue de la Loi 223, Boîte 2, B - 1040 Brussels, Belgium.*

Colombo, Emilio (1920-) Italian politician. Italian Prime Minister 1970-1972. Member of European Parliament 1976-1980. President of the European Parliament 1977-1979. See Genscher-Colombo Initiative.

COM Communist and Allies Group (of the European Parliament).

COM Documents With SEC documents, provide the complete range of the official working documentation of the Commission. COM is an abbreviation of 'Commission'. The documents originate from the Directorates-General of the Commission and have to be submitted to the Secretariat General of the Commission prior to being placed on the agenda for a meeting of the Commission proper. They fall into three categories: (1) Proposals for legislation; (2) Broad policy documents; (3) Reports on the implementaton of policies.

Common Carrier Legislation EC Legislation requiring that transmissions systems (e.g. pipelines or electricity grids) have to carry energy between any third party supplier and the customer at a reasonable tariff.

COM Programme New strategic industrial system of communication. FAST II programme.

COMAC Concerted Action Committee. See, for instance, BIO-COMAC and BME-COMAC.

COMANDOS Construction and Management of Distributed Office Systems. ESPRIT project approved 1985.

COMEL Coordinating Committee for EC Associations of Manufacturers of Rotating Electrical Machinery. *C/o REMA, 8, Leicester Street, London WC2H 7BN, United Kingdom.*

COMETT Community Programme in Education and Training for Technology. Approved by the Council in December 1985, designed to strengthen cooperation between universities and other higher education institutions and industry in the area of advanced training for new technology. A second programme, COMETT II, is proposed as a follow-up (1990-1994). *Comett Office, 71 Avenue de Cortenberg, B - 1040 Brussels, Belgium.*

COMEXT Statistical Office databank of external trade statistics. Access via WEFA and Business Trade Statistics.

COMIS Standardization of Coding of Moving Images on Digital Storage Media. ESPRIT approved 1988.

COMITEXTIL Coordination Committee for the Textile Industries of the **EC.** Represents national textile manufacturers in the EC at Community level. DG III. *Rue Montoyer 24, B - 1040 Brussels, Belgium.*

Commission, European The executive arm of the Community headquartered in Brussels. Functions are to ensure compliance with existing Treaties; to propose new Community laws; to administer common policies; and to act as a watchdog. Consists of 17 commissioners nominated by the 12 Member States who are elected for a four-year term, together with a supporting staff of some 11,000 in 1986. The Commission is divided up into Directorates - General (DG), and operates on a system of majority voting. See Introduction for further details.

Committee for European Research and Development See CERD.

Committee of Agricultural Organizations in the EC See COPA.

Committee on European Cooperation in the Field of Scientific and Technical Research See CERD.

Committee on Scientific and Technical Research See CREST.

Common Agricultural Policy See CAP.

Community Committee for the Coordination of Fraud Prevention Set up by the Commission to find ways of combating fraud in Europe in preparation for 1992.

Community Energy Demonstration Programme (1986-1989) Involved research into energy saving measures for the future, and the formation of a single energy market.

Community Law Arises from the EC constitutions as set up by the Treaty of Paris and the Treaty of Rome.

Community Preference Refers to the situation when the price of domestic agricultural products falls below that of imported products. DG VI.

Comparability of Transactions Term originating in the **ECSC,** means that buyers who produce similar goods or who perform the same functions should have equal access to the sources of production, thus eradicating preferential treatment for some buyers.

Competition Policy A general term for a mechanism aimed at achieving a satisfactory balance between necessary restrictions on competition and the prevention of harmful restrictive practices which hamper the integration of markets.

COMPEX System of Compensation under Lomé Conventions by which EC offsets losses in export earnings of LDCs.

COMPRO Committee for the Simplification of International Trade Procedures in the European Community.

Confederation of Industries of the EC See **UNICE**.

Consultative Council of Social and Regional Authorities Attached to the Commission, it consists of 42 members, and is consulted on matters of regional development.

Continental Shelf That area of seabed over which individual coastal nations are held to have sovereign rights under the 1958 Geneva Convention.

Control of Concentrations between Undertakings Regulation which came into force September 1990 with the introduction of a new mergers system. Enables the Commission to have sole power over big mergers with a combined turnover of at least Ecus 5 billion, while Member States have control over smaller mergers. There are three exceptions: the Commission can examine smaller mergers if requested to do so by a state that has no mergers body of its own; if competition in local markets is threatened; if the national interest is at stake. DG IV.

Coordination Committee for the Textile Industries in the EC. See **COMITEXTIL.**

COPA Committee for Agricultural Organizations in the EC Provides a forum for farmers' views in the EC. DG VI. *Rue de la Science 23-25, Boîte 3, B - 1040 Brussels, Belgium.*

Copenhagen Report Published in 1973, this related to political cooperation between the nine Member States.

COPENUR Standing Committee on Uranium Enrichment.

COPMEC Committee of Small and Medium-Sized Commercial Enterprises of the EC Countries. *Rue du Congrés 33, B - 1000 Brussels, Belgium.*

COPOL Comparison of National and Community Policies.

CORDIS Advisory Committee in Industrial Research and Development. Also runs an online database displaying summary information on current projects.

CORECOM Ad hoc Advisory Committee on the Reprocessing of Irradiated Nuclear Fuels.

COREPER Committee of Permanent Representatives. Comprises national officials from Member States, whose task is to consider all proposals from the Commission, to identify areas of disagreement and harmony, and to prepare discussion material for the Council of Ministers.

COREU Correspondence Européenne. Network of telex communications amongst EC foreign ministries. An institution of EPC.

CORINE Programme A project set up with the objective of collecting and coordinating data on the natural environment, in the **EC** (1985 -1988).

Corporation Tax A system of taxation of unit trusts, prevalent in the **UK**, in which the underlying funds are taxed. A potential problem for European fiscal and financial integration, in view of practices elsewhere in **EC**. See 'Flow Through' Principle.

COSA Agriculture and fisheries domain on the CRONOS data base.

COSEMCO Seed Committee of the EC. *Avenue de la Joyeuse Entrée 1-5, Boîte 19, B - 1040 Brussels, Belgium.*

COSINE Cooperation for OSI Networking in Europe. EUREKA approved November 1985.

COSMOS Cost Management with Metrics of Specification. ESPRIT approved 1988.

COST Committee on European Cooperation in the field of Scientific and Technical Research. Has responsibility for the scientific and technical research in a wide range of fields, in 19 European countries, including the EC states. DG XII *Rue de la Loi 170, B - 1048 Brussels, Belgium.*

COTANCE Confederation of National Associations of Tanners and Dressers of the European Community. *Bd Louis Schmidt 57 (2e étage), Boîte 4, B - 1040 Brussels, Belgium.*

COTREL Committee of Associations of Transformer Manufacturers in the Common Market.

Stressemannallee 19, D - 6000 Frankfurt am Main 70, Germany.

Coudenhave-Kalergi, Count Richard   (1894-1972) Founder and President of the European Union, 1940. Secretary-General of the European Parliamentary Union. First recipient of the Charlemagne Prize 1954.

Council of Ministers   Composed of ministers from each member government. The Minister present depends on the subject under discussion. The Council is the main decision-making body, and takes final decisions on the laws to be applied throughout the EC. It operates a system of qualified majority voting with weighting given to France, Germany, Italy and the UK. The Council meets usually in Brussels, and also in Luxembourg. The presidency is held on a rotational basis. For further information see Introduction.   *Rue de la Loi 170, B - 1040 Brussels, Belgium.*

Council of Ministers, Secretariat   Services the Council of Ministers. Smaller than the European Commission, it possesses no powers of proposal or execution. It is divided into six Directorates-General responsible for the main areas of EC activity.

Court of Auditors   Also known as European Court of Auditors. Based in Luxembourg, set up in July 1975, has 12 members. Responsible for auditing the Community's revenue and expenditure. Examines whether all revenue has been received, and all expenditure incurred has been done so in a lawful and regular manner, and whether the financial management has been sound.   *29 Rue Aldringen, L 1118 Luxembourg.*

Council of Europe   Arose out of the Congress of Europe in 1948, came into being in July 1949.

Membership restricted to European states which 'accept the principles of the rule of law and of the enjoyment by all persons within (their) jurisdiction of human rights and fundamental freedoms'. There are at present 23 members. It has no defence function, and tends to concentrate on cultural and social issues.

Court of First Instance Also known as European Court of First Instance (**CFI**). Established in September 1989 to ease the workload of the European Court of Justice by assuming responsibility for EC staff cases, competition cases, steel quota and levy cases. Staffed by 12 judges. OJ L 319 25/11/1988.

Couve de Murville, Maurice (1907-) French politician. Minister for Foreign Affairs, 1958-1968. Prime Minister, 1968-1969. Supported the French President de Gaulle in opposing extending EC membership to those countries who applied in 1967, especially the UK.

CPC Community Patent Convention. Held with the aim of agreeing conditions for a pan-European patent; to be fully in force by 1992.

CPCCI Permanent Conference of Chambers of Commerce and Industry of the EC. *Square Ambiorix 30, Boîte 57, B - 1040 Brussels, Belgium.*

CPIV Standing Committee of Glass Industries of the EC. *Avenue Louise 89, B - 1050 Brussels, Belgium.*

CPIV Permanent International Vinegar Committee for the EC. *Rue de L'Iscy 8, F - 75008 Paris, France.*

CPMR Conference of Peripheral Maritime Regions. *Bd de la Liberté 35, F - 35100 Rennes, France.*

CPR Regional Policy Committee.

CPSA Standing Committee on Agricultural Structures.

CRAFT Cooperative Research Action for Technology. A new Commission scheme encouraging SMEs to collaborate in commissioning research for third parties. DG XXIII.

CRE Congress of the Regions of Europe. *Immeuble Europe, Place des Halles 20, 67000 Strasbourg, France.*

CREST Committee for Research in Science and Technology. The Committee to which CIDST reports. Established in 1974, has responsibility for coordinating national research and development policies, and keeping the Council and the Commission informed on new research projects. DG XII.

CRM Committee for Medical and Public Health Research. A sub-committee of CREST. DG XII.

Crocodile Group Cross-party group of MEPs (formed in 1980) who drew up proposals to reform the institutions of the EC. Founded by Alltiero Spinelli and Felice Ippolito. Acquired its name from the Crocodile Restaurant where its members met. Strongly pro-federalist.

CRONOS One of the databases of EUROSTAT, it provides information on foreign trade statistics; monthly, quarterly and annual industrial statistics; and employment and unemployment figures on a standardized basis, collected by member countries. Access through DATACENTRALEN / GSI-ECO / CISI Wharton.

CRS Computerized Reservation Systems (for air travel). Governed by a code of conduct within the framework of the European Civil Aviation Conference, agreed with the EC, aimed at preventing non-discriminatory use of CRS and denial of access to them.

CSCE Conference on Security and Cooperation in Europe. 35 state membership. Commonly known until recently as the 'Helsinki Process' in view of the fact that the original CSCE was held in Helsinki and concluded with the signing of the Helsinki Final Act of 1975. Prior to 1989 the main forum for high-level debate between NATO and the Warsaw Pact countries.

CSF Community Support Framework. A key element in the reform of the Structural Funds. Adopted by the Commission to establish the priorities for EC financial assistance.

CSP Confederation of Socialist Parties. An internal organization of the Socialist Parties' group in the European Parliament.

CST Statistical and Tariff Classification for International Trade.

CSTID See CIDST.

CT Community Transit System.

CTS Conformance Testing Services.

CTMO Community Trade Marks Office.

CTU Community Tuberculin Unit.

CUBE Concertation Unit Biotechnology in Europe (Commission unit for coordinating biotechnology policy).

CUC Central Accounting Unit (DG XIX of the Commission).

CUS Customs Union Service (of the Commission).

Customs Duties The EC comprises a customs union and all imported goods are charged at a uniform rate regardless of which state they enter. The CCT (Common Customs Tariff) averages around 6%. However, in view of the GSP and other agreements, exported goods from some Third World countries enter the EC market at lower rates.

Customs Duties on Beef and Cattle These are 16% on imported live cattle, and from between 20% and 26 % on imported beef, depending on variety. DG VI.

CYO Community Youth Opera. OJ C 167 27/6/1988.

DAB Digital Audio Broadcasting System. EUREKA project approved December 1986.

Dahrendorf, Ralf (1929) Politician, academic and writer from the Federal Republic of Germany. Secretary of State for Foreign Affairs, 1969. EC Commissioner, 1970-1974, with special responsibility, first, for external relations and trade; and second, for research, science and technology, the JRC and the Statistical Office. Resigned in 1974 to become Director of the London School of Economics.

Dangerous Substances Directives 67/548/EEC, OJ L 196, 16.8.67; and 84/449/EEC, OJ L 251, 19.9.84. Designed to ensure that all EC Member States apply common procedures in packaging and labelling dangerous commodities. They also ensure that the appropriate authorities are notified when new substances come on the market.

DATACENTRALEN Database host. *6-8 Retortvej, DK 2500 Valby, Denmark.*

Data Protection Rules Proposed by the Commission to form the centrepiece of a single market in information and telecommunications services, which would make it illegal for personal data of any description to be transferred without an individual's knowledge or consent.

Davignon Report 1970 Promoted harmonization of foreign policy, and emphasized the need for joint decisions on foreign policy on issues that concerned Europe. The proposals which were adopted provided for six-monthly meetings of EC Foreign Ministers to discuss matters for 'political cooperation'.

Davignon, Viscount Etienne (1932-) Belgian diplomat, and Belgian Foreign Minister. As an EC Commissioner, he was requested by the Hague summit of 1969 to select a team of foreign policy officials who would find ways of achieving a commonality of foreign policy views. See Davignon Report.

Decisions EC Decisions, usually of the Commission, to be distinguished from Regulations and Directives; the most specific and most binding form of executive act. These are binding in their entirety on those to whom they are directed.

De Gaulle, Charles (1890-1970) French soldier and politician. Major-general in Second World War. From 1940, led the 'Free French' in Britain, and governed France briefly following the liberation. In 1958, he returned to politics and became President of the Fifth Republic until resignation in 1969. Throughout his time in office, emphasized France's independence. Withdrew France from NATO's integrated military structure in 1966. Supported the EC as a means of furthering France's interests, particularly developing closer ties between France and Germany. Opposed to UK membership because of UK close ties with America.

Dehousse, Fernand (1906) Belgian Socialist politician. Member of the EP, 1958. President of the Saar Commission of Western European Union, 1955-1956. President of the Consultative Assembly of the Council of Europe, 1956-1959.

Dehousse Report May 1967 Concerned the rules of association between the EC and non-member states. Two central points were that there should be some relaxation of the qualifications for association; and that preferential arrangements being accorded to countries without membership or association should be considered.

Delors Commission (First) 1988 Responsible for EC Commission's 'Progress Report' on the internal market, showing that the EC was on course to complete the Single European Market by 1992, but also that the removal of financial and physical barriers was not sufficiently advanced.

Delors Community Charter of Fundamental Social Rights of Workers 1989, also known as Social Charter. Statement of rights and objectives aimed at providing social dimension to the integration process. Ratified with substantial amendments by ED Council of Ministers, 1990. Main provisions of original charter:

(1) Freedom of movement and equal treatment for workers throughout the EC.

(2) Sufficient pay to provide a 'decent standard of living'.

(3) The right to a weekly rest period and annual paid leave.

(4) Freedom to join or not join trade unions without suffering any loss.

(5) The right to strike, except for armed forces, police and Civil Services.

(6) The right to collective bargaining between employers and workers.

(7) Access to vocational training throughout working life.

(8) Information, consultation and participation for workers in decisions by employers.

(9) No employment below fifteen years of age; no night work under eighteen years of age.

(10) New measures to provide jobs for the disabled.

Delors Plan   A proposal on 'Making a Success of the Single Act'. 1987. Details of this appear in COM (87) 100.

Delors, Jacques (1925) French university professor and politician; Special Assistant to Gaullist Prime Minister J. Chaban-Delmas, 1969-1972. From 1981-1983, Minister for Economy and Finance. MEP 1979-

1981; Commissioner for Monetary Affairs in the EC from 1985. President of the EC Commission from 1985. Strongly in favour of enhanced political integration. Associated particularly with two Commissions, a Plan and a Report.

DELTA Developing European Learning through Technological Advance (1987). Project designed to develop and improve the use of IT a n d telecommunications through cooperation between users and manufacturers in the field of education.

DEM European Democratic Alliance (Conservatives and Alliance Popular of the European Parliament).

DEMETER Digital Electronic Mapping of European territory. EUREKA approved December 1986.

DEMO Prototype Fusion Reactor.

Democratic Deficit Term used to refer to the relative absence of control over EC policies and laws by Europe's elected representatives, particularly by supporters of political integration.

Denaturing The practice of making a foodstuff unfit for human consumption, through the use of premiums, so that it can be used for animal feed, for instance. Associated with the price support mechanisms of the CAP.

Deniau, Jean François (1928-) French Gaullist politican. Secretary of State for Foreign Affairs, 1973. Director of Commission on Countries seeking association with the EC (1959-1961). Head of delegation to the Conference with States seeking membership of the EC, 1961-1963. Commissioner for Development Aid, EC, 1969-1973.

DEP European Depository Library. Collections of EC documentation designed primarily for use by the general public. Less complete than the EDC.

DEP Group of European Progressive Democrats (of the European Parliament).

Derogations Exemptions from implementation of an EC Directive for special circumstances, for a period of years.

DESIRE Development of an all dry single-layer photolithography technology for sub-micron devices. EUREKA approved 1986.

Deutsch Foundation European Prize (Switzerland) Created in 1963 by Dr Hans Deutsch, an Austrian publisher, awarded for achievements aimed at making Europe a single cultural and political entity.

Development Funds, European See EDF.

DG Directorate General. The departmental unit of organisation in the Commission covering all aspects of the EC's activities. Sub-divided into Divisions which are the basic internal administrative unit. Each DG is the responsibility of a Commissioner, who may however have more than one DG. List of DGs and policy responsibilities:

DG I   External Relations

DG II   Economic and Financial Affairs

DG III   Internal Market and Industry

DG IV   Competition

DG V   Employment, Social Affairs, Education

DG VI   Agriculture

DG VII   Transport

DG VIII   Development

DG IX   Personnel and Administration

DG X   Information and Culture

DG XI   Environment, Consumer Protection, Nuclear
            Safety

DG XII   Science and Research

DG XIII   Telecommunications, Information Industries,
            Innovation

DG XIV   Fisheries

DG XV   Financial Institutions and Company Law

DG XVI   Regional Policy

DG XVII   Energy

DG XVIII   Credits and Investments

DG XIX   Budgets

DG XX   Financial Control

DG XXI   Customs Union and Indirect Taxation

DG XXII   Coordination of Structural Instruments

DG XXIII Enterprise Policy

DIAMANT A database for translation request.

DIAMOND Development and integration of operators in numerical data processing.

DIANE   Automatic integrated system for neutronography. EUREKA approved 1986.

DIANE Guide A description of data bases available on Euronet Diane. Free access via ECHO.

DIANE See **EURONET DIANE.**

Digest of Community Case Law As yet unfinished systematic summary of Court of Justice (ECJ) case law. Divided into four series A-D. Available through OOPEC.

DIME Development of Integrated Monetary Electronics (not yet operational). Project designed to develop and improve the use of IT and telecommunications through cooperation between users and manufacturers in the area of monetary electronics.

DIMUN Distributed Manufacturing using existing and developing networks.

Directives EC laws adopted by the Council of Ministers on a proposal from the Commission. Enforceable by EC law, though their implementation is left to the discretion of each Member State. Implementation should normally take place within 18 months unless Derogation is allowed.

Discrimination   Term referring to the application of restrictive trade measures to one country at the expense of another, particularly within the EC.

DOCDED   Programme covering a number of infrastructure activities in the agricultural databases. CADDIA programme.

DOCDEL   Electronic Document Delivery and Electronic Publishing Programme (1984-1985); aimed at the implementation of a common information market. See also **EURODOCDEL; TRANSDOC.**

DOEOIS   Design and Operational Evaluation of Distributed Office Information Servers.   ESPRIT approved 1984.

DOMIS   On-line Directory of Materials Data Information Sources.   Access via ECHO.

Dooge Report 1985   Ad hoc Committee on Institutional Affairs set up by the Council of Ministers under the chairmanship of James Dooge, Irish Foreign Minister, to improve political cooperation throughout the EC.   The interim and final reports recommended that an Intergovernmental Conference (IGC) should be convened soon to negotiate a Draft European Union Treaty.

DOSE   European Parliament internal database for the management of Working Documents.   No longer in use. Replaced by PARDOC.

DOSES   Development of Statistical Expert Systems. OJ C 9   20/4/89.

Double Disapproval   Term used to refer to system of regulating air fares in which airlines are allowed to work out their own air charges subject to the veto of ministers at either end of the journey. Subject to debate between European Civil Aviation Conference and the EC.

DUNDIS　On-line Directory of United Nations Databases and Information Systems. Free access via ECHO.

DRIVE　Dedicated Road Safety Systems and Intelligent Vehicles in Europe (not yet operational). Project designed to develop and improve the use of IT and telecommunications through cooperation between users and manufacturers in the field of road safety.

Dublin Foundation　European Foundation for the Improvement of Living and Working Conditions. *Loughlinstown House, Shankill, Co. Dublin, Ireland.*

Dumping　Term used to refer to the practice of selling goods overseas at prices below the exporter's domestic price.

E Numbers　Pan-European code numbers for various food additives, e.g. antioxidants, colouring and preservatives, as specified in Council Directives.

EAA　European Asssociation of Advertising Agencies. Founded in 1959, and has expanded to include multinational agencies. Officially recognized by the Council of Europe. *28 Avenue de Barbeaau, B-1160 Brussels, Belgium.*

EAB　ESPRIT Advisory Board.

EABS　Database of Euroabstracts. Concerned with the business of publicizing, protecting and utilizing, research results in the Communities. Free access via ECHO.

EAC European Accident Code (JRC - reactor safety programme).

EAC European Association for Cooperation. *Rue Archimede 17A, Boîte 10, B - 1040 Brussels, Belgium.*

EACEM European Association of Consumer Electronics Manufacturers.

EADP European Association of Directory Publishers. A body which protects the interests of directory and index publishers. Operates an official membership scheme. *Square Marie-Louise 18 (Boîte 25-27) B-1040 Brussels, Belgium.*

EAEC See EURATOM.

EAGGF European Agricultural Guidance and Guarantee Fund, established to finance agricultural needs and, in particular, to give support to farming in the less well-off, and environmentally sensitive, areas, by assisting with modernization of methods and equipment. Also referred to as FEOGA, one of the most important and sizeable intervention instruments of the CAP.

EAGLE European Association for Grey Literature Exploitation. *C/o Mr M. Maurice, Rue Auguste Neyen 39, 2233 Luxembourg* and *Dr D.N.Wood, British Library Document Supply Centre, Boston Spa, Wetherby, LS23 7BQ, United Kingdom.*

EAO European Architects' Organization. *Rue Chaiclot 7, F - 75116, Paris, France.*

EAPS European Association for Population Studies. Founded in 1983 to further work in this field. *Lange*

Houtstraaat 19, PO Box 11676, 2502AR, The Hague, The Netherlands.

EARN European Academic Research Network. *Dr P. Bryant, Rutherford Computing Division, Rutherford Appleton Laboratories, CMI LTO, Didcot, OX11 0QZ, United Kingdom.*

EAST Advanced Software Technology under EUREKA. Development of software factories incorporating software engineering. EUREKA approved June 1986.

EAT European Asociation of Teachers.

EAVE Entrepreneurs of Europe's Audiovisual Area. *Rue Thérèsienne 8, B - 1000 Brussels, Belgium.*

EBA ECU Bank Association. *Rue de la Paix 4, 75002 Paris, France.*

EBIC Centres set up in the UK initially, in 1987, as part of a pilot scheme to provide business-oriented information. Aimed to expand to 200 centres throughout the EC.

EBN European Business and Innovation Centres Network. Set up in 1984 by BICs, provides an international service to support the firms it caters for through BIC. *Rue Froissart 89, B - 1040 Brussels, Belgium.*

EBP European Business Programme (begun 1987), intended to train management specialists at Business Institutes in the EC.

EBRD   European Bank for Reconstruction and Development. Created to finance the revival of private enterprise in Eastern Europe.

EBU European Broadcasting Union. Founded in 1950, and encourages international broadcasting cooperation and joint ventures. *Ancienne Route 17a, 1218 Grand-Saconnex (Geneva), Switzerland.*

EC 1992 Database available via INFOTRADE (Brussels based host) possibly through DIALOG in future.

ECAC European Civil Aviation Conference. Oversees the orderly growth and operation of airways in Europe. *3 bis villa Emile-Bergerat, 92522 Neuilly sur Seine, France.*

ECA European Claimants' Association. *C/o Postbox 458, 6200 AL Maastricht, Netherlands.*

ECBA European Communities Biologists' Association. *Universitetsparken 13, DK - 2100 Kobenhavn, Denmark.*

ECCLAS   European Conference of Ministers of Transports. Oversees the development of Europe's overland transport systems. *19 rue de Franqueville, 75775 Paris, Cedex 16, France.*

ECCOFEX   European Commission Coordinating Committee for Options and Future Exchanges.

ECCSEC Ecumenical Commission for Church and Society in the European Community. A representative body of the non-Catholic churches in Europe concerning the way the activities of the EC reflect on the Church. *Rue Joseph II, 174, B - 1040 Brussels.*

ECCT European Council for Certification and Testing. Mr R. Brockway, British Standards Insitution, 2 Park Street, London W1A 2BS, United Kingdom.

ECDIN Environmental Chemicals Data and Information Network. Access via DATACENTRALEN.

ECDOC European Communities Documentation. No longer in use. See **ECOI**.

ECDVT European Centre for the Development of Vocational Training. See **CEDEFOP**.

ECE The Economic Commission for Europe. An agency of the United Nations set up in 1947, having five Committees of the Commission and a yearly plenary session. *Palais des Nations, 1211 Geneva 10, Switzerland.*

ECF See **EFEC**.

ECFI European Confederation of the Footwear Industry. *Rue du Luxembourg 19, PO Box 14, B - 1040, Brussels, Belgium.*

ECFTU European Confederation of Free Trade Unions in the Community. See **ETUC**.

ECG No longer in use. See **EEIG**.

ECGD Export Credit Guarantee Department. Part of UK Government Department of Trade and Industry, provides protection for UK firms selling goods and services abroad, and may also supply finance for export sales.

ECHO Service European Community Host Organization. Host to a number of Commission databases. *Route d'Esch 177, L - 1471 Luxembourg.*

ECI EURATOM Classified Information.

ECISS European Committee for Iron and Steel Standardization. Set up in 1986, superseded the Iron and Steel Nomenclature and Coordinating Committee. ECISS Euronorms set iron and steel standards that supplant national standards. *C/o CEN, Rue Brederode 2, Boîte 5, B - 1000 Brussels, Belgium.*

ECLAIR European Collaborative Linkage of Agriculture and Industry through Research. Programme adopted by the Council in 1989 as part of the EC research and technological development policy in the field of biotechnology based agro-industries.

ECLAS European Commissioners' Library Automated System. A new bibliographical database of the Commission Library in Brussels now opened to the public. Contains publications based on those available in the Commission's library.

ECMT European Conference of Ministers of Transport. Oversees the development of Europe's overland transport systems. *19 rue de Franqueville, 75775 Paris, Cedex 16, France.*

ECO-Counsellors Counsellors appointed in 12 EC towns during EYE to advise on environmental issues.

Ecofin EC Council of Ministers when composed of Economic and Financial Ministers of Member States.

ECOI (formerly **ECDOC**). The Commission's system for controlling internal documentation. Objective is to provide on file all the documents relating to the agenda of meetings of the Commission, in addition to other documents. Superseded ECDOC 1970.

ECOIN European Core Inventory (Chemicals).

Economic and Social Committee (ECOSOC) An advisory body, headquarters in Brussels. Composed of 189 members who represent three groups: employers, trades unions and consumer organizations. Must be formally consulted by the Commission on proposals relating to economic and social affairs. Produces a Bulletin, available from OOPEC. *2 rue Ravenstein, B - 1000, Brussels.*

ECOSOC See **Economic and Social Committee.**

ECPSA European Consumer Product Safety Association. *C/o Dutch Consumer Safety Institute, PO Box 5169 AD - Amsterdam, Netherlands.*

ECR European Commercial Register. A list of firms in the EC, held by the European Court of Justice.

ECR European Court Reports (Reports of Cases before the European Court of Justice).

ECS European Company Statute. Proposal for a common European Company Statute, such that any firm which incorporated itself under the statute would be exempted from the company laws of Member States.

ECSC European Coal and Steel Community. Came into being in August 1952 with the aim of promoting economic expansion, growth of employment, and a rising standard of living in Member States, through policies pursued in the coal and steel sector. The ECSC provides loans and grants to promote a high level of productivity in the coal and steel industries, while safeguarding employment and preventing unfair competition. *Bâtiment Jean Monnet, Boîte Postale 1907, Luxembourg.*

ECTS European Community Course Credit Transfer System. To enable students to complete one degree at various universities in the EC (set up under ERASMUS).

ECU European Currency Unit. One of three major elements of the EMS, its value is calculated on the basis of a basket of EMS currencies, taking into consideration such aspects as the relative GNP of EC members, together with the significance of their trade and currencies for short-term finance at the time when the amounts are set. Provides a common currency for dealings by the European Community institutions, and has some wider uses in European financial markets. Daily ECU exchange rates database. Access via ECHO. DG II.

ECVP European Community's Visitors' Programme. Set up by the Commission and the European Parliament, enables young people from the Americas, Australasia, and Japan, to visit EC countries.

ECYEB EC Youth Exchange Bureau. *Rue de la Concorde 51, B - 1050 Brussels, Belgium.*

ECYO European Community Youth Orchestra.

ED European Democratic Group (of the European Parliament).

ED European Documentation (series of publications).

EDA European Democratic Alliance (of the European Parliament) of Gaullists, Fianna Fail and Scottish Nationalists.

EDC European Documentation Centre. These centres, of which there are more than 40 in the UK, and 300 throughout the world, house the documents and publications from the EC. Their aim is to promote the teaching and research of the EC, in the academic institutions in which they are based. Sometimes associated with Euroguichet.

EDD See **EURODOCDEL.**

EDF European Development Fund. Established in 1958 to provide financial aid to the dependencies of the six founder EC members, and was renewed a number of times under the Yaoundé Agreements and the Lomé Conventions. The Fund has undergone certain changes over the years and become more flexible, but its fundamental principles have remained the same. The Commission (DG VIII) is responsible for administering the fund.

EDI Electronic Data Interchange Project. Project aimed at establishing electronic linkage between EC chemical industries and trading partners.

EDIFACT Electronic Data Interchange for Administration, Commerce and Transport.

EEB European Environmental Bureau. *Rue Vautier 29, B - 1040 Brussels, Belgium.*

EEIG European Economic Interest Grouping (formerly **ECG**). A loose form of partnership set up under EC law to facilitate cross border joint ventures with companies employing less than 500 people. Adopted by the Council 25.7.85 (OJ L199, 31.7.85).

EES   European Economic Space. Proposed new economic and trading zone incorporating 19 states and some 350 million people in Europe, and including EC and EFTA members. Aiming for free movement of goods, capital, people and services within virtually the whole of Western Europe. Adopted by the EC at the summit of 1989.

EEZS   Exclusive Economic Zone. Relates to the international laws of the sea and fisheries limits.

EF   European File (series of publications).

EFA   European Federation of Agricultural Workers Unions. *Rue Fosse-aux-Loups 38, Boîte 8, B - 1000 Brussels, Belgium.*

EFCI   European Federation of Cleaning Industries representing leading organizations in the EC. *27 Quai aux Pierres de Taille, B - 1000 Brussels, Belgium.*

EFDO   European Film Distribution Office. *Friedensallee 14-16, D - 2000 Hamburg 50, Germany.*

EFEC   European Financial Engineering Company. *Bd Royal 10, Luxembourg.*

EFEC   European Fashion Export Council, *Rue Montoyer 24, B - 1040, Brussels, Belgium.*

EFER   European Foundation for Entrepreneurship. *Rue Washington 40, B - 1040, Brussels, Belgium.*

EFMD   European Foundation for Management Development. *Rue Washington 40, B 1050, Brussels, Belgium.*

EEFPIA   Europeaan Fereration of Pharmaceutical Industry's Associations. *Avenue Louise 250, Boîte 91, 1050 Brussels, Belgium.*

EFQM   European Foundation for Quality Management. *Building Reaal, Fellenoord 3953, 5612 AA Eindhoven, Netherlands.*

EFTA   European Free Trade Association. Includes Austria, Finland, Iceland, Norway, Sweden and Switzerland and was set up in 1960 as a counter to the EC. The UK was the foremost member. When the UK, Ireland and Denmark left EFTA to join the EC in 1973, a free-trade agreement was established between the remaining EFTA countries and the EC; and by 1984, import duties had been eliminated between the two organisations. *Rue de Varembe 9-11, 1211 Geneva 20, Switzerland.*

EIA   Environmental Impact Assessment.

EIB   European Investment Bank. Has headquarters in Luxembourg, lends money to finance capital investments projects within the Community. *Boulevard Konrad Adenauer 100, L-2950 Luxembourg.*

EIESP   European Institute of Education and Social Policy. *Rue de la Concorde 51, B - 1050 Brussels, Belgium.*

EIIA   European Information Industry Association. *PO Box 19, Wilmslow, Cheshire, SK9 2DZ, United Kingdom.*

EINECS European Inventory of Existing Chemical Substances.

EIPA European Institute for Public Administration. Assists public servants in the administration of EC policy. *OL Vrouweplein 22, PO Box 1229, 6201 BE, Maastricht, The Netherlands.*

EIPG Energy Investment Promotion Group.

EIS Export Intelligence Service.

EIS/Baden project Commission energy information data base currently being set up.

EIT European Institute of Technology.

ELD Federation of European Liberals and Democrats. Internal organization of the Liberal and Democratic Parties group in the European Parliament.

ELDBUS Communications architecture based on local area networks for real time control of industrial processes and machines. EUREKA project approved June 1986. See **EUREKA**.

ELISE European Network for the Exchange of Information on Local Employment Initiatives. Set up in 1985 by the Commission as part of the employment policy designed to promote jobs for young people. *Rue Vilain XIV 38, B - 1050 Brussels, Belgium.*

EM European Movement. A Pro-federalist lobby group. *Rue de Toulouse 47-49, B - 1040 Brussels, Belgium* also at *1a, Whitehall Place, London SW1, United Kingdom.*

EMBO   European Molecular Biology Laboratory. *Postfach 102209, D - 6900 Heidelberg, Germany.*

EMC ESPRIT Management Committee.

EMCF European Monetary Cooperation Fund. The third central element of the EMS. Manages the exchange rate mechanism and the intervention mechanism of the EMS. In exchange for issuing the central banks with ECUs, it receives 20% of each Member State's gold and dollar reserves. The ECUs may be used to meet certain debts incurred by the central banks operating in the EMS. The Fund also has responsibility for advancing credit facilities in the short to medium term.

EMEP Cooperative Programme for the Monitoring and Evaluation of the long-range Transmission of Air Pollutants in Europe. Published in OJ L 181/86.

EMF European Monetary Fund. A committee of European central bankers dedicated to the provision and maintenance of a stable pan-European single currency, free from inflation.

Employment, Standing Committee on Established in 1970, the Committee advises the Council of Ministers and the Commission on all facets of employment policy. It comprises trades union representatives, employers' representatives, and ministers of labour from each Member State.

EMS European Monetary System. Set up on 12 March 1979 with the objective of achieving more stable exchange rates within the Community. Further aims of the EMS include a closer correlation of national economic policies and, eventually, total monetary integration within the EC. Comprises ERM, EMCF and Intervention Fund.

EMSU European Medium and Small Businesses Union. *Hochhaus Am Tulpenfeld 606, D - 5300 Bonn 1, Germany.*

EMU European Monetary Union (1972-1974). A short-lived attempt to fix exchange rates in the EC following the breakdown of the Bretton Woods system.

EMUA European Monetary Unit of Account. A precursor of the ECU.

ENBRI European Network of Building Research Institutes. *Rue du Lombard 41, B - 1000 Brussels, Belgium.*

ENDOC On-line directory giving environmental details relating to Member States. Ceased to function in June 1989.

ENDS European Nuclear Documentation System.

ENERGY BUS Project aimed at providing information and advice on energy conservation through use of a mobile vehicle (1980-).

Energy Research Programmes Two of these programmes have been adopted by the EC since 1975. Their central concern has been with investigating the alternatives for maintaining EC energy supplies. DG XII

ENEX Database of environmental research in EC countries, held by the Commission.

Engineers' Directive   Proposed Directive for the general acceptance and recognition of engineering qualifications (first proposed in 1969).

ENGUIDE   Commission database providing information on EC bibliographical databases relating to the environment.

ENIG   Permanent Working Group 'Information on the Environment'.

Enlargement of the Community   As laid down in the Treaties, the EC can be enlarged if applicants are unanimously accepted by the existing members. Membership negotiations can be protracted and difficult: the applicant has to be economically and politically suitable. Existing members may suffer economically when new members join.

ENLEX   A forthcoming database of information concerning environmental legislation and case law on the environment in the EC. Access via Corte suprema di Cassazione, Centro elettronic: di documentazione.

ENOS   European Network of Ocean Stations (COST action project).

ENREP   On-line guide to programmes on environmental research in EC countries. Free access via ECHO.

ENTECH   Energy Technology: the newsletter of the EC non-nuclear R & D programme. From Directorate E of DG XII.

Enterprise Europe   A campaign aimed at promoting the successful operation of the internal market in the EC, by the UK European Movement.

ENVIREG The Commission's Regional Environmental Action Programme, approved 1989. Designed to run for ten years, and to intervene initially to clean up coastal areas, especially in the Mediterranean.

Environmental action In July 1973, the Council of Ministers adopted an initial two-year programme on this issue.

ENW European Network of Women. *C/o Centre for Research on European Women, rue Stevin 38, B - 1040 Brussels, Belgium.*

EOQC European Organization for Quality Control.

EORTC European Organization for Research and Treatment of Cancer.

EP See **European Parliament.**

EP Document Working Document of the European Parliament.

EPC Economic Policy Committee.

EPC European Political Cooperation. Procedures created after 1970 aimed at improving both political cooperation between Member States and debates on, and reporting of, Ministers' decisions within the European Parliament. The system operates, in the main, through the Conference of Foreign Ministers which meets usually once a month.

EPI European Association of National Productivity Centres. Established in 1966 to facilitate and increase exchange of information and experiences with regards to productivity. *Rue de la Concorde 60, 1050-Brussels, Belgium.*

EPIC   European Parliament Industry Council.

EPID COMAC   Epidemiology Concerted Action Committee.

EPO   European Patent Office. *Erhardstrasse 27, D - 8000 München 2, Germany.*

EPOCH   European Programme on Climatology and Natural Hazards. One of two programmes adopted by the Council in 1990 in the field of the environment.

EPOQUE   European Parliament On-line Query System. An internal database of the European Parliament, containing reports, speeches, debates and questions. It replaces PARDOC and PARQ (see also **SYSDOC**). It holds references to all documents produced by the EP in addition to the Catalogue of the Parliament Library.

EPP   European People's Party (Christian Democrats, Fine Gael of the European Parliament).

EPQ   European Parliamentary Question.

EPROM   Study and development and industrialization of integrated circuit non-volatile memory having storage capacity of 16 Mbit (EUREKA project approved December 1986). See **EUREKA.**

EPU   European Payments Union. *No longer in being.*

EPU   European Police Union, which has a membership of 0.5 million police officers.

EPU   European Political Union.

ER Group of the European Right (of the European Parliament).

ERASMUS European Community Active Scheme for the Mobility of University Students. Set up in 1987, this programme is designed to increase the number of student exchanges between Member Countries' universities. The currently available budget is intended to allow 5% of students to spend part of their higher education courses in another Member Country. The programme will run for three years initially, with an intended starting date as 1990. *ERASMUS Office, 15 Rue d'Arlon, B - 1050 Brussels.*

Erasmus Prize (The Netherlands) Established in 1958 by Prince Bernhard of the Netherlands, it is awarded yearly to a person or institution who has been judged to have best contributed to European unity in the cultural, social or scientific spheres.

ERC European Reference Centre. Refers to collections of basic EC documentation usually situated in academic institutions. DG X.

ERDA European Renewal and Democratic Alliance (Gaullists, Fianna Fail, Scottish National Party of the European Parliament).

ERDF European Regional Development Fund. Set up in 1975 to finance the development and restructuring of underdeveloped and declining industrial areas in the Community. Controls nearly 9% of the EC budget. It has been responsible for creating and maintaining nearly 764 thousand jobs.

ERDS   European Reliability Data System (JRC - reactor safety). See also **AORS; CEDB; GRPDS, OUSR.**

ERF European Reserve Fund. Proposed as part of Stage I and Stage II of the Delors Report (12/13 April 1989) on economic and monetary union in the EC.

ERM Exchange Rate Mechanism. Another important element of the EMS, it is a system whereby participants have their exchange rates fixed within the margins of +/- 2.25% (+/- 6.0% for the Lira). Central banks are required to maintain the value of their currency within these limits.

ERMES The European Radio Messaging system. A proposed paging service that would cover the whole of the EC and EFTA countries due to introduced into use, January 1992. It will enable Europeans to bleep each other on a 169.4 - 169.8 MHz frequency.

EROS 2000 European River Ocean System. A long-term programme of research in connection with DG XII of the Commission.

ERT European Round Table of Industrialists. A group of leading industrialists aiming to strengthen Europe's industrial position. *Rue Guimard 15, 1040 Brussels, Belgium.*

ERTIS European Road Transport Information Services (EUREKA project approved December 1986).

ES2 Automatic design and production of custom chips using direct printing on silicon (EUREKA project approved June 1986). See **EUREKA.**

ESA European Space Agency. *Rue Mario Nikis 8-10, F - 75738 Paris Cedex 15, France.*

ESA Euratom Supply Agency. An organization set up in 1958, the ESA alone has the power to sign contracts regarding the import and export of nuclear materials within the EC. It also has responsibility for ensuring that nuclear materials are not used for other than peaceful purposes. *Rue de la Loi 200, B - 1040 Brussels, Belgium.*

ESA European System of Integrated Economic Accounts. Established to promote the development of a European information system ready for 1992.

ESA-IRS European Space Agency Information Retrieval Services. *Via Galileo Galilei, Frascati, Italy.*

ESC see **ECOSOC**.

ESCB European Central Bank System. A proposed pan-European banking system that would entail acceptance by national banks and finance ministries of the abdication of their right to formulate national monetary policies. It has been recommended that this system be set up at the beginning of stage two of European monetary union, to include a European Monetary Fund to be owned and run by the central banks.

ESF European Science Foundation. Set up to promote research in Europe.

ESF European Social Fund. Intended to provide funds for organizations implementing schemes for vocational training, retraining and job creation. It has concentrated little on health and social welfare.

ESIF European Service Industries Forum. *Zeepstraat 55, B - 2850 Keerbergen, Belgium.*

ESPRIT European Strategic Programme for Research and Development in Information Technology. Begun in December 1982, it involves firms from 12 Member States. It aims to consolidate and strengthen the EC's R&D work in science and technology; to bridge the high technology gap between Europe and Japan and the USA; and to coordinate national science and technology policies. Second phase of ESPRIT programme, 1987-1991.

ESPRIT-IES-DC Esprit Information Exchange System Data Collection. Free access via ECHO.

ESRA European Safety and Reliability Association. Set up in 1986 to provide a framework for the systematic exchange of information on advanced analytical techniques used in a variety of industrial activities where a high standard of safety and reliability is required. *Mr B. Tolley, Arts 02-3, Commission of the European Communities, Rue de la Loi 200, B - 1040 Brussels, Belgium.*

ESSOR Complex at ISPRA (JRC establishment).

ESSPROS European System of Integrated Social Protection Statistics.

ESTI European Solar Test Installation at ISPRA (JRC establishment). A standardised form of social statistics developed by Eurostat.

ESTI European Society of Transport Institutes, *Rue de la Charite 15, Boite 6, B - 1040 Brussels, Belgium.*

ESU European Size Unit.

ETAG Permanent Working Group "Technical and Economic Aspects of EURONET Development". See EURONET.

ETC European Technology Community.

ETL European Test Laboratory at PETTEN (JRC establishment).

ETP Executive Training Programme (for young EC executives in Japan 1979).

ETSA European Telecommunications Services Association.

ETSI European Telecommunications Standards Institute. Established in March 1987, it was designed to harmonise European technical specifications.

ETUC European Trades Union Confederation. Represents some 44 million workers, and was set up in 1952 as an organisation of the Free Trade Unions of the six founder Member States of the ECSC and later on of the EC. *rue Montagne-aux-Herbes-Potageres 37, B - 1000 Brussels, Belgium.*

ETUI European Trade Union Institute. Set up in 1978, it is the research, information and educational arm of the European trade union movement. Its aim is to provide workers in the EC with the information and advice regarding the economical, social and political changes likely to affect them.

EUA European Unit of Account. *NO LONGER IN USE. See ECU.*

EUCOFEL European Union of the Fruit and Vegetable Wholesale Import and Export Trade. *Ave de la Brabanconne 18, Boite 8, B - 1040 Brussels, Belgium.*

EUCOMED European Confederation of Medical Supplies Associations.

EUDISED European Documentation and Information System for Education. Access via ESA-IRS.

EUI European University Institute. *Badia Fiesolana, Via dei Roccettini 5, I - 50016 San Domenico di Fiesola, Florence, Italy.*

EUPRIO European Association of Public Relations and University Information Officers. *c/o Dr. L. Beets, University of Leiden Stationsweg 46, 2313 AV, Leiden, Netherlands.*

EUR 12 (10;9) Twelve (Ten; Nine) countries of the EC. The EC had 6 members from 1958 to 1972, 9 from 1975 to 1980, 10 from 1981 to 1985 and 12 from January 1986.

EUR Series of scientific and technical reports.

EURAGRITOUR European Office for Green Tourism. *c/o COPA-COGECA, Rue de la Science 23-25, B - 1040, Brussels, Belgium.*

EURAM Raw Materials Research (1978-).

EURATOM The European Atomic Energy Community. Established in January 1958, its function has been to encourage common efforts between its members in the development of nuclear energy for peaceful purposes. Also referred to as EAEC..*rue de la Loi 200, B - 1049 Brussels, Belgium.*

EUREAU Union of the Water Supply Associations from Countries of the European Communities. *ch de Waterloo 255, Boite 6, B - 1060 Brussels, Belgium.*

EURED European Unified Research on Educational Development.

EUREDATA A forthcoming data bank on reliability.

EUREGIO Trans-frontier cooperation associations.

EUREKA A data bank of Research on European Integration. Access via EURONET.

EUREKA European Programme for high-technology research and development. A French initiative for non-military industrial research in advanced technology in Europe; begun 1985. The aim of Eureka projects is to 'extend and complement existing European technological cooperation in the context of programmes such as COST and CERN' The programme has closer links with private enterprise than with the state. *Secretariat: ave des Arts 19H, B - 1040 Brussels, Belgium.*

EURET European Research for Transport.

EURING Environmental data base.

EURISTOTE On-line directory of university theses and studies on European integration. Free access via ECHO.

Euro Abstracts A journal of the Commission, published monthly by **OOPEC** on behalf of DG XIII. It presents summaries of reports, Commission documents, scientific articles and conference papers, relating to the EC. Can be used to trace documents issued in the EUR series of scientific and technical reports.

Euro-Barometer Series of public opinion polls on basic themes and issues relating to European integration carried out by the EC Commission. Published every Spring and Autumn. *rue de la Loi 200, B - 1049 Brussels, Belgium.*

Eurobases Database distribution service of the Commission of the EC. *ARL 03/04, 200 Rue de la Loi, B - 1049 Brussels, Belgium.*

EUROBIO Group of EUREKA projects. See **EUREKA.**

Eurobonds. Long term bonds sold in denominations other than the currency of the country of the country in which they are sold. A major part of the so-called EUROMARKET. Used by banks increasingly to avoid national governmental restrictions on the access of foreign issuers to national markets. Most popular denominations is the US$, followed by the DM, the Yen and the ECU.

EUROBOT Group of EUREKA projects. See EUREKA.

EUROCARE European project of conservation and restoration (EUREKA project approved December 1986). See **EUREKA.**

EUROCERT An organisation based in Brussels, set up in 1988, made up of national inspection groups from the UK, Belgium, France, Luxembourg, Portugal, Spain, Sweden and Switzerland, aimed at ensuring that the provisions of the 1985 Treaty relating to Common Market products, are honoured by each country.

EUROCHAMBRES Association of European Chambers of Commerce and Industry.Founded in 1958 to lobby the official decision-makers of the EC. *rue Archimede 5, B - 1040 Brussels, Belgium.*

EUROCIM Flexible automated factory for electronic cards, including preparation of circuits and quality control of products (EUREKA project approved June 1986).

Eurocodes.Common European codes for the construction industry, aiming to eventually to replace national technical regulations so as to promote exchange of construction materials, skills and personnel, in the EC. DG III.

EUROCOFIN See EFEC.

EUROCOM Group of EUREKA projects. See EUREKA.

Eurocontrol A system for management of air traffic flow under the auspices of the European Organisation for Safety of Air Navigation, designed to increase the capacity of existing airport runways. *rue de la Loi 72, 1040 Brussels, Belgium.*

EURO COOP European Community of Consumer Cooperatives. *PO Box 2, rue Archimede 17, Boite 2, B - 1040 Brussels, Belgium.*

EUROCOTON Committee of the Cotton and Allied Textile Industries of the EEC. *rue Montoyer 24, B - 1040 Brussels, Belgium.*

Eurocrat A European civil servant in colloquial parlance.

Eurocurrencies provide funds for the international short term capital market which are highly volatile and respond to movements in interest rates.   See Eurodollars.

EURODICAUTOM On-line terminology data bank of the EC. Free access via ECHO. A means of transfering information between languages.

EURODOCDEL A document delivery project for EC documents (1984-1985). See also DOCDEL

Eurodollars Dollar balances belonging to individuals and firms in European banks. They provide a stock of international currency outside of government controls. The system came into operation about the time of the Suez crisis, in 1957. Other currencies also fulfil this role and this has led to the notion of eurocurrencies. See Eurocurrencies and Eurobonds.

EURODUCA Group of EUREKA projects. See EUREKA.

EURODYN High technology gas turbine engine demonstrator programme (EUREKA project approved December 1986).

EUROENERGY Group of EUREKA projects. See **EUREKA.**

EUROENV Group of EUREKA projects. See **EUREKA.**

EUROFARM A data base on farm structures within the CADDIA programme.

Eurofed Nickname of the proposed Central Bank for Europe to accompany monetary union, whose task it would be to 'formulate and implement policy and issuance of the Ecu'.

Eurofer European Federation of the Iron and Steel Industry. *square de Meeus 5, Boite 9, B - 1040 Brussels, Belgium.*

EUROFOR Automation and computerisation of a drilling apparatus for the petroleum industry (EUREKA project approved December 1986)

Euroform Initiative Launched to improve employment opportunities.

EUROGLACES Association of the Ice Cream Industries of the EEC. *Rue de Logelbach 3, 75017 Paris, France.*

Euro-Info-Centres The Commission's Offices established to facilitate greater and prompter access to all Community publications. For further details, contact *Commission of the European Communities, DG XXIII, rue de la Loi 200, B - 1049, Brussels, Belgium.*

Euro-issues Bonds and shares marketed outside the countries of the currencies in which they are issued.

EUROKOM ESPRIT teleconferencing facility and electronic mail and message system which includes details of organisations seeking cross-frontier partners for ESPRIT and EUREKA projects. Access via IT Task Force DG XIII of the Commission.

EUROLASER Evaluation and development of high power laser systems (CO_2, solid state and excimer lasers) for materials processing and production engineering (EUREKA project approved November 1985). See EUREKA

Eurolicence An optional driving licence available to EC citizens from 1976.

EUROLEX European Law Centre data base of EC legislation. *NO LONGER IN USE.*

EUROLOC Locate in Europe Information Retrieval System. A data base of funds available from the EC. Access via University of Strathclyde.

EUROMAISERS Maize Industry Association Group of the EEC countries._ *ave de la Joyeuse Entree 12, Boite 9, B - 1040 Brussels, Belgium*

EUROMALT Working Committee of the EEC Malting Industries. *rue de l'Orme 19, B - 1040 Brussels, Belgium.*

EUROMAR A programme involving the examination of ecological changes and relations in the oceans of Europe through the application of new technologies.(EUREKA project approved June 1986). See EUREKA.

Euromarkets Markets that for the past twenty years have provided offshore conduits for capital, free from the restrictions of individual states' regulations and taxes.

EUROMAT Group of EUREKA projects. See **EUREKA.**

EUROMATIC Group of EUREKA projects. See EUREKA

Euromessage Europe's first Multinational Paging Service involving the UK, France, Italy and West Germany : due to commence 1990. The project will enable businessmen in all four countries to contact one another whether their pager is tone, numeric or alphanumeric.

EURONET Diane Direct Information Access Network for Europe, set up in 1980, with a tansmission network (Euronet) connecting Amsterdam, Brussels, Copenhagen, Dublin, Frankfurt, London, Luxembourg and Paris. Euronet Diane news provides up-to-date information on developments in EURONET. (DG XIII).

EURONET European On-Line Information Network. Its purpose is 'to make scientific and technical information accessible as rapidly and cheaply as possible to all Community enquirers'.

Euronews An up-to-date and in depth electronic information retrieval service for EC Member States. It holds information on Commission statements on R & D projects, such as ESPRIT; and Council of Ministers' decisions on EC R & D proposals. DG XIII.

Europa The term put forward by the Federal Trust for a parallel European currency.

Europa Houses Institutions set up in certain European countries with the task of disseminating information on European matters. Students, academics, trades union representatives and professional people, are drawn together to discuss European affairs, organised by the International Federation of Europa Houses.

Europa Nostra A group of international non-governmental bodies protecting and furthering Europe's natural and cultural interests. *35 Lange Voorhout, 2514-EC, The Hague, The Netherlands.*

Europa Prize Awarded yearly 1967-1971 by five financial publications for outstanding services in the European economic and financial spheres.

EUROPATENT The Community Patent, which also relates to European countries outside the EC. See also Patents.

European Bureau for Lesser Used Languages A partially funded EC body providig lesser used languages within the EC. Founded after the Arfe Report   OJ C 287 9/11/81. *7 Cearnog Mhuirfean, Dublin 2, Ireland.*

European Centre for Vocational Training   Opened in March 1977 in West Berlin, has responsibilty for encouraging the development of uniform vocational training within the EC.

European Coal and Steel Community Consultative Committee A committee set up in 1974 to advise the EC Commission on the broad aims and programmes for the coal and steel industries.

European Communities' Glossary Series of volumes compiled by the Terminology Service of DG IV to enable translation of key concepts of EC legislation.

European Company Statute First initiated in 1970, the intention has been to create an optional system of company law (instead of using national law) for European firms engaged in business in two or more Member States. (DG III).

European Committee for Electrotechnical Standardisation. See CENELEC.

European Committee for Standardisation See CEN.

European Council Since 1974, summit meetings between heads of governments of Member States have been referred to as meetings of the European Council, and occur on a regular basis three times a year. Effectively the highest decision making body in the EC. See also Council of Ministers. Not to be confused with the Council of Europe.

European Court of Human Rights. Established in 1950 together with the European Commission of Human Rights, following the signing of the European Convention on Human Rights. Examines grievances submitted by states or individuals relating to breaches of the Convention, passed on by the Commission of Human Rights.

European Court of Justice. (ECJ) Consists of 13 judges appointed by agreement of the governments of the Member States for a term of six years. Final Court of Appeal on matters of Community Law, dealing mainly with economic issues. Has very limited powers of enforcement but provides an important source of authoritative interpretation on matters of principle. *Boite 96, Plateau du Kirchberg, Luxembourg.*

European Cultural Foundation A private organisation promoting pan-European cultural activities. *Jan van Goyenkade 5, 1075HN Amsterdam, Netherlands.*

European Economic Community (EEC) 1957 Set up by the Treaty of Rome in March 1957, it included Belgium, France, West Germany, Italy, Luxembourg and the Netherlands. The central aim of the EEC was to bring Europe into closer union by dismantling the barriers between member states which were hindering greater economic and social progress. The institutions created by the Treaty of Rome included an Assembly, a Council of Ministers, a Commission and a Court of Justice

European Economic Interest Grouping Set up to facilitate easier cooperation between Member States on joint projects and enterprises.

European Development Fund. See EDF.

European Financial Area. An attempt to bring about the liberalisation of capital movements through provision of medium-term financial assistance for Member States' balance of payments. Part of the drive towards EMU. OJ L 178 8/7/88.

European Foundation An organisation set up in 1977 to: encourage European integration; increase mutual understanding in the EC; and deepen knowledge of Europe's cultural heritage. DG V.

European Information Market Develpoment Group *177 Route d'Esch, L-1471 Luxembourg.*

European Institute for the Media Centre of research into the mass media. The University, Manchester M13 9PL, UK.

European Parliament A directly-elected body of 518 members from EC states. Members are elected on a five-yearly basis. The administration of the Parliament is in Luxembourg, but the Parliament's plenary sessions are held in Strasbourg, and its committee meetings in Brussels. The Parliament's formal consultation is required on many proposals before they can be adopted by the Council. The Parliament can question the Commission, and has the power to dismiss it by a two-thirds majority. However, it cannot introduce legislation, nor does it have the ultimate say in passing laws. *Plateau du Kirchberg, Case Postale 1601, Luxembourg* and *Palais de l'Europe, 67006 Strasbourg, France.*

European Plan A hotel guest system whereby the customer pays for his room and services separately from payment for meals, as distinct from the American system whereby the cutomer pays a fixed daily rate for room, meals and service.

European Regional Development Fund See ERDF.

European Recovery Programme Known also as the Marshall Plan after its creator, General George Marshall, in 1947, it proposed American financial assistance for European economic recovery once the Europeans had reached agreement on their needs and how they would respond effectively to the offer.

European Trade Union Confederation See ETUC.

European University Institute Established in 1976 in Florence in order to assist gifted students in advanced research in the humanities and social sciences; and to work together with other institutions of learning in order to gain further knowledge and undestanding of current problems as they affect the EC.

EUROPECHE Association of National Organisations of Fishing Enterprises of the EEC. *rue de la Science 23-25, B - 1040 Brussels, Belgium.*

Europension The outcome of a proposed scheme by Leon Brittan, EC commissioner for competition and financial services, that would facilitate cross-border membership, management, and investment, of European pension funds.

Europe Prize   Awarded yearly 1956-1960 by the Consultative Assembly of the Council of Europe for services to European cooperation and unity.
Europe Prize Created in 1955, and awarded yearly by the Committee of Local Authorities of the Council of Europe in Strasbourg, to towns which have most contributed to European unity and promoted greater links between the peoples of Europe. The award must be spent on promoting youth exchanges.

EUROPMI European Committee for Small and Medium-Sized Industries. *rue de Stalle 90, B - 1180 Brussels, Belgium.*

EUROPOLIS A programme using the latest intelligent control systems to assist the flow of heavy urban traffic and to provide an advanced means of access to information, and control. (EUREKA project approved June 1986). See EUREKA.

Europoort Built in 1958 in the Netherlands, for the storage of iron ores and oil, transhipment, engineering, shipbuilding and chemicals, it covers some 4,000 acres.

Eurosecurities Internationally traded and issued bonds and shares.   See also Eurobonds, Eurocurrencies, Eurodollars, Euromarkets.

EUROSTAT A series of statistics from the SOEC. To date, it has compiled three databanks: CRONOS, REGIO, COMEXT. *Batiment Jean Monnet, Plateau du Kirchberg, L-2920 Luxembourg.*

Eurosyndicat Index An index number for European Stock Exchange Securities

EUROTEC A regular journal issued by DG X on recent R&D news.

EUROTECH ALERT European Information Service for the Results of National Research. A project set up by the Consultative Committee on Innovation and Technology Transfer to analyse public sector research results, technology fairs, industrial design, and information on national research results.

EUROTECH Capital A pilot scheme to promote the financing of internatonal high technology projects. Made firms eligible for various EC funded services if they satisfied certain requirements (investment capacity of at least ECU50m., of which at least 20 % must be levied for international high-tech projects).

EuroTecnet Commission network of innovative projects on vocational training and new information technologies. Set up 1985.

EURO-TOQUES European Community of Cooks. *Sheraton Towers, Place Rogier 3-29, B - 1210 Brussels, Belgium.*

EUROTRA Machine translation system of advanced design set up in 1982. It covers all the official languages and was developed through collaboration between the Translation Directorate and the Directorate General for Telecommunications Information Industry and Innovation.

EUROTRAC European experiment on transport and transformation of environmentally relevant trace constituents in the troposphere over Europe (EUREKA project approved November 1985). See EUREKA.

EUROTRANS Group of EUREKA projects. See EUREKA.

EUROVISE European Vision System Economic (EUREKA project approved December 1986). See EUREKA.

EUROVOC Multilingual thesaurus of standardized terms for OOPEC.

Eurowatch EC information profile service launched in 1988 by Micro Data Solutions in conjunction with University of Reading, United Kingdom.

EUR Reports A major series of reports concerned with the results of EC research activities. Specialist and technical in nature.

EURYCLEE Network regrouping national information centres which specialise in Information Technology.

EURYDICE Education Information Network in the European Community (A data base with limited access via the EURYDICE Central Unit in the Commission).

EUs Euronorms. The standards produced by the **ECSC** which cover all areas of steel standardisation in terms of quality, dimensions and tolerances, methods of testing, and glossaries of terms. The EUs are published by the Office of Official Publications in Luxembourg, and appear at intervals in the Ofical Journal. A complete set of **EUs** is held in the British Library Science Reference Library.

EUSIDIC European Association of Information Services. *PO Box 429, London W4 1UJ, United Kingdom*

EVCA European Venture Capital Association. Set up in 1983 as part of the EC's industrial policy to promote the development of a venture capital sector along

American lines. Linked up with the Commission to launch a pilot project called "Venture Consort", the aim being to increase finance for SMEs involved in new

EWEA European Wind Energy Association. A body for the furthering of the development of wind energy in Europe.

Explosive Atmospheres Directives Council Directives 76/117/EEC and 79/196/EEC relating to the use of electrical equipment in potentially explosive situations. (published in OJ L24/76 and OJ L43/79).

Export Restitution Payments Under the CAP, these are subsidies paid to exporters from the Export Fund to plug the gap between high EC prices and lower world prices.

Extensification Refers to the practice of reducing intensity of farming, balancing losses due to lower output against gains due to savings on expenditure on fertilizers and pesticides.

EYE European Year of the Environment (1987-1988).

FA database of EAGGF forecasting (a project within the CADDIA programme).

FACE Federation of Hunting Associations of the EC. *Rue de la Science 23-25, B - 1040 Brussels, Belgium.*

FADN Farm Accountancy Data Network. A source of economic information on the situation of agricultural holdings used in the drafting of various Commission reports. It handles individual and confidential data on the accounts of agricultural holdings. The sample now includes over 55,000 such holdings selected by Member

States to represent commercial agriculture in the EC. It submits annual reports.

FAE numbers Code numbers for antioxidants, colouring matter and preservatives in foodstuffs as specified in various Council Directives.

FAEP Federation of Associations of Periodical Publishers in the EC. *Bd Charlemagne 92, Boîte 9, B - Brussels, Belgium*; and *Suite 19, Grosvenor Gardens, London, SW1 0BS, United Kingdom.*

FALEC Association of Concentrated and Powdered Milk Manufacturers of the EEC.

FAMOS Identification and selection of flexible automated assembly proposals for development into industrial pilot projects, generating enabling technologies which will benefit future assembly systems (EUREKA project approved December 1986).

FAO Food and Agricultural Organization (UN).

FAOR Functional Analysis of Office Requirements (ESPRIT project approved 1984).

FAP Final Abandonment Premium.

FAP Forestry Action Programme.

FAR Fisheries and Aquaculture Research (1988-1992).

Farm Fund See **FEOGA.**

FARO Fuel Melting and Release Oven (JRC - reactor safety programme).

FAST Forecasting and Assessment in Science and Technology. A research programme, of which there have been two, that, broadly speaking, is concerned with the effects of technological change on work and employment and the implications of this for the future of the EC. DG XII. *200 Rue de la Loi, B - 1040 Brussels, Belgium.*

FASTCAT High speed multilingual computer assisted translation system (EUREKA project approved December 1986).

FBF A database of EAGGF for forecasting (within CADDIA).

FBUFOC Association of Fodder Seed Producer Houses in the EC.

FEDEMAC Federation of the Common Market Furniture Removing Enterprises. *Schulstrasse 53, D - 6234 Hattersheim - Main 1, Germany.*

FEDIOL EEC Seed Crushers' and Oil Processors' Federation. *Rue de la Loi 74, Boîte 4, B - 1040 Brussels, Belgium.*

FEDOLIVE Federation of the Olive Oil Industry of the EEC. *Via de Governo Vecchio 3, I - 00186 Rome, Italy.*

FEE Federation of European Accounting Experts. *Rue de la Loi 83, B - 1040, Brussels, Belgium.*

FEEE Foundation for Environmental Education. *Avenue Voltaire 154, B - 1040 Brussels, Belgium.*

FEFAF European Federation of Women in the Home. *Avenue de Tervueren 66, Boîte 1, B - 1040 Brussels, Belgium.*

FEOGA Fond Européen d'Orientation et de Garantie Agricole. Under the CAP (Regulation (EEC) 355/77), the Farm Fund can assist the processing and marketing of agricultural products as long as they are part of national or regional programmes.

FEOPAY A project engaged in a review of the system of payments for the guidance section of the EAGGF (a project within the CADDIA programme).

FEORI A project engaged in setting up a database for applications for assistance under the guidance section of the EAGGF (a project within the CADDIA programme).

FEPF European Federation of the Industries of Earthenware and China Tableware and Ornamental Ware. *C/o Ceramie Unie, Rue des Colonies 18-24, Boîte 17, B - 1000 Brussels, Belgium.*

FEWITA Federation of European Wholesale and International Trade Associations. *Avenue de la Joyeuse Entrée 11, B - 1040 Brussels, Belgium.*

FIMCEE EEC Marble Industry Federation. *Avenue Henri Dunant 2, Boîte 15, B - 1040 Brussels, Belgium.*

FINA Financial accounts domain on the CRONOS database.

FIPACE International Federation of Self-generating Industrial Users of Electricity. *40 Avenue Albert-Elisabeth, B - 1200 Brussels, Belgium.*

FIPMEC International Federation of Small and Medium-sized Enterprises. *Congresstraat 33, B - 1000 Brussels, Belgium.*

FIS Fast Information System to establish a computer infrastructure for the horizontal utilization of the AMIS database (a project within the CADDIA programme).

FISH Fisheries domain on the CRONOS database.

FITCE Federation of Telecommunication Engineers of the European Community. *Rue des Palais 42, B - 1030 Brussels, Belgium.*

FLAIR Food-Linked Agro-Industrial Research, 1989-1992. Programme adopted by the Council in 1989 as part of the EC research and technological development policy. It is concerned wiith the improvement of food quality and hygiene, safety and toxicological aspects.

'Flow Through' Principle A system of taxation of collective investment vehicles, common in Europe, under which the fund itself is not taxed but the liabilities are passed on to the individual investor. See, in contrast, **Corporation Tax.**

Fontainebleau Agreement Established in 1984, it provided a series of measures directed to overcoming the EC budgetary problems of a shortage of funds, and increasingly bitter disputes associated with the budgetary process. The measures, which included the raising of VAT contributions, and a decision on refunds for the UK, were insufficient to prevent another budgetary crisis in 1987.

FOPS Falling Object Protective Structures.

FORMEX　Formalized Exchange of Electronic Publications (COPEC).

'Fortress Europe'　Refers to a potential situation created by the 1992 Single European Market, where preferential treatment is accorded to European companies over US or Japanese competitors. This has been declared undesirable by the EC.

Fouchet Plans I and II - 1961　Attempted to bring about economic and political union in the EC, and recommended a joint foreign policy. The plans foundered owing to de Gaulle's strong opposition to them on the grounds that national sovereignty would be seriously eroded.

Fourchette　The top and bottom price levels between which Member States must fix their agricultural prices. The scheme was established in the first instance for cereals.

FOWM　Fibre Optic Well Monitoring System. (EUREKA approved 1987).

Framework Programme　Science and Technology Framework Programme (1984-1987 and 1987-1991).

FRCC　Fast Reactors Coordinating Committee.

Free Mover　Programme supplying grants to students independent of the ERASMUS scheme.

Free trade area　A region consisting of two or more states where duties and other trade restrictions are abolished on the majority of trade between the two or more members.

Fresco Report Reported on the general considerations of the problems of enlargement of the Community (1978). Appears in Bulletin of the EC Supplement 1/78.

FRIC External trade domain on the CRONOS database.

FRRMEX Formalised Exchange of Electronic Publications (OOPEC).

FRSWG Fast Reactor Safety Working Group.

FSSRS Farm Structure Survey Retrieval System.

FTAs Free Trade Areas. These are entirely tariff-free.

FTSC Fusion Technology Steering Committee.

FUNCODE Ensuring intercompatibility between high quality videotelephones and HDTV (RACE project).

FURS Functional Urban Regions.

GAC General Advisory Committee (of the JRC).

GALC European Booksellers Association. *C/o Ter Borchtlaan 75, B - 2520 Edegem, Belgium.*

GALENO 2000 Development of 'non-invasive' diagnostic equipment for medical purposes. (EUREKA approved June 1986).

GAP Analyses and Forecasting Group.

Gasperi, Alcide de (1881-1954) An Italian politician from 1911. Italian Prime Minister 1946-1954. Supported the French plan to establish a European

Assembly, 1948. Led Italy into the **Council of Europe** as a founder member, 1949.

GATS General Agreement on Trade in Services. A proposed mechanism for liberating international trade in services such as shipping, aviation, banking insurance and telecommunications.

GATT General Agreement on Tariffs and Trade. Was established in 1947 to promote the liberalization of trade, and to lay down international rules for trading world-wide. *Centre William Rappard, Rue de Lausanne 154, CH-1211 Geneva 21, Switzerland.*

GBOP Balance of payments domain on CRONOS database.

GCAC General Concerted Action Committee.

GCC Gulf Cooperation Council. Includes countries of the Gulf and the Arabian Peninsula with those of the EC.

GCECEE Savings Bank Group of the EC. *Avenue de la Renaissance 12, B - 1040 Brussels, Belgium.*

GCOP Balance of payments domain on the CRONOS database.

GEEL JRC establishment. *Steeweg op Retie, 2440 Geel, Belgium.*

GELC Book Publishers Group of the European Communities. *Avenue du Parc 111, B - 1060 Brussels, Belgium.*

GEMU German Monetary Union.

Generalized System of Preferences See **GSP**.

Genscher, Hans Dietrich Born 1927. West German politician. Member of Free Democratic Party (FDP) since 1956. Minister of Foreign Affairs since 1974.

Genscher-Colombo Initiative For a draft European Act 1981. Aimed at making constitutional reforms of the EC. This Bonn-Rome initiative originating from the Foreign Ministers of Germany and Italy proposed to invigorate the EC by strengthening political and security cooperation as a means of achieving European union.

GENST Standard Goods Nomenclature for Transport Statistics. Links up with NIMEXE.

GEONOM Geonomenclature (country nomenclature for external trade statistics).

GEQ Working Party (Group) on Economic Questions.

GINTRAP European guide to Industrial Trading Regulations and Practice. This forms a database on EC consumer protection legislation and trading standards, available both in print and on line, from 1990.

GIPE Generation of Interactive Programming Environments (ESPRIT project approved 1984).

GIRP International Group for Pharmaceutical Distribution in the Countries of the EC. *Rue St Bernard 60, B - 1060 Brussels, Belgium.*

GLOBE Global Legislators Organization for a Balanced Environment. A joint venture between European and American MPs to improve the environment.

GLP   Good laboratory practices.   CEN/CENELEC produce European standards for the verification and inspection of laboratories for GLP.   OJ L 145 1/6/1988.

Golden Triangle   The region of the EC bounded by Paris, the Ruhr and Milan, comprising the area of economic growth.

GPRMC   Reinforced Plastics Group of the Common Market.   *C/o Fabrimetal, Rue des Drapiers 21, B - 1050 Brussels, Belgium.*

Green Currencies   A mechanism for maintaining common prices for agricultural goods despite fluctuating exchange rates.   Under the CAP, common support prices are set yearly in ECUs, but in reality farmers receive income from the Farm Fund in their own currencies, calculated at favourable exchange rates or 'green currencies'.

Green Labelling Scheme   One element of the Commission's proposed scheme to promote environmental best practice throughout the EC. Companies would be encouraged to append environment-friendly labels (eco-labels) to products which had passed certain specified tests.

Grey   List (of dangerous substances discharged into the aquatic environment) Council Directive 76/464/EEC (published in OJ L129/76).

GRIPS   General Relation based Information Processing. (No more information.)

Groupes de Travail   Working groups which are sub-committees created to look into specialised areas, and then report back to a Committee.   A part of the system set up to assist the Brussels administration in its work.

GROUPISOL Association of the EEC Manufacturers of Technical Ceramics for Electronic, Electrical, Mechanical and other Applications. *Rue des Colonies 18-24, B - 1000 Brussels, Belgium.*

GRULA A group of Latin American countries.

GSP Generalised System of Preferences. A wide-area scheme designed to give tariff-free access to EC markets for selected semi-manufactured and manufactured goods, but with imposed quotas, to developing countries..

GUD Gestion de l'Union Douaniere. Section of the EC Commission that administrates the customs union.

Guest Worker Refers generally to a person originating from a non-EC Member State who has come to work in the EC. He is not allowed to remain permanently, nor to bring any dependants.

Guide Price The price offered to farmers for beef and veal under the CAP. It is equivalent to the Target Price; and a single rate operates throughout the EC.

GVA Gross Value Added.

Hague Agreement on the **Common Fisheries Policy** July 1976. (Council Resolution published in OJ C105/81).

Hallstein, Walter (1901-1982) West German politician; Secretary of State for Foreign Affairs, 1951-1958. President of the EC Commission, 1958-1967. President of the European Movement, 1968-1974 Awarded the Robert Schuman Prize, 1969.

HANDYAIDS An index of technical aids available in Europe for the handicapped (not yet operational).

HANDYCE An EC information system for the handicapped consisting of HANDYLEX and HANDYCOM.

HANDYLEX EC and national legislation concerned with the handicapped (not yet operational).

HANDYNET An information exchange network on the handicapped in the EC (not yet operational).

HANDYSEARCH Directory of current research into technical aids for the handicapped in the EC.

HANDYTEC An information system on technical aids for the handicapped .

HANDYWHO A European index of organisations associated with technical aids for the handicapped (not yet operational).

HARD Hardware Resources for Development (a project within the CADDIA programme). See **CADDIA.**

'Hard' Ecu Originates from the British proposal for a strong ecu running alongside other individual EC currencies, and a Eurpean Monetary Fund, as opposed to the Delors plan for a single currency (ecu), and an EC Central Bank.

HASS Home Accident Surveillance System.

HDTV High definition television.

Heath, Edward (1916) British politician since 1950. .Prime Minister 1970-1974. Led Britain into the EC in

1973. Awarded the Charlemagne Prize, 1963, and the Stresemann Medal, 1971.

HELIOS Handicapped People in the European Community Living Independently in an Open Society. 1988-1991. An action programme set up in 1988 to promote social and economic integration and an independent way of life for disabled people. OJ L 104 23/4/88.

HERCULE Application of robotics to the construction industry (EUREKA project approved June 1986). See EUREKA.

HERMES A European model which analyses the interrelationships between energy and the economy. DG XII.

HERODE Handling of mixed text/image/voice documents based on a standardized office document architecture (ESPRIT project approved 1984). See **ESPRIT.**

HFR High Flux Reactor at PETTEN (JRC establishment).

HIDCIM Holographic labelling used for automatic identification in CIM environments.

HIVITS High quality videophone HDTV systems.

HORIZON Initiative to promote the integration of the handicapped.

HSR Harmonized Commodity Description and Coding System. A compilation of statistics regarding commodity description and coding. Published in OJ L 198/87.

HSR COMAC Health Service Research Concerted Action Committee.

HTDS Host Target Development System (ESPRIT project approved 1985). See **ESPRIT**.

HUFIT Human Factor Laboratories in Information Technologies (ESPRIT project approved 1984).

IAP Integrated Action Programme. (No further information).

IAEA International Atomic Energy Agency (UN).

IBASS Intelligent Business Applications Support System (ESPRIT project).

IBC Integrated broadband communication. The creation of a European reference model for the IBC was sought under the RACE programme in 1985.

ICEF Coordinating Committee of Chemical and General Workers Unions in the EC. *Königsworther Platz 6, Postfach 3047, D - 3000, Hanover, Germany.*

ICG Eurostatus General statistics domain on the CRONOS database. See **CRONOS**.

ICONE Comparative Index of National and European Standards.

ICP Inter-University Cooperation Programmes (related to ERASMUS).

IDES Interactive Data Entry System (a project within the CADDIA programme).

IDMS Integrated Data Management System.

IDN Integrated Digital Network.

IDO Integrated Development Operation (1979). A programme aimed at improving the EC's ecnomic and social cohesion.

IDP Integrated Development Programme (EC agricultural programme in the Western Isles of Scotland 1981).

IDRIS Intelligent Drive for Shop Floor Systems (ESPRIT approved 1988).

IDS Information Dissemination System. Designed to facilitate access to, and dissemination of, the information contained in the automated data processing systems. Part of the INSIS programme.

IDST Scientific and Technical Information and Documentation.

IES-DC Information Exchange System Data Collections. A directory and reference service of Information Technology in Europe. Free access via ECHO.

IFA Internal Financial Agreement (Internal agreement on the financing and administration of EC aid).

IFAPLAN An organization set up in the 1970s to coordinate the EC's Action Programmes to study the education and training needs of young people. The two programmes so far have run: 1976-1983; 1983-1987. Details published in Programme News, *32 Square Ambiorix, B - 10 40 Brussels, Belgium.* DG V.

IFC Internal data base of SII on EC financial instruments.

IEA International Energy Association (OECD).

IGADD Intergovernmental Authority on Drought and Development.

IGAF Functional Analysis Group for Management and Financial Administration.

IGC Intergovernmental Conference. Agenda includes economic and monetary union (EMU), and the Social Charter. To be declared open December 1990.

IHS Integrated Home Systems. A project involved in the creation of a communications system for domestic use (EUREKA project approved December 1986).

IKAROS Intelligence and Knowledge Aided Recognition of Speech (ESPRIT project).

ILE Isotopic Lead Experiment (environmental research programme).

IM Information Market. Relates to the activities of DG XIII. Covers areas such videotex, teletex, telefax, broadband communications and knowledge systems. *177 Route d'Esch, L - 1471 Luxembourg.*

IMACE Association of the Margarine Industries of the EEC countries. *Rue de la Loi 74, Boîte 3, B - 1040 Brussels, Belgium.*

'Immigration Group' Refers to officials from the twelve Member States and a Commission observer who are involved in the search for effective measures for the establishment of an EC passport union.

IMPs Integrated Mediterranean Programmes. Created in 1985, they aim to give assistance to the development of the Mediterranean areas of Greece, Italy and France. Currently under expansion. Each IMP lasts from five to seven years. Run in conjunction with local/national authorities.

IMPACT Information Market Policy Actions.

Impact Directive Abreviated title for Council Directive 85/337/EC on Environmental Impact Assessment.

IMPROFEED Development of new methods for the improvement of the feed value of raw materials and feeds (EUREKA project approved December 1986).

INCA Integrated Network Architecture for Office Communications (ESPRIT project approved 1984).

Incoterms International rules covering the definition of terms appearing in foreign commercial contracts.

Independents MEPs in the European Parliament not attached to any of the main political groups.

INDE Energy and industry domain on the CRONOS database.

INDIS Interbourse Data Information Service. A project implemented by the Commission in 1985, designed to link the various stock exchanges in the EC.

I N D O C Intelligent Documents Production Demonstrator.

INDUSER   An EC project to promote on-line information awareness. *c/o G.Hall, Online Information Consultants, 7 Southlands, Holmes Chapel, Cheshire CW4 7EU.*

INFO 1992 A new database set up by the Commission to provide concise information on the measures planned or adopted under the White Paper programme, and national incoporation measures.   Access via EUROBASES.   Available in all languages except Greek.   Cost ECU 10 per hour on-line.

INSEM Inter-institutional Service of Electronic Mail.

Insider Dealing Directive Adopted November 1989. OJ L 334 18.11.89.   Aimed at assisting the securities markets to operate smoothly by making illegal the fraudulent usage of inside information.

INSIS   Inter-institutional Integrated Services Information System.   An electronic mail service used for Parliamentary questions,   and the exchange of monetary documents between the EC institutions and Member States, government departments, and other message handling services that can be managed electronically.

INSTIL   Integration of Symbolic and Numeric Learning Techniques.

INTERACT An EC information system to coordinate measures at local level to achieve the social and economic integration of handicapped and old people.

INTERLAINE Committee for the Wool Industries of the EC. *Rue du Luxembourg 19, Boîte 14, B - 1040 Brussels, Belgium.*

International Textile, Garment and Leatherworkers Federation Covers 75 countries, and is associated with the ICFTU. *8 Rue Joseph Stevens, 1000 Brussels, Belgium.*

Intervention Agency Under the CAP rules, a body that may intervene to buy in produce when market prices fall below a fixed price, known as the Intervention Price. See introduction, **EAGGF**.

Intervention Price Under the CAP, the price fixed for agricultural commodities. Once market prices fall below this price, the Intervention Agency acts to buy in produce.

INTRASTAT A statistical collection system compiling figures relating to trade between Member States.

Investment Securities Directive Approved September 1989 OJ C 298 27.11.89. Due to come into force 1993, it is intended to provide a 'single passport' to a firm authorized in one Member State, enabling it to sell its services in any other Member State without having to acquire further authorization, while ensuring proper standards of solvency and investor protection.

IPE Individual Protection Equipment.

IPM Integrated Pest Management.

IPR Intellectual Property Rights.

IQ Intelligent Quattro to develop intelligent mechatronic automation and a remote control system for hydraulically operated vehicles which gives possibilities to wide range applications (EUREKA project approved December 1986).

IRCC International Radio Consultative Committee.

IRDAC Industrial Research and Development Advisory Committee.

IRIS Stimulation of Use of Information Technologies. A scheme set up by the Commission in 1988 to provide a network of demonstration projects on vocational training for women, as part of the EC's equal opportunities programme.

IR-SOFT An on-line directory of software packages currently on the market. Free Access via ECHO.

ISDN Integrated Services Digital Network. An improvement of the quality of traditional communication services (e.g. telephone, telex, etc.), with addition of new ones (e.g. hi-speed fax, videotex etc.)

ISG Internal Steering Group.

ISIS Integrated Standards Information System. Makes available information on safety standardization from CEN and CENELEC and ICONE.

ISO International Organization for Standardization.

ISPG Information Service Providers Group.

ISPRA JRC establishment. *21020 Ispra (Varesse), Italy.*

ISTI Indices of production, turnover, new order, wages, etc. on the CRONOS database.

ISUG Information Services Users Group.

IT Information Technologies.

ITER International Thermonuclear Experimental Reactor. The project to design an ITER was set up as part of the EC's research and training programme in the field of controlled thermonuclear fusion (1988-1992). Japan, USA and USSR also involved.

ITO International Trade Organization.

I T T T F Information Technology and Telecommunications Task.

IULA International Union of Local Authorities. *Wassenaarseweg 41, 2596 CG, The Netherlands*; also at *35, Great Smith Street, London SW1P 3BJ, United Kingdom.*

IVICO Integrated Video Codec (RACE project approved February 1986).

IVIS Integrated Vacuum Instrumentation System (EUREKA approved 1987).

JAF COST Working party on legal, administrative and financial questions. See **COST**.

JANUS The title of a journal from DG V. It aims to encourage an exchange of information between interested parties.

Jean Monnet Project 220 subsidies made available (as a pilot) for the teaching of European integration in Univesity curricula.

JENDRPC Joint EURATOM Nuclear Data and Reactor Physics Committee.

Jenkins, Roy (1920-) British politician and writer, he was a Labour MP 1948-1977, and an SDP MP, 1982-1987. He was Chancellor of the Exchequer 1967-1970; deputy leader of the Labour Party 1970-1972. He was President of the Commission of the EC 1977-1981; and Chancellor of Oxford University from 1988. In 1972, he won the Robert Schuman prize.

JESSI Joint European Submicron Silicon.   A programme set up by the Commission to strengthen Europe's electronic industry, and particularly the semiconductor industries (EUREKA project approved December 1986).

JET Joint European Torus.   JET is a vessel for engaging in research into fusion, occurring in the inside of the sun.   The aim of JET has been to build such a machine, and it is the centrepiece of the EC Fusion Programme. DG XII.

JET-SB Joint European Supervisory Board.

JICS The Joint Interpreting and Conference Service. A language service operated by the EC and established in 1985 that helps to provide training for conference interpreters.

JOULE Joint Opportunities for Unconventional or Long-Term Energy Supply. Programme adopted by the Council, 1989 as part of the EC's research and technological development policy.

JRC Joint Research Council. *Rue de la Loi 200, B - 1040 Brussels, Belgium.* Establishments at **GEEL** (Belgium); **ISPRA** (Italy); **KARLSRUHE** (Germany) and **PETTEN** (Netherlands). The council engages in research for the EC, mainly in the area of nuclear energy, but also solar energy. In future the JRC is set to be less financially dependent on the EC and more dependent on industrial contracts. DG XII.

JSP Joint Study Programmes (1976).

Jumbo Council ECO/FIN and Social Affairs Councils of Ministers joint meeting of 16.11.82 on the economic and social situation in the EC.

JUSLETTER Database with records and weekly summaries of decisions taken by various organs of the EC. It monitors developments of initiatives and decisions of EC institutions. Access via ECHO.

JWP Joint Working Party.

Kangaroo Group Formed in 1983, aimed at combating the barriers to trade within the EC. *Millbank Tower, Millbank, London, SW1P 4QS, United Kingdom.*

KARLSRUHE JRC establishment. *7500 Karlsruhe, Postfach 2340, Germany.*

KIWI KBS User Friendly System for Information Bases (ESPRIT project).

KRITIC Knowledge Representation and Inference Techniques in Industrial Control (ESPRIT project approved 1984).

LDCs Less Developed Countries.

LDR Liberal and Democratic Group (Liberals, Social Democrats and Republicans of the European Parliament).

LDTF Large Dynamic Test Facility (JRC - reactor safety programme).

LEDA   Local Employment Development Action Programme. Set up in 1984 by the Commission to help combat regional unemployment, and extended in 1988. OJ C 161 21/6/1984.

LEI Local Employment Initiatives.

LENO 2000 Development of automatic non-invasive medical diagnostic equipment based on new sensors and AI (EUREKA project approved June 1986).

Levies on Beef and Beef Cattle   These are fixed each week and are made up of the difference between the imported price (plus duties) and the guide price. Paid by Member States into the EC's own resources.

Liability for Defective Products Directive Council Directive EC7/8-1985 concerning liability for defective products, based on the principle of the manufacturer's strict liabiity.

LIB-2 Studies on the impact of new information technologies in libraries.

LIDAR Light Detection and Ranging (environmental research programme).

LINAC   Linear Accelerator at **GEEL**   (J R C establishment).

Linear-Tariff Cuts Refers to a uniform reduction in tariffs, either in respect to certain sections of a national tariff, or to the tariffs of all other countries concerned.

LINGUA Programme to improve linguistic fluency in the EC, 1990-1994. It runs an exchange scheme for pupils and teachers in secondary education, and also staff of businesses. Lingua Assistance Team, *2-3 Place du Luxembourg, B - 10 40 Brussels, Belgium.*

LION Local Integrated Optical Network (ESPRIT project approved 1984).

LOBI Loop Blowdown Investigation (JRC - reactor safety programme).

LOC Proposed Statistical Office databank on Community aid from the structural funds to local authorities.

LOCA Loss of coolant accidents. These occur as a result of small breaks in the primary circuit of a light water reactor. The Lob-Mod 2 integral test facility financed by the JRC investigated this problem in 1985.

LOGIMAX Development of second generation information and transport network throughout Europe. (EUREKA approved 1987).

Lomé Conventions There have been four Lomé Conventions to date, the first beginning in 1975 and the fourth beginning in 1990. They apply to those countries of Africa, the Caribbean and the Pacific, and enable them to have tariff-reduced access to EC markets on a non-reciprocal basis. (Lomé I in OJ L 25/96; Lomé II in OJ L 347/80; Lomé III in OJ L 86/86)

London Report On European political cooperation (published by HMSO as Cmnd 8424 in 1981).

LORINE Limited Rate Imagery Network Elements (RACE project approved February 1986).

Low Voltage Directive   Council Directive 73/23/EEC relating to electrical equipment designed for use within certain voltage limits (published in OJ L77/73).

Luxembourg Compromise   Came into being in 1966 in response to French complaints regarding the erosion of national sovereignty. Allows members to agree to disagree over a certain proposal; the proposal is then left on one side unadopted.

Luxembourg Convention   (1975) Between EC Member States only, aimed at furthering provisions (regarding a European patent) of the Munich convention.

Luxembourg Report   Related to political union in the EC, and appeared in 1970. Published in Bulletin of EC 11/1970.

Macmillan, Harold   (1894-198) British Member of Parliament from 1924. Secretary of State for Foreign Affairs, 1955; Chancellor of the Exchequer, 1955-1957; and Prime Minister 1957-1963. British delegate to the first consultative assembly of the Council of Europe, 1949.

MACNET Programme to develop a network of medical centres for consultation (1987-1991).

MACpacket family   Refers to a single package of standards for transmission and reception for satellite broadcasting. (Commission's White Paper, 1985.)

MACS   Maintenance Assistance Capability for Software (ESPRIT approved 1988).

MADRAS Modular Approach to Definition of RACE Subscriber Premises Network (RACE project approved February 1986).

MAGHREB countries Collective term for countries in the western part of the south Mediterranean, particuarly Morocco, Algeria, Tunisia.

Mansholt Plan Concerned the reform of agriculture, 1969. A ten-year plan authored by Dr Sicco Mansholt, then a vice-president of the EC Commission, was agreed which aimed to restructure agriculture in a manner that would raise the living standards of farmers, and diminish the increase in the CAP's costs.

Mansholt, Sicco (1908) Dutch politician. Minister of Agriculture, Fisheries and Food, 1945-1948; 1951-1952; 1956-1958. Engaged in the negotiations to etablish Benelux Union, 1946. Vice-President of the EC Commission, 1958-1967. President of the combined executives of EC, ECSC and Euratom, 1972-1973. Awarded the Robert Schuman Prize in 1968.

MAP Mediterranean Action Plan.

MAP Multi-Annual Programe.

Marlia Reports A device whereby the President of the Council presents the General Affairs Council with a progress report on outstanding business from other councils.

Marshall, George (1880-1959) Member of United States Army and politician. Chief of Staff, 1939-1945; Secretary of State, 1947-1949; and author of the Marshall Plan for the economic recovery of Western Europe after the Second World War.

Marshall Plan See **European Recovery Programme.**

MASHREQ Countries Collective term for countries at the eastern end of the southern Mediterranean, particuarly Syria, Jordan, Egypt, Lebanon.

MAST Marine Science and Technology research and development programme (1989-1992).   The four elements are: 1. Basic Applied marine science.   2. Coastal bore science.   3. Marine technology.   4. Supporting initiatives.

Matthaeus Programme Adopted by the Commission, April 1989, for the training of national customs officials to prepare them for the completion of the internal market.

MAX Metropolitan Area Communication System (ESPRIT approved in 1988).

MC Management Committee Set up to enable the Commission to ensure the smooth functioning and development of EC policies in different areas.

MCAs Monetary Compensatory Amounts. A system of border subsidies and taxes introduced under the CAP to prevent the movement of grain from the lowest-priced markets to the highest-priced markets. DG VI.

MCAC Management and Coordination Advisory Committees.

MDNS Managed Data Network Systems. A proposed joint venture company intended to improve on Europe's poor record in the fast growing market for data communicatios that are deemed vital for modern business. It would enable customers to buy enhanced pan-European data services from a single outlet.

MEC Special Committee of Enquiry.

MECU Million European Currency Units.

MEDIA Measures for Encouraging the Development of the Audiovisual Production Industry Programme (1987). Research covers distribution, production and financing.

Medical Care EC residents are entitled to free, or reduced rates of, medical care in all EC Member States. In general, the costs are borne by the EC country where the worker or holidaymaker is insured, but in certain countries, payment is required towards the medical costs.

Medspa Protection of the environment in the Mediterranean region. A proposed Regulation by the Commission as part of its management of environmental resources.

MENTOR Expert system for dealing with major plant failures and security control (EUREKA project approved June 1986).

MEP Member of European Parliament.

Merger Treaty 1965 Provided for the establishment of a single Council of Ministers to replace the three existing Councils of Ministers, and for a single Commission to replace the Commissions of the EC, Euratom and the High Authority of the ECSC. Came into force in July 1967.

MERMAID Metrication and Resource Modelling Aid (ESPRIT project approved in 1988).

MESA group Mutual ECU Settlement Account (financial body dealing in ECUs).

Messina Conference On 2-4 June 1955, the Foreign Ministers of the six ECSC Member States met at Messina to discuss plans for further European economic integration. The outcome of the meeting was the Messina Resolution.

Messina Resolution Result of the Messina Conference in June 1955, undertook to take further measures to establish a united Europe by expanding joint instituions; gradually integrating national economies; establishing a common market; and combining social policies. Led to the negatiations resulting, eventually, in the 1957 Treaty of Rome.

METEOR An integrated formal approach to industrial software development (ESPRIT project approved 1984).
METKIT Metrics Education Toolkit (ESPRIT project approved 1988).

METRE Measurements, standards and reference techniques.

MFAs Multi-Fibre Arrangements. Measures taken to safeguard Community manufacturers in textiles from competition by countries with cheap labour costs. Due to be gradually phased out beginning 1991 when the textile industry will be brought under the umbrella of GATT.

MFTA Medium-term financial assistance.

MGQ Maximum Guaranteed Quantity. Part of the EC's management of the CAP. An agricultural stabilizer aimed at improving the planning of production and conversion of leaf tobacco.

MIDAS Management Information Dissemination Administrative System. In conjunction with SYSDOC it acts as an internal database within the European Parliament.

MINSTREL New information models for office filing retrieval (ESPRIT project approved 1984).

Mirage Migration of Radioisotopes in the Geosphere (programme dealing with radioactive waste).

MIS Multilingual Information System (ESPRIT approved).

MISEP Mutual Information System on Employment Policies. Set up by the Commission in 1985 as a means of providing a network for the collection of information on the legislative background to employment problems, and attempts to deal with them, in Member States. DG V. *PO Box 3073, NL - 6202 NB Maastricht, The Netherlands.*

MITHRA Development, industrialization and the sale of mobile robots for use in tele-surveillance (EUREKA project approved June 1986).

MLTS Medium and Long-term Translation Service.

MNE Multinational Enterprise.

MOBIDICK Multivariable On-line Bilingual Dictionary Kit (EUREKA project approved December 1986).

MODESTI Mould design and manufacturing optimization by development, standardisation and extensive use of CAD/CAM procedures (BRITE project approved 1985).

Monetary Committee A committee comprising two members from each Member State and two members from the Commission, whose task is to enhance coordination of monetary policies in Member States to facilitate the smooth functioning of the EC.

Monetary Compensatory Amounts See MCAs.

MONITOR Research programme on strategic analysis, forecasting and assessment in research and technology. Adopted by the Council in 1989 as part of the EC's research and technological development policy (1988-1992).

Monnet, Jean (1888 1979), Monnet was one of the founding fathers of the EC, and, perhaps, the main driving force behind its creation. He was motivated by French concern that, in the aftermath of the Second World War, Germany would once again attempt to dominate Europe through its holdings of coal and iron in the Saarland. Monnet was responsible for promoting the Schuman Plan for the ECSC, which came into being in August 1952 with Monnet as its chairman. He was a central figure behind the Treaty of Rome, signed in 1957, which brought the EC into being.

Monnet Committee See **Action Committee for United States of Europe.**

Montant de Soutien The amount of financial support offered to farmers for a specific commodity under the Mansholt proposals.

Montant Forfaitaire The amount by which the levy on imports from one Member State to another is reduced in order to give EC suppliers an advantage over outside suppliers.

MOSES Development of new generation of multi-media database services with integration of the multimedia features in the whole chain of equipment (EUREKA project approved June 1986).

Most Favoured Nation Status A term that was created by GATT, and refers to the privilege bestowed by one country on another by way of an advantage, benefit or immunity, in its trading facilities.

MOU Memorandum of Understanding.

Mountain When prices for certain commodities, particularly butter and beef, have been set high, under the CAP, this has encouraged over-production. The result has been heavy EC intervention buying to support the price, and a mountain of the product in question has been the consequence.

MS Member States of the EC.

MTFA Medium term financial assistance.

MTN Multinational trade negotiations.

Multifibre Agreements See **MFA**.

MULTOS Multimedia filing system (ESPRIT project approved 1984).

Multilateral Deregulation A device to bolster competition that would enable airlines from one EC country to compete on routes between two others.

Munich Convention (1973) Agreed on a pan-European system for the granting of patents. Involved non-EC countries as well.

MUSIP Multisensor Image Processor (ESPRIT approved 1988).

MUST Next Generation Data Base Management System Development (ESPRIT project).

NABS Nomenclature for the Analysis and Comparison of Scientific Programmes and Budgets.

NACE General Industrial Classification of Economic Activities within the European Communities (formerly NICE). Part of the Commission's standardization programme for 1992, operating through EUROSTAT.

NADC Non-associated Developing Countries.

NAFO The Regulatory Area of the North West Atlantic Fisheries Organizations. An area of controlled fishing designated by the Council.

NARIC National Academic Recognition Information Centres of the EC (inaugurated in 1982 and controlled by the Commission through national centres).

NCE Non-compulsory Expenditure.

NCI New Community Instrument. Also known as the 'Ortoli facility' after the Commissioner who proposed it, the NCI is the finance mechanism through which the Commission funds programmes of technological development and innovation by small businesses within the EC, in conjunction with the EIB.

NCPI New Commercial Policy Instrument.

NEPTUNE New European Programme for Technology Utilization in Education.

NET Next European Torus. The second stage of the Vokamak programme in the field of controlled thermonuclear fusion, formed by the JET project. Detailed design to begin in 1991.

NETT Network for Environmental Technology Transfer. Funded by the Commission. *Square de Meeus, B - 1040 Brussels, Belgium.*

NGAA National Grant Awarding Authority. Operates within the ERASMUS programme.

NGO Non-governmental Organization.

NIC Newly industrializing country.

NIMEXE Nomenclature of goods for the external trade statistics of the Community and statistics of trade between Member States. The body which provides a uniform classification for the application of customs duties throughout the Community. From 1988 merged to form CN.

NIPRO Common Nomenclature of Industrial Products. Body classifying goods according to the industry which manufactures them, and identifies their position in NIMEXE.

NITS New Information Technologies in Education. (1983).

Non-Affiliated Refers to those members of the EP that belong to no special grouping.

Non-Associated States Those countries that have no special links with the EC.

Norm Price The price which the producer of tobacco is guaranteed under the CAP.

NPCI National Programme of Community Interest.

NST/R A revised version of NST - the Uniform Nomenclature of Goods for Transport Statistics.

NT New Technologies.

NTB Non-Tariff Barriers. Set up to ensure the free movement of goods throughout the EC. DG III.

NUTS Nomenclature of Territorial Units for Statistics.

NVA Net Value Added.

Nyborg Agreement Reached in September 1987 by Ministers for Economic and Financial Affairs. Dealt successfully with the after effects of the October 1987 stocmarket crash.

OASIS Open and Secure Information Systems (EUREKA project approved December 1986).

Ockrent Report of 1957 represented the Community's proposals for the creation of a Free Trade Area covering the six Member States and the seven non-member countries. In 1958, the French government threw out the plan altogether.

OCA Optimum currency area. Area covered by a group of countries linked through fixed rates of exchange.

OCTS Overseas countries and territories (dependencies of Member States).

ODAS Ocean Data Acquisition System (COST action project). See **COST**.

ODETTE A project launched by the European motor industry with the aim of replacing paperwork by electronic data interchange.

OECD Organization for Economic Cooperation and Development. The OECD replaced the OEEC (Organization for European Economic Cooperation) in September 1961. It has 25 members. Its objectives are to enhance economic and social welfare throughout the OECD area by assisting its members' governments in the formulation and coordination of policies directed towards that end; and to encourage members' efforts in favour of developing countries. *Rue André-Pascal 2, 75116 Paris, France.*

OEITFL Association of European Fruit and Vegetable Processing Industries. *Avenue de Cortenburg 172, Boîte 6, B - 1040 Brussels, Belgium.*

Official Journal of the European Communities See **OJ**.

OFCA Organization of Manufacturers of Cellulose Products for Foodstuffs in the EC. *PO Box 661, 2280 AR Rijswijk, The Netherlands.*

OFPPT Office for Vocational Training and Employment Promotion. Blue Flag scheme, in connection with EYE, a scheme to identify EC beaches which attain basic levels of health, hygiene and safety.

OJ   Official Journal of the EC, published daily by OOPEC in all the official languages.   There are three series: 'L' - legislation; 'C' - information and notices; 'S' - supplement.   Available from EDCs.

OOPEC   Office for Official Publications of the European Communities.   Established in 1969, the Office is an organisation that prints, sells and distributes material coming from the the EC institutions.   *Rue Mercier 2, 2985 Luxembourg.*

Open Network Provision   (ONP)   A technical project seeking to harmonize tariff conditions, technical standards, and conditions of access to telecommunications networks across the EC.

ORGANIGRAMME   Directory of the Commission of the EC.

Origin Principle   A system of tax collection whereby tax would be collected on goods during the course of production.   Due to be implemented in the EC in 1996.

Ortoli Facility   See **NCI.**

Ortoli, François-Xavier   (1925)   Italian tax inspector. Secretary-General of the Franco-Italian Committee of the EC, 1955.   Director-General of Internal Market Division of the EC, 1958.   President of the EC Commission, 1972-1976.

OSI   Open Systems Interconnection.   A standard format for information interchange via information technology (IT).

OSIRIS Mechanised system for the production of statistical tables.

OSIS Open Shops for Information Systems (COST action project).

Oslo Declaration Signed in March 1989 by the EFTA countries as a reaffirmation of their own strong links, and their desire for good relations with the EC.

OSSAD Office Suppport System Analysis and Design (ESPRIT project approved 1984).

OT Overseas Territories.

OUSR Operating Unit Status Report which acts as a component of ERDS.

OVIDE Organisation Videotex pour les Deputés. Currently an internal video conferencing and video information service for MEPs and staff of the EP concerning the work of Parliament and its various sub-committees.

Own Resources A formula for financing the Community Budget that does not rely on the direct contributions from Member States. Instead, the contributions are collected by Member governments and passed on to the Commission in the form of (1) customs duties; (2) agricultural levies; and (3) up to 1.4% of VAT. Adopted by the EC in 1970. DG IX.

PABLI An on-line version of current EC development projects DG VIII. Access via ECHO.

PACE European Programme of Advanced Continuing Education (American/EC initiative not yet operational).

Pagis Performance Assessment of Geological Isolation System (research into aspects of radioactive waste programme).

PALABRE Integration of artificial intelligence, vocal input-output and natural language dialogue - application to directory services (ESPRIT project approved 1985).

PAN(N5) Manufacturer of pilot equipment to produce then prove the feasibility of manufacturing flow-line style, high pressure sub-sea pipes (EUREKA project approved 1986).

PANGLOSS Parallel Architecture for Networking Gateways linking OSI Systems (an ESPRIT Project).

Pannenbourg Report A report compiled by the ESPRIT Review Board evaluating the progress of the ESPRIT programme.

PANORAMA of EC INDUSTRY Reference source published by OOPEC. Covers the manufacturing and services industries, with analysis.

PAP Priority Action Plan.

PARADI Automatic production management system using AI developments (EUREKA project approved 1986).

PARDOC European Parliament Documents. A European Parliament internal database which replaced DOSE and is being replaced by EPOQUE.

Paris Treaty The establishment of the ECSC on 23 July 1952.

PARQ An internal European Parliament data base of parliamentary questions which is being repace by EPoque.

Patents European Patent Law and procedures are governed by the Community Patent Convention (CPC), 1975, and the European Patent Convention (EPC), 1973. Between them, these two conventions established the EC as one uniform bloc to be covered by one set of patent procedures; created one central office for administering patents; and provided a 20 year protection period. DG XIII.

Paul Finet Foundation Established in 1965 by the High Authority of te ECSC to commemorate its former President, its objective is to provide funds to the orphans of workers in the coal, iron ore mining and steel industries of the ECSC who died after June 1965 of industrial accidents or work-related diseases. The money is designed to help with education and training.

PCERT Parliamentary Committee on Energy Research and Technology.

PDB Preliminary Draft Budget.

PEDIP Programme for the Development of Portuguese Industry.

PEGASE An internal database of the European Parliament library catalogue (see also **SYSDOC**).

Pentagonal Initiative An attempt by Italy, Austria, Hungary, Yugoslavia and Czechoslovakia at regional cooperation in political and economic matters in 1990, as a modest counterweight to the political and economic power of an united Germany.

PERINORM   A compact disc produced monthly showing UK, German, French, European and international standards and technical regulations (including CEN and CENELEC). *BSI Database, Linford Wood, Milton Keynes, MK4 6LE.*

Perla Performance Calibration and Training Laboratory (JRC - fissile materials safeguards and management programme).

PERSEE Internal database of SII showing decision-making processes between the Commission and other Community Institutions.

PERT Professional Electronics and Research Technology (not yet operational).

PETRA Project of Equipment for the Treatment of Radioactive Waste in ADECO (JRC - safety of nuclear materials programme).

PETRA Programme for the vocational training of young people preparing them for adult working life. (1988-1992). *Petra Support Office, IFAPLAN, 32 Square Ambiorix, B - 1040 Brussels.*

PETTEN JRC establishment. *Westerduinweg 3, Postbus Nr 2, 1755 ZG Petten, The Netherlands.*

Pietro Adonnino Report   1985 Set forth proposals aimed at reforming the Community for the benefit of its citizens.   Among the issues covered were those concerned with driving licences, a European ombudsman, travel, educational qualifications, cross-border television, and a more uniform electoral system.

PHOEBUS A solar power demonstration plant with a capacity of 30 megawatts (EUREKA approved, 1987).

PIMS Project Integrated Management Systems (ESPRIT project approved 1985).

PINC Illustrative Nuclear Programme for the Community (1966).

PIP Priority Information Programme. Established by the Commission in 1989 to publicize the priorities in its annual programme.

PISC Project for the Inspection of Steel Components (JRC project). See **JRC.**

Plating Directive Council Directive 76/114/EEC relating to statutory plates and inscriptions for motor vehicles (published in OJ L1555/78).

Plumber Regulations Council Directive 3/84 introducing arrangements for movement within the EC of goods sent from one Member State for temporary use in one or more other Member States. Appears in OJ L 2/84.

p.m. Pour Mémoire (a token entry in the Budget - no money has been allocated but it is expected in due course).

PMG Project Management Group.

PMS Project Management Services.

PODA Piloting of the Office Document Architecture (ESPRIT project approved 1985).

Pompidou Group Established in 1971 within the Council of Europe to counter drug abuse.

Pompidou, Georges, Jean Raymond   (1911-1974) French politician.   Prime Minister of France, 1962-1968; President of France, 1969-1974.   In contrast to President de Gaulle, he overturned the French veto on British membership of the EC.

Ponsonby Rule   Relates to the UK's system of ratifying treaties, or amendments or enlargements to the original EC treaties.   In general, it requires that, subsequent to the text being placed before Parliament, a twenty-one day period must elapse before the government proceeds with ratification.

POP   Refers to Regulation 4028/86 detailing measures to improve and adapt fisheries and aquaculture.

POSEIDOM   Programme of options specific to the remote and insular nature of the overseas departments.

PPS   Purchasing power standard: a common unit representing an identical volume of goods and services for each country.

PRAG   Agriculture and fisheries domain on the CRONOS database.

PRC   An internal data base of SII, it is regarded as the most politically sensitive file.   It contains an examination of the proposals, recommendations and communications set before the Council, and Council decisions.

Preference   An advantage awarded to the trade of a state, or of a group of states.

Press Agencies, European Alliance of   Established in 1957 with headquarters in Brussels, Belgium.

Price Index   The EC publishes a Consumer Price Index in EUROSTAT, on a monthly basis, in which price changes in the EC, Japan and the US are monitored and compared.

Production Grouping   An association of agricultural producers who have an important role to play in the regulation of the EC market through intervention buying. It is their duty to plan the production and distribution of certain produce and to dispose of the income.

Product Liability Directive   85/374/EEC (OJ L 210, 7.8.1985). Came into force in 1988. Established in order to bring uniformity to national laws for liability of substandard goods, and to protect the consumer from having to prove the manufacturer's error. The Directive ensures that the manufacturer or importer of defective goods, accepts liability. DG III.

Project 1992   A proposed joint treaty to integrate the six EFTA states fully into the EC's single market, but without offering full EC membership.

PROMAN   Commission internal database on the management of contracts for energy projects receiving EC support.

PROMETHEUS   To create concepts and solutions which will point the way to a road traffic system with greater efficiency, economy and with reduced impact on the environment (EUREKA project approved June 1986).

PROSPECTRA   Programme Development by Specification and Transformation (ESPRIT project approved 1984).

Protective Measures   Those which a Member State is entitled to take under Article 109, when faced with a sudden balance of payments crisis, in a situation where the Council has not rendered any assistance.

PROVA   Commission internal database on the management of invitations to submit proposals for energy demonstration projects.

p.s.r.   (quality sparkling wines) produced in specific regions.

PTF   Preliminary Task Force.

PTO   Public telecommunications operator.

PTTs   State-controlled telecommunications monopolies.

Publications Bulletin   Annual list of all publications of the JRC.

Public Procurement Directives   Since 1978 a series of EC directives have specified with increasing vigour that public contracts worth 200,000 ECUs or more must be publicized throughout the EC in the Official Journal of the European Communities.   Exceptions include contracts connected with water, telecommunications, transport and security matters.   DG III.

Public Supply Contracts   Since 1978, such contracts worth 200,000 ECUs or more, must be publicized throughout the EC in the Official Journal of the European Communities.   Exceptions include contracts connected with water, energy, telecommunications, transport and security matters.   DG III.

Public Works Contracts Directive (72/277EEC) Stipulates that there must be a uniform procedure for publicizing and granting public sector construction contracts where the estimated cost amounts to one million ECUs or more. Exceptions include such areas as transport, water and energy. DG III.

RACE Research and Development in Advanced Communication Technology for Europe Programme. Initiated in 1985, it was intended to keep the EC in the forefront of the telecommunications industry. Responsible for coordination of research into Integrated Broadband Communication (IBC) among other subjects.

RAINBOW group See **ARC**.

RAISE Rigorous Approach to Industrial Software Engineering (ESPRIT project approved 1984).

RAPID A new database containing information on the complete texts of press releases from the Commission's Spokesman's Service. In addition, certain speeches by members of the Commission are also included. It covers material from January 1985 to the present. For further information, contact: *Commission of the* EC, *Eurobases, 200 Rue de la Loi, B - 1049 Brussels, Belgium.*

RARE Associated Networks for European Research.

RBW Rainbow Group of the European Parliament (which includes the Greens).

RDE European Renewal and Democratic Alliance (of the European Parliament).

RDP Regional Development Programme.

Recommendations   These are not enforceable.

RECHAR   Programme to assist the conversion of coalmining areas. An ECSC Consultative Committee programme, 1989.

REDO   Maintenance, reliability, re-usability and documentation of software systems (ESPRIT approved 1988).

Reference Price   This refers to the Community reference price which is derived from the representative market prices for food and vegetables calculated in each Member State that are then averaged. Should the import price of these foodstuffs be lower than the reference price, then a levy is added to make the prices equal.

Regie   A status that when applied to a company means that it cannot be declared bankrupt.

REGIO EUROSTAT   Statistical Office databank of regional statistics, mainly concerning economic aspects. Access via WEFA-CEIS.

Regional Fund   See **ERDF**.

Regional Fund Committee   Set up by a Council Decision of 1975 (OJ L 73, 21.3.1975) to provide the Commission with support in the examination of applications for regional aid, and in making awards from the Regional Fund. DG XVI.

Regional Policy Committee   Set up by a Council Decision of 1975 (OJ L 73, 21.3.1975) to provide the Commission with assistance in allocating the Regional Fund, particularly with respect to the larger projects. It also has the task of coordinating national, regional and EC policies. DG XVI.

Regulations Directly applicable to all Member States. A regulation takes precedence over existing national law and does not have to be confirmed by national Parliaments.

REM Radioactivity Environmental Monitoring. A database under the auspices of the JRC at Ispra.

RENAVAL Programme to assist the conversion of shipbuilding areas. An ECSC Consultative Committee programme, 1988-1990.

Representative Organizations Multinational interest organisations that have been set up in Brussels with the aim of influencing EC policy. Their task is to articulate the concerns of their members to the Commission, and to respond to the Commission's proposals for legislation and change.

REQUEST Reliability and Quality of European Software (ESPRIT project appproved 1984).

RES Integrated Development of Renewable Natural Resources (FAST II programme).

RESEAU European Environmental, Agricultural and Urban Development Monitoring Network (a database of environmental statistics within the CADDIA programme).

RESIDER Programme to assist the conversion of steel areas. An ECSC Consultative Committee programme (1988-1990).

Residence (or Worldwide) Principle Means that residents are taxed on their income at the same rate regardless of source.

Resolutions   are not legally binding but represent either agreement on a principle or a willingness to act, and are adopted by the Council of Ministers, having been recommended by the Commission.

Restitution Payments   Under the CAP, financial support paid on exports of agricultural products on the difference between the global price and the (higher) domestic price in the exporting country in the EC.

RETI Association of Traditional Industrial Regions of Europe.   An industrial pressure group aiming to direct flows of funding towards member regions. *Rue de Bethune 57, Boîte 20 35, F - 59014 Lille, France;* or, *Mr M. Gregg, Strathclyde Regional Council, Strathclyde House, 20 India Street, Glasgow G2 4PF, United Kingdom.*

REWARD   Recycling of waste R&D.

Rey, Jean (1902-) Belgian lawyer.   Delegate to Consultative Assembly of Council of Europe, 1949-1953.   Minister of Economic Affairs, 1954-1958. President of the EC Commission, 1967-1970.

Rey Report   A report produced in 1980 by a Committee set up by the European Parliament and chaired by Jean Rey.   The aim was to consider how EC institutions could be improved.   The central recommendation was that the Commission should have a more political role, and that there should be closer liaison between the European Parliament and the Commission.   Other recommendations were that Advisory bodies should remain advisory and not try to usurp the Commission's role.   Also, that women should be adequately represented on the Commission.

RGMG Representatives of the Governments of the Member States.

RICA A system developed to transfer data under **FADN** (CADDIA programme project).

RICHE European information and communication networks for hospitals (ESPRIT approved 1988).

Right of Establishment Refers to a number of directives (DG III) adopted firstly in 1963, that establish the rights of individuals in one Member State to work in agricultural sectors in other Member States.

Ritter List Commission list of pending proposals published in June and October annually as a COM document.

RMC RACE management committee.

Rome Treaty Signed by France, West Germany, Italy, The Netherlands, Belgium and Luxembourg, establishing the EEC, which came into force in January 1958.

ROPS Roll-Over Protective Structures.

ROSE Research Open Systems for Europe (ESPRIT project). See **ESPRIT.**

Rowindows Proposed agencies to inform SMEs of EC information.

RSUP RACE strategy for verification.

RTI Road transport informatics.

RUBRIC   Rule Based Approach to Information Systems Development (ESPRIT project).

RUE Rational Use of Energy.

Rules of Competition   These cover such issues as restrictive trade practices; kinds of trade agreements that are forbidden and allowed; monopolies and mergers.

SA Societas Europea.   The proposed European company which would transcend national company law by operating on a system of EC law only.

SAD Single Administration Document.   Introduced in January 1988 to facilitate trading in the EC by enabling all Member States to use the same documentation and a common integrated tariff.

SAID Simulation for Agro-Industrial Development.

SARA Simulation of Reactor Accident.

SAST Strategic analysis in the field of science and technology (Part of the MONITOR Programme).

SC Standing Committee.

SCA Shared-Cost Action.

SCAR Standing Committee on Agricultural Research

SCAD Automated Central Documentation Service.

SCAD Bibliographical database on current events, official publications, periodical articles etc. developed by SCAD. Bulletins published weekly. Access via EUROBASES.

SCAP   Social Action Programme, 1974. A wide ranging document aimed at achieving full and better employment; improved living and working conditions; and the increased participation of employers and workers in EC decisions.

SCAR   Standing Committee on Agricultural Research.

SCE   Standing Committee on Employment.

SCENT   System for a customs enforcement network. Designed for the passage of urgent electronic mail messages in cases of fraud.

SCF   Scientific Committee for Food. Set up in 1974 to advise the Commission in relation to food products and their impact on human health, it also has responsibilities with regard to the composition of food products, the use of additives, the detection of contaminants; and it prepares occasional reports.

Schengen Agreement   A border-free treaty designed to end frontier controls between France, West Germany and the Benelux countries (the Schengen Group). Broke down in December 1989 owing to France's misgivings at the flood of refugees and immigrants arriving in West Germany from the German Democratic Republic and elsewhere in Eastern Europe, but revived a few months later and signed in June 1990. The Schengen Group members now seek to lock their currencies together, and it is possible that they will move towards full monetary union on their own in future.

Schmidt, Helmut (1918-)   German politician; chairman of SPD in Bundestag, 1967-1969. Minister of Defence, 1969-1972. German Federal Chancellor, 1974-19 .

Schuman Plan (1950) Introduced by Robert Schuman, then French Foreign Minister, in a speech he made in May 1950. The Plan embodied a scheme for bringing together Europe's coal and steel resources, and was eventually included in the Treaty which established the ECSC in 1951.

Schuman Prize (Federal Republic of Germany) Created in 1966 by Bonn University and awarded yearly to honour prominent Europeans who have benefited the cause of European unity.

Schuman Prize (France)   Created in 1967, and awarded yearly, by the Foundation and Association of the Friends of Robert Schuman, this Gold Medal is presented for outstanding contributions to European unity.

Schuman, Robert (1886-1963) A French politician, Schuman was both Foreign Minister and Prime Minister. He is perhaps best known for his plan in 1950 for pooling the coal and steel industries of France and West Germany, which was to lead to the establishment of the ECSC. Schuman was a passionate advocate of the movement towards European integration and recommended that it should be based on the surrender of national sovereignty to a supranational body.

SCIENCE   Plan to stimulate the international cooperation and interchange necessary for European researchers (1988-1992).

SCOPE Software certification on Program in Europe (ESPRIT project 1988).

SCP Single Cell Protein (COST action project).

SCRIPT Support for Creative Independent Production Talent (1988-).

SD Special Directive.

SDIM System for Documentation and Information in Metallurgy. Acces via FIZ Karlsruhe.

SDR Special Drawing Rights.

SE European Company.

SEA The Single European Act. Agreed at the Luxembourg European Council of December 1985, it came into being on 1 July 1987. The Act defines the single market as, 'an area without internal frontiers in which free movement of goods, persons, services and capital, is ensured in accordance with the provision of the Treaty'. The Act requires EC members to work progressively towards establishing a single market to be realized by 31 December 1992. In addition, the Act urges members to strive towards improving the quality of the environment; strengthening the scientific and technological industrial base; enhancing economic and social cohesion; cooperation in economic and monetary policy; and better relations in the work place. OJ L 169 29/6/1987.

SEAQI The screen-based quotation system for international equities. An international equity market run by the London Stock Exchange widely considered to be the prototype for a pan-European stock market.

SEC documents SEC is an abbreviation for 'Secretary-General'. SEC documents in conjunction with the COM documents form a major part of Commission business. SEC documents are less formal than the COM documents and consist of interim reports, draft resolutions, discussion documents, etc. They generally emanate from earlier in the working process of the Commission than COM documents.

SECA   National accounts domain on the CRONOS data- base (formerly SEC1).

SECB National accounts domain on the CRONOS database (formerly ZCN2).

Second Banking Directive   Adopted December 1989 OJ L 386 30/12/89.   Laid down a formula for the introduction of a single banking licence which once issued to a Member State would be valid in all other Member States.   Provisions are in place to ensure that licence holders are suitably qualified and supervised.

SECS   National accounts domain on the CRONOS data- base (formerly AMP1).

SEDOC   European system for the International Clearing of Vacancies and Applications for Employment.

SEDOS   Software Environment for the Design of Open Distributed Systems (ESPRIT project approved 1984).

Segre Report   A report produced for the Commission in 1966, on the European capital market.   It recommended the adoption of fixed exchange rates to help offset the weaknesses in the market.

SEM   South and Eastern Mediterranean Countries.

SEPLIS   European Secretariat of the Liberal, Independent and Social Professions.   *Rue du Congrès, B - 1000 Brussels, Belgium.*

SERV   Service activities and technological change (FAST II programme) See **FAST**.

SESAME   An on-line Commission database on hydrocarbon technology and energy demonstration projects. Access via DATACENTRALEN.

Set aside Taking land out of production.

Seveso I Directive   Council Directive 82/501/EEC on the major accident hazards of certain industrial activities (published in OJ L 230/82). Amended in OJ L 85/87 and OJ L 336/88.

Seveso II Directive   Council Directive 84/631/EEC on the supervision and control within the EC of the transfrontier shipment of hazardous wastes (published in OJ L326/84 and OJ L181/86).

SFAC Social Fund Advisory Committee.

SFINX   Software Factory Integration and Experimentation (ESPRIT project approved 1985).

SG Secretariat-General of the Commission.

SGM Standard Gross Margin.

SHIFT Project A system of health control of imports from third countries at frontier inspection posts.

SIAP Service Infrastructure Action Plan (proposals not yet published).

SIDIC European Association of Information Services.

SIDR Energy and industry domain on the CRONOS database.

SIENA Databank of external trade statistics. Access via SOEC.

SIGLE System for Information on Grey Literature in Europe. Access via BLAISE.

SII Integrated Information Systems. Formerly CIRCE. Coordinating organization for managing databases internal to the Comminssion, under DG IX.

SIMPER Structured Information Management Processing and Effective Retrieval (ESPRIT project approved 1988).

SINCOM Computerized Accounting and Financial Management for the Commission.

Single Banking Licence Enables banks established in one Member State to set up and operate branches throughout the EC.

SIPS Population and social conditions domain on the CRONOS data base.

SIRENE A databank concerning energy currently being created by the SOEC and DG XVII (formerly known as EIS/Baden).

SITC Standard international trade classification developed by the United Nations.

SLOM A set of provisions adopted by the Council in 1989 to enable adjustment of the milk quota system and related measures.

Sluicegate Price Similar to the threshold price, this covers pigmeat, eggs and poultry, and is the price set

within the EC for these products. Imports of these
foodstuffs entering the EC below this price are subject
to a levy which will raise them to the sluicegate price.

SME   Small and Medium Enterprise Task Force.
Established in 1986 with the aim of improving the
business environment within the EC, it supplies
information and assistance to SMEs and is responsible
for overseeing the Community's 'Fiche d'Impact' System,
whereby all Commission proposals must be assessed for
their likely effect on Community SME business. DG
XXIII.

SMU Small and Medium-sized Undertaking.

SMUK   Supplementary Measure in favour of the
United Kingdom.

Snake The snake was the nickname for a parity club of
stable exchange rates with 2.25% margins. A number
of EC Member States joined; however, the UK and Eire
did not, and Italy and France subsequently left under the
pressure of the 1973 Oil Crisis. Superseded by EMS.

SOAG Senior Officials Advisory Group (internal
working party to assist the Commission in implementing
measures for a common imformation market).

Soames, Sir Christopher (1920-) British politician
and diplomat. Member of Parliament, 1950-1966.
Ambassador to France, 1968-1972. Vice President of
the EC Commission, 1973-1976.

SOC Socialist group of the European Parliament.

SOCI Population and social conditions domain on the
CRONOS database.

Social Dumping The process whereby manufacturers shift production from high to low wage areas in the EC.

Social Fund See ESF.

Social Fund Advisory Committee Provides advice to the Commission on the allocation of the Social Fund (ESF), and comprises members of governments, trades unions, and employers' organizations.

SOEC Statistical Office of the European Communities. One of the departments of the EC Commission, based in Brussels. *Bâtiment Jean Monnet, Rue Alcide de Gasperi, 2920 Luxembourg.*

Soft Terms The name given to aid which is granted at less than the cost of its provision by the donor state.

SOGITS Senior Officials Group for Information Technology Standardisation.

Solidarity Principle of Solidarity.

Solvency Ratio Directive (19.6.89) Sets out the legally binding capital requirements for banks in the EC. Its central provision is a minimum risk asset ratio of eight%, including off balance sheet assets.

SOMIW Secure Open Multimedia Integrated Work-station (ESPRIT project approved 1984).

Sonning Prize (Denmark) Presented for contributions to European culture.

Source (or Territorial) Principle Means that income is taxed at varying rates depending upon its source.

Spaak Report Rationale of the Report was that political integration naturally follows closer economic cooperation between the EC's Member States. 1956.

Spaak, Paul-Henri (1899-1972). Belgian Socialist politician. Prime Minister twice (1938-1939); (1947-1949). A founding father of the UN and first president of the General Assembly (1946-1947). Became Secretary-General of NATO (1957-1961).

SPAG Standards Promotion and Application Group. *Avenue Marnix 28, B - 1050 Brussels, Belgium.*

SPEAR Support Programme for a European Assessment of Research (1988-1992) (Subsidiary of MONITOR).

SPECS Specification Environment for Communication Software (RACE project approved February 1986).

SPEL A model of agricultural prices (a project within the CADDIA programme).

SPEM Software Production Evaluation Model.

SPES Stimulation Plan for Economic Science. Programme adopted by the Council in 1989 as part of the EC's research and technological development policy. OJ C 306 1/12/88.

Spierenburg Report Put forward 'Proposals for the Reform of the Commission of the European Communities and its Services' (1979). The five-man team responsible for the preparation of the Report met under the Chairmanship of Dirk Spierenburg, a former Dutch Permanent Representative. They constituted an Independent Review Body set up by the Commission to look into the organization and staffing of the Commission.

SPIN Speech Interface at Office Workstations (ESPRIT project approved 1984).

Spinelli Report Put forward 'Proposals for the Reform of the Commission of the European Communities and its Services' (1979). The five-man team responsible for the preparation of the Report met under the Chairmanship of Dirk Spierenburg, a former Dutch Permanent Representative. They constituted and Independent Review Body set up by the Commission to look into the organisation and staffing of the Commission.

Spinelli, Altiero (1907-) Italian politician. From July 19484 Chairman of the European Parliament Committee on Industrial Affairs. EEC Commissioner 1970-1976, with responsibilities for industrial policy. Member of Italian Chamber of Deputies since 1976. A co-founder of the Crocodile Group.

SPMMS Software Production and Maintenance Management Support (ESPRIT project approved 1984).

Spokesman's Service Group under the authority of the President of the Commission who supply the media with Community and Commission news and developments.

SPRINT Strategic Programme for Innovation and Technology Transfer (1983-1993).

SPRINT Software Programme for Research in Telecommunications (RACE project approved February 1986).

SSID   Specialized Service for Documentary Data Processing.

SSV Short Study Visits (1977-1987). Now part of ERASMUS.

STABEX Stability in Export Revenue   Established under Lomé Convention I with the intention of offsetting the worst effects on producers in the ACP states of sudden falls in their incomes as the result of fluctuating world prices, or a heavy drop in production caused by the weather and other influences (DG VIII).

Stabiliser A means for controlling farm output.

STABINE   Development of an advanced power generation system, compounding a diesel cycle to that of an industrial gas turbine (EUREKA project approved June 1986).

STADIUM   Statistical Data Interchange Universal Monitor.

Standards Directives 83/189/EEC (OJ L 109, 26.4.1983). Established a routine for providing advance warning of intention to introduce new technical standards and regulations. The aim of the Directive is to prevent Member States from using standards as non-tariff barriers to trade, by enhancing the European standard consultation framework. DG III.

Standing Committee on Employment   Set up in 1970 (OJ L 273, 17.12.70), it has responsibility for enforcing contact between employers and workers at the EC level, to promote employment DG III.

Standstill A term which means that Member States refrain from adopting laws that could hinder movements between countries in the EC.

STANORM Statistical Normalization. To enable comparison and data exchange between various types of data processors.

STAR Special telecommunications action for regional development. A Community programme set up to assist the development of less well off areas of the EC by providing improved access to advanced telecommunications services (1986-).

STARCOM Tariff and Trade Statistics.

STC Scientific and Technical Committee (EURATOM).

STC Scientific and Technical Cooperation.

STD Science and Technology for Development (1983-1991).

STECLA Standing Technological Conference of European Local Authorities. *12, Old Park Ridings, London N21 2EU, United Kingdom.*

STEP Science and Technology for Environmental Protection. One of two research programmes adopted by the Council in 1990 in relation to the environment (1989-1992).

STFC Scientific and Technical Fisheries Committee.

STID Scientific and Technical Information and Documentation.

Stimulation Programme Action to Stimulate the Efficacy of the EC's Scientific and Technical Potential (1983-). DG XII.

STM Supplementary Trade Mechanism.

STMS Short-Term Monetary Support.

STOA Scientific and Technological Options Assessment (European Parliament Committee established in 1987).

Stockholm Convention Responsible for creating EFTA which came into force in May 1960.

STRADA Electronic mail system between the Institutions and the Member States.

Stresa Conference Met in 1958 to consider the particular problems of agriculture in the EC. It laid down guidelines for the formulation of a common agricultural policy.

Stresemann Prize (Federal Republic of Germany) A gold medal presented by the Gustav Stresemann Society, Mainz, for special contributions to European politics.

STRIDE Science and Technology for Regional Innovation and Development in Europe. A programme launched in 1989 designed to promote research and development in the poorer regions of the EC.

Structural Funds See EAGGF (Guidance Section); ERDF; ESF. Intention is to spread the benefits of 1992 as evenly as possible throughout the EC.

Subsidiarity   The principle that political decisions should be taken at the lowest practicable level.

Summits (EC) 1983-1990 Held every 6 months:

Stuttgart, June 1983 (West German Presidency): Agreed to reform budget, particularly in response to the coming enlargement, and also to bring the CAP into line with market needs.

Athens, December 1983 (Greek Presidency): Stuttgart declaration reaffirmed.

Fontainebleau, June 1984 (French Presidency): Principles of budgetary discipline agreed; agreement on British budget rebate.

Dublin, December 1984 (Irish Presidency): Established internal market without frontiers and the key to growth and jobs.

Milan, June 1985 (Italian Presidency): Disagreement over Single European Act giving European Parliament more power and setting 1992 as date for completion of internal market.

Luxembourg, December 1985 (Luxembourg Presidency): Single European Act finally agreed.

The Hague, June 1986 (Dutch Presidency): Limited sanctions against South Africa. Budget reform deferred.

London, December 1986 (British Presidency): Further progress on internal market; and Community agreement to combat terrorism.

Brussels, June 1987 (Belgian Presidency): Disagreement (Thatcher veto) over proposed budget reform based on

proposals put forward by Jacques Delors, the President
of the European Commission. Britain complained of
too weak farm controls.

Copenhagen, December 1987 (Danish Presidency):
Further modifications to Delors reforms, but still not
sufficient for British support. Agreement to hold
extraordinary summit in Brussels in February 1988, to
rectify the situation before the Hanover summit of June
1988 and the passing of the Presidency to Greece.

Brussels, February 1988 (West German Presidency):
Delors reforms agreed. *Hanover,* June 1988 (West
German Presidency): Delors Committee on Economic
and Monetary Union set up. 1992 declared
'irreversible'. Delors confirmed as President of the
European Commission for a second term.

Rhodes, December 1988 (Greek Presidency):
Presentation of European Commission's mid-term report
on progress towards the completion of the internal
market by 1992. 'Slippage' named as growing cause for
concern.

Madrid, December 1989 (Spanish Presidency): Delors
Committee reports on European Central Bank.

Dublin April 1990 (Irish Presidency): Agreement on a
four-stage programme towards political union within the
EC.

SUNDIAL Speech, Understanding and Dialogue.

SUNSTAR Integration and design of speech
comprehending interfaces.

Super 301 Countries An American listing of 'priority'
states with the most numerous trade barriers which are

then targeted for special investigation and negotiation under Section 301 of the Omnibus Trade Act.

SUPERNODE Operating systems and programmes for parallel computers (ESPRIT approved 1988).

SUPER SUBSEA To develop standardized modular subsea production systems (EUREKA project approved December 1986).

Support Measurement Unit One common measure of support covering export refunds, deficiency payments and price guarantees.

SVC Standing Veterinary Committee.

SWPI Standing Working Party on Investment.

Synthetic Index of regions measuring the relative intensity of regional problems in the EC (published in COM(84) 40 Table 7.1.1).

SYSDOC programme European Parliament document system programme comprising **PEGASE; MIDAS** and EPOQUE.

Sysmin System for Safeguarding and Developing Mineral production. Developed under Lomé II to aid mineral production in ACP countries.

Systran Coordination of National Policies Relating to Machine or Machine-Assisted Translation. Currently being extended to cover more languages.

TABAN Table Analysis Project. Begun in 1980 by EUROSTAT to review the collection and distribution of statistical tables.

TAC Total Allowable Catch. A device for managing the EC's fisheries policy.

Tachograph Equipment placed in commercial vehicles that records driving time, speed and distance travelled, required by Regulation 1463/70, issued under the Common Market Transport Policy. DG VII.

TAI Terminology and Computer Applications (Department within DG IX of the Commission).

TAP Temporary Abandonment Premium.

TAP Telecommunications Action programme, set up in 1984. It oversees projects such as RACE and TEDIS.

Target Price Under the CAP The basic price set annually for each commodity by the Council of Ministers. EC price support for farmers is calculated with reference to the target price.

TARIC Integrated Customs Tariff. Came into being in January 1988. Similar to CCT but contains additional matter on preferences, quotas and duty suspensions. Classified using CN. DG XXI.

Tariffication The process which converts variable levies, such as the Community's import levies, into fixed tariffs as a prelude to their dismantling.

Taxation Classical System of One embraced by the Netherlands, Luxembourg and the United States, in which corporate profits are taxed twice: dividends paid to shareholders are subject to tax without any credit against corporate tax.

Taxation Imputation System of One embraced by the United Kingdom whereby corporate tax is charged at one rate regardless of the destination of the profits: if profits are distributed via dividends, shareholders are given a tax credit which limits their liability to personal tax.

Taxation Split-Rate System of   One employed by West Germany whereby distributed corporate profits are subject to a lower rate of corporation tax than undistributed ones.

TBB Transnational Broadband Backbone Project. A major project launched under the EC's telecommunications policy in 1985 in the field of broadband communications.

TC Technical Committee.

TECNET A database of programmes demonstrating the scope of projects in Information Technologies and Vocational Training, as part of the EuroTechnet. Free access via ECHO.

TED   Tenders Electronic Daily.   An electronic information service that carries   details of Member States' public procurement contracts awarded by national and local authorities in instances where bidding is open to suppliers throughout the EC.   An OOPEC databank of EC Tenders. Access via ECHO. *15 Avenue de la Faiencerie, Luxembourg.*

TEDIS   The Trade Electronic Data Interchange Services Programme. Designed to enhance electronic data interchange throughout the EC.

TEDUC   Transfer of Commercial Data Using Commercial Networks programme (not yet operational).

TELEMAN   Research and training programme on remote handling in hazardous or disordered nuclear environments. Programme adopted by the Council in 1989 as part of the EC's research and technological development policy. (1989-1993)

TEMPUS   A programme launched by the EC to support higher education and training in Poland and Hungary. One aspect of the programme is the establishment of a European Training Foundation, and support for East European students and academics to study in EC countries.

TERA   Research into the development of high performance and high capacity optical disk storage systems for use as data libraries (EUREKA approved 1987).

TERMINALS guide A database giving descriptions of terminals with the addresses of suppliers and service operators on Europe. Free access via ECHO.

TF Task Force of the Commission.

THERMIE Programme for the promotion of energy technology in Europe.   A ECSC Consultative Committee programe concerning loans to Hungary and Poland (1990-1994).

THESAURI An on-line analytical inventory of current structured vocabularies which have appeared in at least one of the official ED languages.   Free access via ECHO.

Thirtieth of May Mandate Declaration following the Congress of Europe held in Paris in May 1980, to celebrate the 30th anniversary of the Schuman Plan (organized by the European Movement).

Thomson Report Report on the 'Regional Problems in the Enlarged Community', May 1973.

Thomson, Lord George Morgan of Monifieth (1921-). British journalist. Labour politician 1952-1972. Deputy Foreign Secretary (1969-1970) with special responsibility for European affairs and Common Market negotiations. Chairman of Labour Committee for Europe 1972-1973. Member of Committee of European Communities, with special responsibility for Regional Policy, 1973-1976.

Three Wise Men Report Report on European institutions published by the Commission in 1979. The Committee preparing the Report was composed of Barend Biesheuvel (Dutch); Edmund Dell (British) and Robert Marjolin (French). This 'Committee of Three' was set up by the Council to investigate what adjustments were necessary to the machinery and procedures of the institutions for an effective operation of the Community on the basis of the Treaties, and to progress towards European union. Published in OJ C9/88.

Threshold Price Under the CAP, the minimum price fixed for cereals, milk products and sugar. Imports of such foodstuffs arriving from non-EC countries at a lesser price are subject to a levy to raise them to the threshold price level. In contrast to the target price, the threshold price includes the transportation costs from the port of entry to the internal destination. DG VI.

TIC Terminal Independence Consultation manual for the domains of CRONOS.

TII European Association for the Transfer of Technologies Innovation and Industrial Information.

Rue Alcide de Gasperi 7, Boîte Postale 1704, 1017 Luxembourg.

Tindemans Plan (1976) Developed by Leo Tindemans, the then Belgian Prime Minister, this plan sought to combine the Fouchet and Werner plans for a joint foreign policy and monetary union, but also included a programme of common regional and social policies for a Citizens' Europe. In common with its predecessors, this plan also met with failure.

Tindemans, Leo (1922-) A Belgian politician, Tindemans was Prime Minister 1974-1978. He was an MEP, 1979-1981. In 1980, he won the Robert Schuman Prize. In 1975, he published 'European Union; and, in 1976, 'Europe, Ideal of our Generation'. In 1976, he was the author of the Tindemans Plan.

TIP Technology Integration Project (within ESPRIT programme).

TIR Transport International Routier is a document distributed to international wagon operators that permits loaded lorries to cross international borders.

TIS Terminology Information Service. An internal Council of Ministers database for translators and terminologists.

TNC Trade Negotiating Committee. The governing body for GATT's Uruguay Round of talks aimed at liberalizing trade.

Toxic Effluent Directive 76/464/EEC (OJ L 129, 18.5.76) Established to prevent deterioration of aquatic areas by banning, or limiting, present and future emissions of dangerous and harmful substances. The Directive set standards of water quality restricting (or prohibiting altogether) the amounts of specific substances that can be discharged into rivers and seas. The list of such substances is being continually updated. DG XI.

TOXWASTE   A database of toxic and hazardous wastes in the EC (not yet operational).

TPC Committee on the Adaptation of the Directives to Technical Progress.

TRAIN   A training database using a subset of the EABS file. Free access via ECHO.

TRANSDOC   A project to upgrade a manual database of selected scientific journals, French patents and technical reports (1984-1985).

Trans-Europ-Express A network of fast and luxurious trains which connect the major cities in the EC, enjoying minimum border formalities.

Transitional Period   Refers to the time allowed for the new Member States to adapt to the provisions of the EC Treaty.

TRANSPOTEL   A worldwide reproduceable concept for physical distribution centres where central facilities are offered of which the major provision is an integral data and communications processing system (EUREKA project approved June 1986).

TREND   A database via ECHO which monitors trends in computer hardware and software development.

TREVI Group Member States' Interior Ministers' meeting to discuss terrorism, violence and drugs.

Tripartite Conference A yearly meeting between the Council of Ministers and workers' and employers' organizations designed to bring the latter two groups into closer contact with EC policy making in areas which are of interest to them than would otherwise be possible.

TROIKA Refers to the current Presidency and the following two Presidencies of the Council of Ministers.

TTER Two-Tier Exchange Rate.

TWE The relationship between Technology, Work and Employment (FAST II programme).

Two-Tier Tariff The application of two sets of rates for the same goods in the tariff.

UAA Usable (utilised Agriculrural Area

UACEE Union of Craft Industries and Trades of the EEC. *Rue du Congres 33, B - 1000 Brussels, Belgium.*

UACES University Association for Contemporary European Studies. *C/o King's College, Strand, London WC2R 2LS*

UAS User agent service designed to facilitate accessto, and dissemination of, the information contained in the automated data processing systems. Part of the **INIS** programme.

UCITS Directive Coucil directive 85/611/EEC on the coordination of laws relating to Undertakings, for Collective Investment in Transferable Securities. A set of standards aimed at protecting those who invest in foreign firms. (published in OJ L 375/85). Amended in OJ L 100/88.

UCOL Ultra Wideband Coherent Optical Lan (**ESPRIT** project 1984).

UEAPME European Association of Craft, Small and Medium Sized Enterprises. *Rue de Spa 8, B - 1040 Brussels, Belgium.*

UETP University - Enterprise Training Parnership (**COMETT** project).

UFE Union of Professional Groups of the potato-starch Industry of the **EC** *Oude Boteringstraat 37, Postbox 1105, 9701 BC, Gronigen, The Netherlands.*

UKREP United Kingdom Permanent Representative to the **EC**. See **COREPER,** Permanent Representtive.

UNCTAD United Nations Conference on Trade and Development. Responsible for co-ordinating **GATT** negotiations.

UNESDA Soft Drinks Associations' Union of the **EC** countries. *Avenue General de Gaulle 51, Boîte 5, B - 1050 Brussels, Belgium.*

UNESEM European Union of Natural Mineral Water Sources of the Common Market. *C/o Chmb Synd Eaux Minerales, Rue Clement Marot 10, F - 75008 Paris, France.*

UNICE Union of Industries of the European Communities. Dedicated to economic growth, job creation and improved living standards. *Rue de Loxum 6, Boîte 21, B - 1000 Brussels, Belgium.*

UNISTOCK   Union of Cereal Storage Firms in the
EC. *MAttenwiete 2, D - 2000 Hamburg 11, Germany.*

Uraguay Round (1986-1990) Extended trade talks
within **GATT**, marked at the time by internal dissention
caused by disagreements between the developed world
and **LDCs**. Partial success in 1989; completion aimed
for 1990.

USD US dollars.

Val Duchesse   A chateau near Brussels which has
played host to a number of high level discussions in the
EC.

VALOREN   Exploitation of Indigenous Energy
Potential in certain less-favoured Regions (1986-).

VALUE   Programme for the dissemination and
utilization of research results. Programme adopted by
the Council in 1989 as part of the EC's research and
technological development policy (1989-1992).

VAMAS   International Scientific and Technical
Collaboration on Advanced Materials and Standards.

VAT Value Added Tax. A general, non-uniform, tax
which is applied to the goods and services used by the
consumer.

Vedel Report Looked into the need for policy and
institutional reforms of the EC. 1972. Specifically, it
argued that the European Parliament be given greater
legislative powers and a stronger role.

Vedel, Georges (1910-).   French lawyer. Political
adviser to French delegation at Common Market
negotiations 1956-1957.

VERS Voluntary Export Restraints. Arrangements intended to curtail exports from non-member countries to EC states. Generally apply on a bilateral basis. Tend to be a substitute for more stringent controls.

Veto All Member States can exercise a veto in the Council, but this becomes relevant only where a Treaty stipulates that a vote on a specific matter must be unanimous. In January 1966, the French government insisted that 'where very important interests are at stake the discussion must be continued until unanimous agreement is reached'. The effect of this has been that nearly all Council Acts since 1966 have been the outcome of unanimous agreement.

VISION 1250 Established a trans-national network to bring together those concerned with **HDTV**, under the **EEIG.**

Vredeling Initiative Proposal for a Directive on procedures for informing and consulting the employees of undertakings with complex structures,1981 and 1983. An extension of worker-participation found in some Member States, particularly West Germany and Holland. (Published in Bulletin of EC supplement 3/1980 and revised in 2/1983 and concluded in OJ C 203/86.

VUSEC Voluntary work and employment (Commission study within the Programme of Research and Actions on the Development of the Labour Market in the EC).

Yes for Europe Programme for the promotion of youth exchanges in the EC.

YF Youth Forum. Political arena for national and international European youth organizations. Publishes Youth Opinion in English and French. *Rue de la Science 10, B - 1040 Brussels, Belgium.*

YWU Year - Work - Unit.

ZBP1 Balance of payments domain on the CRONOS database.

ZCA1 External trade of the ACP States domain on the CRONOS database.

ZEN1 Energy and industry domain on the CRONOS database.

ZPA1 Agricultural supply balance sheets and production statistics domain on the CRONOS database.

ZPVD Developing countries domain on the CRONOS database.

ZRDI Research and development domain on the CRONOS database.